Map 1

A THOUSAND YEARS OF JEWISH CULTURE AND COMMUNAL LIFE

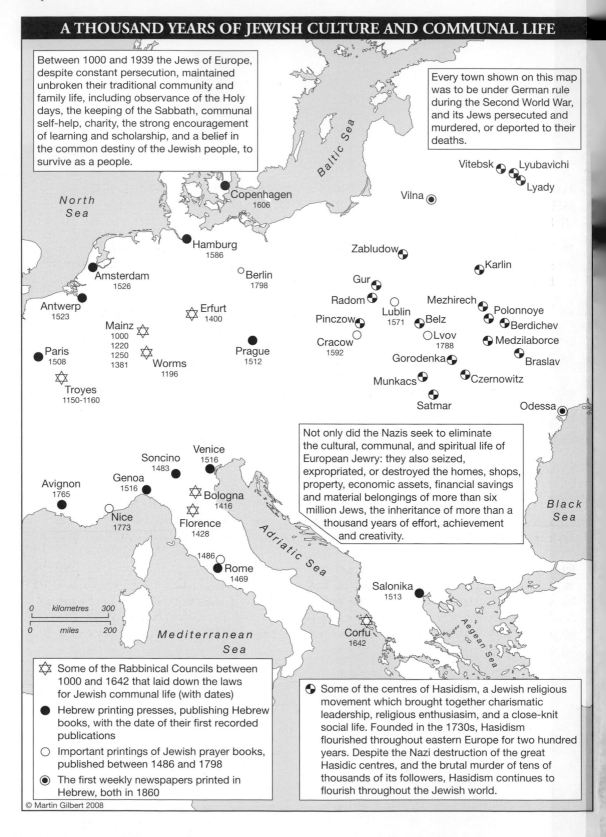

Between 1000 and 1939 the Jews of Europe, despite constant persecution, maintained unbroken their traditional community and family life, including observance of the Holy days, the keeping of the Sabbath, communal self-help, charity, the strong encouragement of learning and scholarship, and a belief in the common destiny of the Jewish people, to survive as a people.

Every town shown on this map was to be under German rule during the Second World War, and its Jews persecuted and murdered, or deported to their deaths.

Not only did the Nazis seek to eliminate the cultural, communal, and spiritual life of European Jewry: they also seized, expropriated, or destroyed the homes, shops, property, economic assets, financial savings and material belongings of more than six million Jews, the inheritance of more than a thousand years of effort, achievement and creativity.

North Sea
Baltic Sea
Black Sea
Adriatic Sea
Aegean Sea
Mediterranean Sea

Copenhagen 1606
Vilna
Vitebsk
Lyubavichi
Lyady
Hamburg 1586
Zabludow
Karlin
Berlin 1798
Gur
Mezhirech
Amsterdam 1526
Radom
Lublin 1571
Polonnoye
Antwerp 1523
Erfurt 1400
Pinczow
Belz
Berdichev
Mainz 1000 1220 1250 1381
Cracow 1592
Lvov 1788
Medzilaborce
Paris 1508
Prague 1512
Worms 1196
Gorodenka
Braslav
Troyes 1150-1160
Munkacs
Czernowitz
Satmar
Odessa

Soncino 1483
Venice 1516
Avignon 1765
Genoa 1516
Bologna 1416
Nice 1773
Florence 1428
1486
Rome 1469
Salonika 1513
Corfu 1642

0	kilometres	300
0	miles	200

Some of the Rabbinical Councils between 1000 and 1642 that laid down the laws for Jewish communal life (with dates)

● Hebrew printing presses, publishing Hebrew books, with the date of their first recorded publications

○ Important printings of Jewish prayer books, published between 1486 and 1798

◉ The first weekly newspapers printed in Hebrew, both in 1860

Some of the centres of Hasidism, a Jewish religious movement which brought together charismatic leadership, religious enthusiasim, and a close-knit social life. Founded in the 1730s, Hasidism flourished throughout eastern Europe for two hundred years. Despite the Nazi destruction of the great Hasidic centres, and the brutal murder of tens of thousands of its followers, Hasidism continues to flourish throughout the Jewish world.

© Martin Gilbert 2008

THE ROUTLEDGE ATLAS OF THE HOLOCAUST

THE GRAPHIC HISTORY OF THE NAZI ATTEMPT TO DESTROY THE JEWS OF EUROPE DURING THE SECOND WORLD WAR IS ILLUSTRATED IN THIS SERIES OF 333 DETAILED MAPS.

The maps, and the text and photographs that accompany them, vividly depict the fate of the Jews between 1933 and 1945, while also setting the chronological story in the wider context of the war itself. The maps include:

- Historical background – from the effects of anti-Jewish violence between 1880 and 1933 to the geography of the existing Jewish communities before the advent of the Nazis
- The beginning of the violence – from the destruction of the synagogues in November 1938 to Jewish migrations and deportations, and the establishment of the concentration camps and death camps throughout German-dominated Europe
- The spread of Nazi rule – the fate of the Jews throughout Europe including Germany, Austria, Poland, Greece, Yugoslavia, Bulgaria, Russia, Denmark, Norway, France, Holland, Belgium, Italy, and the Baltic States
- Jewish revolts and resistance; and the work of Christians in saving Jews
- The death marches, the advance of the Allies to the liberation of the camps, the fate of the survivors, and the final death toll.

This revised edition includes a new section which gives an insight into the layout and organization of some of the most significant places of the Holocaust, including Auschwitz, Treblinka and the Warsaw ghetto, which will be especially useful to those visiting the sites.

Sir Martin Gilbert is one of the leading historians of his generation. An Honorary Fellow of Merton College, Oxford – of which he was a fellow for thirty years – he is the official biographer of Winston Churchill and the author of eighty books, among them *The Routledge Atlas of the Second World War*, *The Holocaust: The Jewish Tragedy*, *The Righteous: The Unsung Heroes of the Holocaust*, and *Churchill and the Jews*. For more information on his books visit http://www.martingilbert.com.

BOOKS BY MARTIN GILBERT

The Routledge Atlas of American History
The Routledge Atlas of the Arab-Israeli Conflict
The Routledge Atlas of British History
The Routledge Atlas of the First World War
The Routledge Atlas of the Holocaust

The Routledge Historical Atlas of Jerusalem
The Routledge Atlas of Jewish History
The Routledge Atlas of Russian History
The Routledge Atlas of the Second World War

The Appeasers (with Richard Gott)
The European Powers, 1900–1945
The Roots of Appeasement
Children's Illustrated Bible Atlas
Atlas of British Charities
The Holocaust: Maps and Photographs
The Jews of Arab Lands: Their History in Maps
The Jews of Russia: Their History in Maps
Sir Horace Rumbold: Portrait of a Diplomat
Jerusalem: Rebirth of a City
Jerusalem in the Twentieth Century
Exile and Return: The Struggle for Jewish
    Statehood
Israel: A History
The Story of Israel
Auschwitz and the Allies
The Jews of Hope: The Plight of Soviet Jewry
    Today
Shcharansky: Hero of Our Time
The Holocaust: The Jewish Tragedy
Kristallnacht: Prelude to Destruction
The Boys: Triumph over Adversity
The First World War

Somme: The Heroism and Horror of War
The Second World War
D-Day
The Day the War Ended
Empires in Conflict: A History of the Twentieth
    Century, 1900–1933
Descent into Barbarism: A History of the
    Twentieth Century, 1934–1951
Challenge to Civilization: A History of the
    Twentieth Century, 1952–1999
Never Again: A History of the Holocaust
The Jews in the Twentieth Century: An
    Illustrated History
Letters to Auntie Fori: The 5,000-Year History
    of the Jewish People and Their Faith
The Righteous: The Unsung Heroes of the
    Holocaust
In Search of Churchill
Churchill and America
Churchill and the Jews
The Will of the People: Churchill and
    Parliamentary Democracy

THE CHURCHILL BIOGRAPHY

Volume III: The Challenge of War, 1914–1916
    Document Volume III (in two parts)
Volume IV: World in Torment, 1917–1922
    Document Volume IV (in three parts)
Volume V: The Coming of War, 1922–1939
    Document Volume V: The Exchequer Years,
    1922–1929
    Document Volume V: The Wilderness Years,
    1929–1935
    Document Volume V: The Coming of War,
    1936–1939
Volume VI: Finest Hour, 1939–1941
    Churchill War Papers I: At the Admiralty,
    September 1939–May 1940
    Churchill War Papers II: Never Surrender,
    May–December 1940
    Churchill War Papers III: The Ever-Widening
    War, 1941

Volume VII: Road to Victory, 1941–1945
Volume VIII: Never Despair, 1945–1965
Churchill: A Photographic Portrait
Churchill: A Life

EDITIONS OF DOCUMENTS

Britain and Germany between the Wars
Plough My Own Furrow: The Life of Lord
    Allen of Hurtwood
Servant of India: Diaries of the Viceroy's Private
    Secretary, 1905–1910
Winston Churchill and Emery Reves:
    Correspondence 1937–1964

THE ROUTLEDGE ATLAS OF
THE HOLOCAUST

4th Edition

Martin Gilbert

Routledge
Taylor & Francis Group

LONDON AND NEW YORK

First published 1982 as *The Atlas of the Holocaust*
by Michael Joseph

Second edition published 1993 as *The Dent Atlas of Jewish History*
by J.M. Dent Ltd

Third edition published 2002 as *The Routledge Atlas of the Holocaust*
by Routledge

Fourth edition published 2009
by Routledge
2 Park Square, Milton Park, Abingdon, Oxon OX14 4RN

Simultaneously published in the USA and Canada
by Routledge
270 Madison Ave, New York, NY 10016

Routledge is an imprint of the Taylor & Francis Group, an informa business

Typeset in Sabon by
Keystroke, 28 High Street, Tettenhall, Wolverhampton
Printed and bound in Great Britain by
MPG Books Ltd, Bodmin

British Library Cataloguing in Publication Data
A catalogue record for this book is available from the British Library

Library of Congress Cataloging in Publication Data
Gilbert, Martin, 1936–
    The routledge atlas of the Holocaust. — 4th ed.
        p. cm.
    1. Holocaust, Jewish (1939–1945)—Maps. 2. Holocaust, Jewish (1939–1945)
    I. Title.
    G1797.21.E29G58 2009
    940.53'180223—dc22   2008043844

ISBN10: 0–415–48481–2 (hbk)
ISBN10: 0–415–48486–3 (pbk)

ISBN13: 978–0–415–48481–7 (hbk)
ISBN13: 978–0–415–48486–2 (pbk)

List of Maps

Special symbols used in this Atlas

00,000	numbers of Jews in a particular country, town or village before the Holocaust, according to the last peace-time census
11,111	number of Jews seeking refuge elsewhere, deported, or confined to a ghetto
22,222	numbers killed, or deported to their deaths
╲	the borders of Greater Germany at the time of any particular map
▲▲▲▲	the front lines at the time of any particular map
✳	acts of resistance or revolt by Jewish groups or individuals

Introduction

The map below shows the birthplaces, places of work, and places of execution of 17 Jews who were murdered during the war years. The text which follows on this page tells, briefly, something of their personal stories. If a similarly short reference were made to each Jew murdered between 1939 and 1945, 353,000 such maps would be needed. To draw these maps at the author's and cartographer's fastest rate of a map a day, would take more than 967 years.

Among the 17 people whom I have chosen for this map is the historian, Simon Dubnow, who had taught at Vilna, Kovno and Berlin, and who was murdered in Riga on 8 December 1941, at the age of 81. Among other Jewish historians murdered by the Nazis was Emanuel Ringelblum, born in Buczacz, who survived the Warsaw ghetto revolt, but was later caught by the Gestapo and murdered, at the age of 44, together with his wife and children *(page 166)*.

Many thousands of doctors, medical men and scientists were also killed, among them the pharmacologist Emil Starckenstein, born in the Bohemian town of Pobezovice, who had made major contributions to preventive medicine, first as a Professor at Prague, and after 1938, as a refugee in Amsterdam. In 1941, at the age of 58, he was deported to Mauthausen and killed *(page 66)*.

Charlotte Salomon was a painter. Born in Berlin, she had fled to France in 1939, at the age of 22. Later she was deported to Auschwitz and gassed. One of her paintings bore the caption: 'I cannot bear this life, I cannot bear these times.' Rudolf Levy, also a painter, was born in Stettin in 1875, and worked with Matisse. In the First World War, as a German soldier, he won the Iron Cross. Fleeing from Berlin to Paris in 1933, from Paris to Florence in 1940, he was deported from Italy to Auschwitz in 1943. That same year, the Munich-born painter Hermann Lismann, who had studied in Lausanne and Rome, was deported from France to Majdanek *(page 142)*.

Harry Baur, a Marseilles dock worker who became known throughout France as 'the king of character actors', died in Berlin in 1943, after being tortured by the Gestapo. A fellow French Jew, René Blum, successor to Diaghilev as director of the Monte Carlo ballet, perished at Auschwitz in 1944.

Many poets were also murdered, among them Mordechai Gebirtig, killed in Cracow *(page 91)*, Samuel Jacob Imber, deported to Belzec *(page 119)*, Yitzhak Katznelson, killed at Auschwitz with one of his sons *(page 170)*, and Miklos Radnoti, a 35-year-old Hungarian who, after more than three years in different slave labour camps, died in October 1944 on a death march from Bor in Yugoslavia to Györ in Hungary *(page 193)*.

Among the hundreds of thousands of teenagers killed was the 15-year-old Yitskhok Rudashevski, who recorded in his diary the day-to-day life and moods of the Vilna ghetto *(page 143)*, and Judit Sandor, from Budapest, who survived both the death camps and the war itself, but was too weak to survive the peace, and died at Karlstad, in Sweden, in September 1945, shortly after her seventeenth birthday *(page 223)*.

Janusz Korczak, writer of children's stories, educator and social worker, was murdered at Treblinka with all 200 children from his Warsaw orphanage. He had insisted on acompanying them to the death camp. Alice Salomon, director of the children's home at La Rose, near Marseilles, also voluntarily joined her children, when they were deported to Auschwitz *(page 142)*.

In all, more than a million Jewish children

Map 2

were murdered by the Nazis, among them the three-year-old Pierre Roth, born in Mulhouse *(page 133)*. Thousands of children were shot in the streets, or separated from their parents for the terrible journey to the death camps. Even the tiniest infants were brutally murdered, many wrenched from their mothers' arms, as both were shot, beaten to death, or gassed.

With the death of so many children, future generations were also destroyed, and the natural descent of generation to generation was unnaturally cut off. We shall never know what these million and more children would have made of their lives, had evil men not marked them out to die.

The 317 maps that follow show, in chronological sequence, the destruction of each of the main Jewish communities of Europe, as well as acts of resistance and revolt, avenues of escape and rescue, and the fate of individuals.

The story told in these maps is not complete, nor can the statistics, however carefully researched, be comprehensive. 'With all the resources in the world', as Professor Yehuda Bauer has said, 'it is impossible to show – or even to know – all that was done.'

For each community whose pre-war strength, or war-time destruction, I have been able to plot on one of these maps, two or three other communities existed, particularly smaller ones, for which there is either no room in this Atlas, or for which there is no evidence beyond the knowledge that they were in fact destroyed. The Nazi aim was to blot out these communities and all they represented of life, heritage and culture. Although the Nazis made no specific effort to record every killing, their general efficiency and sense of order was such that much detailed evidence survives of the killings in progress, often as set down at the time by the killers themselves.

The aim of this Atlas is to trace each phase of Hitler's war against the Jewish people: against all those with Jewish blood or of Jewish descent, wherever they could be found. It therefore traces the German conquest of territory in which Jews had lived for centuries, the first random but brutal killings, the enforced expulsions of ancient communities, the setting up of ghettos, the deliberate starvation of tens of thousands – at least 4,000 a month in Warsaw alone – the round-ups and deportations, the creation and

working of the death camps, the slave labour system, the death marches, and the executions up to the very moment of liberation.

The photographs show the places, and some of the people, against whom this enormous organization and effort of murder was directed. Most of them, tragically, are anonymous. Nevertheless, the people in these photographs were real people. Their faces once meant struggle and sorrow, joy and laughter, to those who knew them.

Although this Atlas is one of Jewish suffering, no book or atlas on any aspect of the Second World War can fail to record that in addition to the six million Jewish men, women and children who were murdered at least an equal number of non-Jews was also killed, not in the heat of battle, not by military siege, aerial bombardment or the harsh conditions of modern war, but by deliberate, planned murder. Hence, even in this Atlas, which traces the Jewish story, mention has frequently been made, often as an integral part of the Jewish fate, of the murder of non-Jews. These include Polish civilians killed after Poland's capitulation *(page 25)*, the first, mostly non-Jewish, victims at Auschwitz *(page 33)*, the tens of thousands of victims of the Nazi euthanasia programme *(page 38)*, the non-Jews killed with Jews in the slave labour camps of the Sahara *(page 43)*, the Serbs killed with Jews in April 1941 and January 1942 *(pages 45 and 74)*, the Czech villagers massacred at Lidice *(page 88)*, the Poles expelled and murdered in the Zamosc province *(page 126)*, the Gypsies deported to the death camps *(page 128)*, the non-Jews killed with Jews in the reprisal action in Rome *(page 168)*, Greeks and Italians taken hostage and drowned with Jews in the Aegean *(page 179)*, the French villagers massacred at Oradour-sur-Glane *(page 182)*, and the tens of thousands of Gypsies, Russian prisoners-of-war, Spanish republicans, Jehovah's Witnesses and homosexuals murdered at Mauthausen *(pages 219–20)*.

I have tried in this Atlas to give a chronological presentation of how the Holocaust evolved, and to show how that evolution was bound up with the changing course of the Second World War. The facts set down here will I hope add to our knowledge of what was done to the Jews, with particular reference to where it was done, in what circumstances, and on what massive a scale throughout every territory which came under Nazi domination.

Acknowledgements

The sources for all the facts shown in this Atlas are given in the Bibliography on pages 251–259. In gathering this material, and in preparing the maps themselves, I was particularly inspired by Rabbi Hugo Gryn, a survivor of Auschwitz, whom I first met in the spring of 1974, when work on the Atlas was beginning. His desire to see the story told in as much detail as possible has been a strong influence on my work; as were his personal encouragement and specific suggestions at every stage in drafting the maps and preparing the text.

For Hugo Gryn, as for many of the survivors who have helped me to collect material, or have encouraged me to map particular events, the act of recollection itself is often painful. They feel strongly, however, that unless the full scale and range of the slaughter is set down, many of its episodes will never be recorded, thus blurring the full enormity of the Holocaust, and reducing it to little more than a footnote to the history of the Second World War.

As the work proceeded, I also gained inspiration from the work of the French lawyer and historian, Serge Klarsfeld, whose father was deported from Paris to Auschwitz and perished there, and whose own comprehensive edition of the deportation lists of Jews from France, first published in 1978, is not only a model of scrupulous historical research, but also provided the basic material for thirty-three of the maps in this Atlas.

For the maps themselves, I am indebted to the cartographic work of Terry Bicknell, who transformed my rough and tentative drafts into maps of the highest quality. The Atlas owes much to his skills and patience.

As the maps evolved, I was helped considerably by the kindness and wisdom of Dr Shmuel Krakowski, the Director of Archives at Yad Vashem, Jerusalem, and himself a survivor, who not only provided me with valuable material, but also encouraged me in my researches: his knowledge of the fate of Polish Jewry in the war years, and of events in many other regions, has been an indispensable help, as has been his own pioneering work on Jewish resistance in Poland between 1942 and 1944.

I am also grateful to Professor Yehuda Bauer, of the Institute of Contemporary Jewry at the Hebrew University of Jerusalem, who scrutinized the maps when they were still in draft, and who gave me important guidance as to themes and sources; some of the most important research work on the Holocaust is being done by his pupils, and under his supervision.

When the maps were already at an advanced stage, they were helped by the critical scrutiny of Dr Arthur Cygielman.

Two institutions, Yad Vashem in Jerusalem and the Wiener Library in London, provided me with considerable help from their own substantial holdings, both published and manuscript. I was also helped in my search for materials, and for other reference works, by the late Dr Chaim Pazner, who not only gave me enormous personal encouragement, but also introduced me to the experts at Yad Vashem, whose assistance has been of considerable value.

I am also grateful to Taffy Sasson, who helped to collate the material once it was assembled, and who translated documents and articles from Hebrew and Yiddish. The typing of the texts was done by Esther Gerber, who came specially from Jerusalem to Oxford for this task, and by Sue Rampton.

In its last phase, the Atlas benefitted from the cartographic corrections of Danuta Trebus, whose work was financed in part by a grant from the Memorial Foundation for Jewish Culture. Work on the original maps was made possible by the generosity of Rex and Deborah Harbour.

My sincere thanks are also due to Frederick A. Praeger, of Westview Press, Boulder, Colorado, for his encouragement of the project in its early stages; to Max J. Holmes, of Holmes and Meier; to Martin Savitt, and the Board of Deputies of British Jews, which published an illustrated 23-map school edition in 1978; to Arthur Wang, of Hill and Wang, who published this school edition in the United States; and to Paul Shaw, then Educational Officer to the Board of Deputies, who gave me good guidance on the presentation and content of many of the maps at this early but important planning stage, and who encouraged me to continue with the present larger work.

I am also grateful to Michael O'Mara, Managing Director of George Rainbird Ltd, whose interest in the project has been a main factor in its fulfilment, as was his appointment of Erica Hunningher as its editor. Her efforts on behalf of the Atlas have been continuous, persistent and substantial.

Many people have written to me with suggestions for specific maps, or have answered my own requests for information. In this regard I should like to thank: Chana Abells; Dr Yitzhak Arad, Chairman of the Directorate, Yad Vashem, Jerusalem; the late Ehud Avriel; Dr Gershon Bacon; Dr Konstantin Bazarov; Professor Shlomo Ben-Ami; Andras Bereznay; Professor Yehuda Blum; John A. Broadwin; Peter Brod; Hyam Corney; Dr Szymon Datner; Professor Dr L. de Jong, Director, Netherlands State Institute for War Documentation; Adina Drechsler; Melvin Durdan; Dr Elizabeth Eppler, Assistant Director, Institute of Jewish Affairs, London; Henning Gehrs, Librarian, Museet For Danmarks Frihedskamp 1940–1945, Copenhagen; Richard Grumberger; Clara Guini, Reference Librarian, Yad Vashen, Jerusalem; Professor Yisrael Gutman; Jerzy Herszberg; Alfred Herzka; Professor Daniel Ivin; Stanislaw Kania, Main Commission for the Investigation of Nazi Crimes in Poland; Hadass Kaufman, Secretary of Archives, Yad Vashem, Jerusalem; Dr Rivka Kauli; Donald Kenrick; Dr J. Kermish, Director of Archives, Yad Vashem; Warren Kimball; Yehudit Kleiman; Erich Kulka; Janet Langmaid; Naomi Laqueur; Curt Leviant; Dr Dov Levin; Karin Levisen, Press and Cultural Department, Royal Danish Embassy, London; Lawrence Litt; Fritz Majer-Leonhard; Hadassa Modlinger; Miriam Novitch; Thomas Orszag-Land; Professor Dr Czeslaw Pilichowski, Director of the Main Commission for the Investigation of Nazi Crimes in Poland; Hayim Pinner; Leon Pommers; Leslie Reggel; Matthew Rinaldi; Dr S. J. Roth, Director, Institute of Jewish Affairs; Dr Livia Rothkirchen, editor of *Yad Vashen Studies*, Jerusalem; Michele Sarfatti, Centro Di Documentazione Ebraica Contemporanea, Milan; Dr. Schulz, Landeshauptarchiv, Koblenz; A. E. Scopelitis, Embassy of Greece, London; Mrs. M. Segall; Tovia Shahar; Dr Shmuel Spector; Jennie Tarabulus; Michael Tregenza; Harold Werner; and K. Zailinger, Director, Service Social Juif, Brussels.

The photographs in this volume come principally from the archives of Yad Vashem, Jerusalem. Others are from Serge Klarsfeld (page 132); The Main Commission for the Investigation of Nazi Crimes in Poland, Warsaw (page 196); The Museum of Denmark's Fight for Freedom 1940–1945, Copenhagen (page 154); I am grateful to those who put these photographic archives at my disposal; and to Tomasz Krasowski, who accompanied me on my own journey through Poland during which I took the photographs on pages 3, 69, 90, 135 and 169. The photograph on page 142 was taken by me in 1976.

As with each of my books, the support and advice of my wife Susie has been of inestimable value, both in terms of the structure of the work, and of her scrutiny of its content at every stage in the long process of evolution; to her are due not only my thanks, but also those of every reader who finds the Atlas of service.

I am most grateful to those who have provided me with extra materials, or have sent in corrections, which I have been able to include in this fourth printing. Special thanks are due to Ben Helfgott, to Professor Gaston L. Schmir, and to Luci Petrovic and A. Mosic (Federation of Jewish Communities in Yugoslavia). Any further material, corrections, or suggestions for new maps, would be much appreciated. My particular thanks are due to the publisher, William Morrow and Company, Inc., and to my editor there, Rose Marie Morse, for giving me the extra pages needed to include an index of the places and of the people mentioned in the atlas. For help in enabling me to compile this index, which will, I hope, add significantly to the usefulness of the atlas, I would like to thank Rachelle Gryn, Kay Thomson, and my son, David.

Martin Gilbert
Merton College
Oxford

22 September 1992

Note to the Fourth Edition

In the six years since the last edition, visits to the concentration camps have become more frequent; I have drawn sixteen new maps, at the end of the atlas, for the use of visitors, and those who are interested in the camps themselves. A new Map 1 *(page ii)* shows a thousand years of Jewish culture and communal life. I have also updated Map 316 *(page 230)*, showing, country by country, the numbers of Christians who saved Jews.

16 September 2008   MARTIN GILBERT

Map 3

ANTI-JEWISH VIOLENCE BEFORE THE FIRST WORLD WAR

Baltic Sea

Dusyata

TSARIST RUSSIA

Siemiatycze **1**
Minsk

Bialystok **80**

Warsaw   WHITE RUSSIA   Mogilev

POLAND   Lodz   Brest-Litovsk   Gomel **12**   Starodub

Siedlce **30**   Pinsk

Czestochowa   Lublin   **THE PALE**   Konotop

VOLHYNIA   Nyezhin

Zhitomir   Kiev

Pereyaslav

PODOLIA   Smyela

Botosani   UKRAINE   Elizavetgrad

Dorohoi   Ekaterinoslav

Burdujeni   Sulita   Ananayev

Tirgul Frumos   Kishinev **49**   Nikolaiev   Melitopol

Jassy

Bacau   Odessa **300**

Sea of Azov

Akkerman   CRIMEA

RUMANIA   Simferopol

Calarasi **60**

Black Sea

© Martin Gilbert 1982

miles 0 — 150
kilometres 0 — 200

Jews had lived throughout Europe for more than a thousand years. But no century had passed without their being attacked, expelled and killed.

Before the First World War, several hundred Jews had been killed in a series of violent attacks, or 'pogroms', in all the towns shown above, throughout western Russia and Rumania. As on each of the maps that follow, the numbers of those killed are shown inside a black box.

The murder of 49 Jews in Kishinev in 1903 led to protests throughout the Christian world; but the pogroms had continued.

Immediately after the First World War, tens of thousands of Jews were murdered in the western Ukraine *(opposite)*. In a single town, Proskurov, the numbers killed far exceeded the total deaths in 40 years of pogroms throughout Tsarist Russia.

Farther killings took place in Hungary in 1919, with the overthrow of the Communist regime, in which some Jews had played a prominent part. In Germany, at Nuremberg, Munich, Rosenheim, Zwickau, Coburg and

Map 4

ANTI-JEWISH VIOLENCE IN EUROPE, 1918-1932

LATVIA

North Sea

MEMEL   LITHUANIA

Baltic Sea

SOVIET UNION

Vilna **80**
April 1919

Berlin
Walter Rathenau   DANZIG

Proskurov
1,700   15 February 1919

Osnabrück

P O L A N D

Zhitomir   Fastov

GERMANY   Kalisz
2
1919

Krefeld   Weimar   Zwickau   **70**   November 1918

Boguslav

Coburg   Lvov   **500**   Berdichev   Tetiev

Braslav   Trostyanets

UKRAINE
85,000
1918-1920

Nuremberg   Holesov
3   GALICIA   Bershad

SAAR   Landsberg   CZECHOSLOVAKIA

Munich   Passau   Czernowitz
1

Rosenheim   Salzburg   Debrecen   Piatra   Jassy

HUNGARY   Oradea

AUSTRIA   Budapest
300
1919   Szeged   Cluj   Targu Ocna

2
1931   R U M A N I A

Bucharest

Black Sea

© Martin Gilbert 1982

Salzburg, Adolf Hitler preached hatred of the Jew as part of his National Socialist, or 'Nazi', philosophy. 'It is our duty', he declared in 1920, 'to arouse, to whip up, and to incite our people to instinctive repugnance of the Jews.'

In Berlin, in 1922, anti-semites murdered Walter Rathenau, the German Foreign Minister, and in 1923 Jewish houses in Berlin were attacked.

In the Moravian town of Holesov, in 1918, three Jews had been murdered. In eastern Poland, in 1918 and 1919, Jews were attacked and killed in Vilna, Lvov and throughout Galicia, where more than 500 Jews were killed.

In Rumania, in December 1922, restrictions were imposed on the percentage of Jewish students at Cluj University; then at universities in Jassy, Bucharest and Czernowitz, where Jewish students were attacked. Three years later at Piatra, synagogues and schools were looted and the Jewish cemetery desecrated. In 1926 a Jewish student was murdered at Czernowitz, and his murderer acquitted. In 1927, during anti-Jewish riots in Oradea, four synagogues were wrecked, while prayer houses were plundered in Jassy, Targu Ocna and Cluj.

But it was in Germany that anti-semitism gained its greatest hold. Between 1922 and 1933 there were 200 instances in Nuremberg alone of desecration of Jewish graves. Also in Nuremberg, the first issue of a vicious anti-semitic newspaper, *Der Stürmer,* was published in 1923. The newspaper proclaimed as its banner slogan 'The Jews are our misfortune'.

Following his unsuccessful attempt to seize power in Munich in 1924, Hitler was imprisoned at Landsberg. From there, on 18 July 1925, he published the first part of *Mein Kampf (My Struggle),* in which he wrote with venom of the Jews. The second part was published on 10 December 1926.

Out of prison, Hitler rebuilt his Nazi party, and at 'Party Day' in Weimar in 1926, and again at Nuremberg in 1927, many speakers advocated driving the Jews out of German life. In 1927 Jewish cemeteries were desecrated by Nazi gangs: at Osnabrück and Krefeld the synagogues were wrecked. In Berlin, on 12 September 1931, the eve of the Jewish New Year, Nazi gangs attacked Jews returning from synagogue.

On 30 January 1933, Adolf Hitler became Chancellor of Germany. He was to rule Germany for nearly twelve years, until his suicide in Berlin on 30 April 1945.

Map 5

TWO THOUSAND YEARS OF JEWISH LIFE IN EUROPE BY 1933

NORWAY
82 years

ESTONIA
600 years

DENMARK
311 years

LATVIA
400 years

HOLLAND
800 years

MEMEL
269 years

LITHUANIA
600 years

BELGIUM
700 years

WHITE RUSSIA
550 years

GERMANY
1,612 years

DANZIG
400 years

POLAND
800 years

• Wlodawa

UKRAINE
816 years

LUXEMBOURG
647 years

SAAR
312 years

CZECHOSLOVAKIA
1,000 years

CRIMEA
1,900 years

AUSTRIA
1,030 years

FRANCE
1,930 years

HUNGARY
1,900 years

RUMANIA
1,800 years

ITALY
2,100 years

YUGOSLAVIA
1,000 years

BULGARIA
1,900 years

GREECE
2,233 years

RHODES
2,000 years

0   miles   300

0   kilometres   400

© Martin Gilbert 1982

From the moment that Hitler became Chancellor of Germany, he worked to transform one of Europe's most civilised states into a totalitarian dictatorship, and to deny Germany's half million Jews the basic rights of citizenship. Yet Jews had lived on German soil since the time of the Roman Empire. Despite often savage persecution in medieval times, and frequent expulsions from town to town, they had continued, over a period of sixteen centuries, to make their contribution to the development of

Map 6

THE JEWS OF GERMANY AND THE TRIUMPH OF NAZISM, 1933-1938

North Sea

Baltic Sea

MEMEL

DANZIG

EAST PRUSSIA

HOLLAND

Hamburg
19,794

Esterwegen
concentration camp
1933

Sachsenhausen
concentration camp
1933

Berlin
172,672

GERMANY

POLAND

BELGIUM

Cologne
16,093

Sachsenburg
concentration camp
1933

Breslau
23,240

UPPER SILESIA

Buchenwald
concentration camp
1937

Leipzig
12,594

Frankfurt
29,385

LUXEMBOURG

SAAR

CZECHOSLOVAKIA

Nuremberg
8,603

FRANCE

Dachau
concentration camp
1933

Munich
10,068

45 *Jews murdered*
1933 · 1935

SWITZERLAND

AUSTRIA

HUNGARY

0   miles   100
0   kilometres   160

© Martin Gilbert 1982

modern Germany. Elsewhere in Europe the earliest Jewish communities dated back even further: the map opposite shows the age of those communities in countries which were to come under German rule or influence between 1933 and 1945.

The photograph, taken in 1980, is of a seventeenth-century synagogue in the present-day Polish town of Wlodawa.

From the very first days of Nazi rule in Germany, concentration camps were set up *(above)*. Critics of the regime were sent to these camps, as were thousands of individuals against whom Nazi hatred was directed, including homosexuals, for whom the law was particularly severe, socialists, dissident clergymen, and Jews. Brutality by guards led to many deaths in these camps from the first days of Hitler's rule.

In July 1935 the *Manchester Guardian*

published the following description of the interrogation of a prisoner at the hands of the Gestapo: 'His head was wrapped in a wet cloth that was knotted so tightly across his mouth that his teeth cut into his lips and his mouth bled profusely. He was held by three assistants while the official and another assistant took turns in beating him with a flexible leather-covered steel rod *(Stahlrute)*. When he fainted from pain and loss of blood he was brought to by means of various other tortures ... He was told that he might write a letter to his wife, as he would never see her again. The assistants fingered their pistols and discussed which of them should shoot the prisoner. But he remained silent. He was released some time afterwards.' Similar press reports appeared regularly outside Germany: by 1935 at least 45 Jews had been murdered in Dachau alone.

Map 7

THE JEWS OF THE SAAR, 1 MARCH 1935

LUXEMBOURG

GERMANY

FRANCE

Sötern
95

Bosen
25

Bettingen
25

Neunkirchen
213

Tholey
41

Brotdorf
26

Hilbringen
28

Merzig
204

Saint
Wendel
130

S A A R

Diefflen
29

Nalbach
29

Ottweiler
55

Dillingen
135

Pachten
3

Saarwellingen
151

Illingen
107

Saarlouis
274

Fraulautern
37

Merchweiler
26

Waldmohr
21

Bous
5

Wadgassen
6

Homburg
128

River Saar

Saint Ingbert
76

Differten
8

Saarbrücken
2,650

Blieskastel
8

0   miles   10

0   kilometres   15

©Martin Gilbert 1982

The first territory outside Hitler's control to be incorporated inside Nazi Germany was the Saar *(above)*. This small but prosperous province had been separated from Germany in 1919, under the Treaty of Versailles, but was then returned, as a result of a plebiscite, overwhelmingly in Germany's favour. The plebiscite, held under the auspices of the League of Nations, took place on 13 January 1935. Jews had lived in the city of Saarbrücken since the fourteenth century. Under the League of Nations administration between 1920 and 1935, their civil, political and personal rights had been protected by the minority statutes of the League. Outside Saarbrücken itself, there were some 25 rural communities with Jewish inhabitants, ranging in size from the 274 Jews of Saarlouis, to single Jewish families.

On 1 March 1935, six weeks after the plebiscite, the Saar became an integral part of Germany *(opposite, below)* and was at once subjected to all the rigours of Nazism, including the anti-Jewish legislation, the rule of the Gestapo, and the concentration camps. Almost all the Jews of the Saar chose French or Belgian citizenship. By 1938, when the Saarbrücken synagogue was burned down during the 'night of broken glass' *(page 13)*, only 177 Jews were still living in the city.

In Upper Silesia *(opposite)*, the first record of a Jewish community dates back to the eleventh century when, in 1060 a synagogue near Ratibor was seized by the town authorities and transformed into a church. There is also a record of Jews being persecuted in Leobschütz a century later, in 1163. Many of the earliest Jewish settlers in this region were poor; fugitives from the crusades or from persecution further east.

Despite more than six centuries of persecution, the Jews of Upper Silesia

THE JEWS OF UPPER SILESIA, 15 JULY 1937

0 — miles — 15
0 — kilometres — 20

P O L A N D

G E R M A N Y

LOWER
SILESIA

Pitschen
31

Landsberg
20

Kreuzburg
160

Rosenberg
102

Jellowa

Königshuld

Hitler
Sea

Guttentag
145

Grottkau
40

Falkenburg
51

Oppeln
607

Malapane

UPPER SILESIA
to Germany

Tworog
5

Niesse
220

Patschkau Ottmachau

Gogolin

Gross
Strehlitz
145

Tost

Beuthen
3,500

Neustadt
100

Ziegenhals

Oberglogau
50

Cosel
80

Peiskretscham
45

Gleiwitz
1,899

Hindenburg
1,200

Stanitz

Leobschütz
111

Bauerwitz
1

Ratibor
640

EAST
UPPER
SILESIA
to Poland

CZECHOSLOVAKIA

Katscher
42

© Martin Gilbert 1982

emerged in the nineteenth century as a small but progressive community. When, after the First World War, the region was returned to Germany, the minority rights of the Jews shown here were protected. This was a result of the German-Polish Convention of 15 May 1922. Even after Hitler came to power in 1933, these minority rights were upheld by the League of Nations, and the imposition of Nazi racial laws was prevented, following a Jewish petition, the 'Bernheim Petition', to the League. But the Convention itself expired on 15 July 1937, bringing the Jews of Upper Silesia, like those of the Saar two years before, within the full rigour of Nazi rule.

THE GERMAN REICH, 1935-1937

North
Sea

Baltic Sea

Sachsenhausen

Berlin
GERMANY

Warsaw

UPPER
SILESIA

SAAR

Dachau

Prague

Cracow

Munich

0 — miles — 200
0 — kilometres — 400

© Martin Gilbert 1982

ANTI-JEWISH RIOTS IN RUMANIA, 1935

POLAND

SOVIET UNION

CZECHOSLOVAKIA

Humenne

Hotin

Czernowitz

Siret

Belz

Radauti

Suceava

Kishinev

Budapest

HUNGARY

Piatra

Tighina

Buhusi

Bacau

Alba Iulia

Panciu

RUMANIA

Timisoara

2

Sinaia

BANAT

Petrovaradin

Bucharest

YUGOSLAVIA

Black Sea

BULGARIA

0 miles 100

0 kilometres 150

Sofia

© Martin Gilbert 1982

ANTI-JEWISH MEASURES, 1935-1939

Leningrad

Reval

Stockholm

SWEDEN

ESTONIA

0 miles 200

0 kilometres 150

Baltic Sea

Riga

LATVIA

LITHUANIA

Memel

Danzig

Kovno

Vilna

SOVIET UNION

Berlin

Warsaw

GERMANY

POLAND

see map opposite

Kiev

Lvov

Prague

CZECHOSLOVAKIA

BESSARABIA

Vienna

Budapest

1 3 February 1939

AUSTRIA

HUNGARY

RUMANIA

BANAT

Bucharest

YUGOSLAVIA

Belgrade

Black Sea

Adriatic Sea

BULGARIA

Sofia

© Martin Gilbert 1982

In the 1930s anti-Jewish violence spread through eastern Europe. It was particularly fierce in Rumania, where attacks on Jews took place in each of the towns shown on the map *(left)*. In universities throughout Rumania, student members of an influential anti-semitic organization, the Iron Guard, prevented Jewish students from attending lectures. From 1934, no new Jewish lawyer were allowed to enter the legal profession. I 1936 the Iron Guard exploded a bomb in a Jewish theatre in Timisoara, killing two Jews, and injuring many more.

In November 1936, at Petrovaradin in Yugoslavia, the editor of an anti-semitic paper modelled on the Nazi *Der Stürmer,* was tried and acquitted. In August 1937, at Humenne in Czechoslavakia, Jews were accused of sacrilege.

In Lithuania *(left, below),* severe restrictions were imposed on the number of Jews allowed to enter universities; in the 1936 university entrance, not a single Jewish student was granted admittance to study medicine.

Anti-Jewish laws now began to appear in the statute books of several countries. On 21 January 1938 Rumania formally abrogated the minority right of Jews, and revoked the citizenship of many Jews who had been resident there since the end of the war.

On 29 May 1938 the Hungarian Government passed its first law specifically restricting the number of Jews in the liberal professions, administration, commerce and industry to 20 per cent, while on 3 May 1939 a second 'Jewish Law' forbade any Hungarian Jew to become a judge, a lawyer, a schoolteacher, or a member of Parliament.

Such laws encouraged anti-semitism and led to violence. On 3 February 1939 a bomb thrown into a Budapest synagogue killed one worshipper and injured many more.

But it was in Poland that violence against the Jews was most widespread between 1935 and 1937. In every town and village shown on the map opposite, Jews were attacked in the streets, and Jewish houses and shops were broken up and looted. It was necessary, a Polish Jesuit periodical asserted in 1936, 'to provide separate schools for Jews, so that our children will not be infected with their lower moralty'. On 29 February 1936 Cardinal Hlond declared in a public letter: 'It is true that the Jews are committing frauds, practising usury, and dealing in white slavery. It is true that in schools, the influence of the Jewish youth upon the

Map 12

LITHUANIA

EAST
PRUSSIA

DANZIG

Suwalki

Grodno

Jasionowka

Lomza

Bialystok

Wysokie
Mazowieckie

Suraz

Bydgoszcz

Dybek

Stok

Bransk

Raciaz

Plonsk

Wloclawek

River Vistula

Serock

Sterdyn

Stoczek

Warsaw

Kaluszyn

Brest-Litovsk

Zyrardow

Otwock

Minsk
Mazowiecki

Lukow

River Bug

Warka

P O L A N D

Nowe Miasto

Odrzywol

Piotrkow

Przytyk

3

Opoczno

Kleszcow

Kamiensk

Lublin

Dzialoszyn

Przedborz

Radomsko

Czestochowa

79

Koniecpol

Jedrzejow

Jews killed
throughout Poland
between 1935 and 1937

Zarki

Imielno

Stawiany

Mierzwin

Stawy

5

Katowice

River Vistula

Lvov

0   miles   40

0   kilometres   60

Myslenice

© Martin Gilbert 1982

Catholic youth is generally evil, from a religious and ethical point of view. But let us be just. Not all Jews are like that. One does well to prefer his own kind in commercial dealings and to avoid Jewish stores and Jewish stalls in the markets, but it is not permissable to demolish Jewish businesses, break windows, torpedo their houses . . .'

On 9 March 1936, in the village of Przytyk *(above)*, the murder of three Jews sent further fears through Poland's three million Jews. A few days later, five Jews were murdered in the village of Stawy. Despite Jewish self-defence, as shown here in the Warsaw region and indicated by the star symbol, 79 Jews were killed, and 500 injured.

During 1937 there were further attacks on Jews throughout Poland: 350 attacks in August alone, and in Katowice bombs were thrown into Jewish-owned shops. Tens of thousands of Polish Jews emigrated: to France, Belgium, Holland and Palestine.

THE JEWS OF EASTERN AUSTRIA, 13 MARCH 1938

CZECHOSLOVAKIA

0   miles   20
0   kilometres   30

Gmund 40
Retz 45
Paysdorf 38
Laa 62
Hohenau 70
Horn 55
Mistelbach 95
Hollabrun 78
Angern 63
Stockerau 104
Krems 99
Klosterneuberg 227
Tulln 72
Vienna 176,034
Melk 10
Kittsee 62
St.Pölten 310
Modling 302
Bruck 42
Ybbs 130
Baden 1,108
Neusiedlersee
Amstetten 28
Bad Vöslau 99
Eisenstadt 225
Wiener Neustadt 685
AUSTRIA
Neunkirchen 204
Fruen-kirchen 386
Mattersburg 511
Kobbersdorf 172
Deutschkreuz 433
HUNGARY
Pinkafeld 34
Liessing 87
Bruck 12
Rechnitz 170
Leoben 130
Oberwart 138
Knittelfeld 26
Güssing 74
Judenburg 50
Graz 1,720

© Martin Gilbert 1982

ANTI-JEWISH RIOTS IN POLAND, APRIL-JUNE 1938

Baltic Sea
LITHUANIA
EAST PRUSSIA
Vilna 29 April
GREATER GERMANY
Warsaw 8 to 15 June
P O L A N D
SOVIET UNION
Dabrowa 15 April
Przemysl 13 June
CZECHOSLOVAKIA
EASTERN GALICIA
Tarnopol 11 and 12 June
0   miles   100
0   kilometres   150
Vienna
© Martin Gilbert 1982

Jews had lived in Austria since Roman time In 1867, following the abolition of all laws based on religious discrimination, Jews had risen to prominence in Austrian life and culture. They had come to Vienna from all over the Austro-Hungarian Empire, especially from the impoverished province of Eastern Galicia.

In 1919 the Treaty of St Germain guaranteed minority rights to the Jews of Austria. Most lived in Vienna (left), but as the map shows, some were to be found in the towns and villages of every region: the Austrian census of 22 March 1934 listed 769 localities with Jewish inhabitants.

Following the violent suppression of the Social Democrat parties in 1934, anti-Jewish discrimination grew, and Austrian Nazism was encouraged by the German Nazis in power across the border.

On 13 March 1938 Germany annexed Austria, and a further 183,000 Jews came under German rule. The activities of all Jewish organizations and congregations wer at once forbidden. Many Jewish leaders were imprisoned; several were taken to Dachau and murdered. The Great Synagogue of Vienna was first desecrated by organized hooligans, then 'occupied' by the German army. Many Jews were forced to turn their property over to the Gestapo. Individual Jews were seized in the streets, beaten, and even killed. More then 500 Jews, driven to despair, committed suicide.

In Poland a further spate of anti-Jewish activity broke out within three weeks of the imposition of Nazi rule in Austria (left, below). Starting in Dabrowa on April 15, hundreds of Jews had been injured, and much Jewish property destroyed.

From Poland, and from Greater Germany, which now included Austria, tens of thousands of Jews sought safety elsewhere (opposite, above). More than 85,000 Austrian Jews found havens in Britain, the United States, and in countries which were later to fall under Nazi rule. From Germany almost half of the country's 500,000 Jews emigrated or fled abroad (opposite, above), including more than 33,000 to Palestine, where they joined tens of thousands of recent Jewish immigrants from Poland. But on 5 July 1938, with the opening of the Evian Conference, it became clear that more and more countries wanted to restrict the number of Jewish refugees. The Australian delegate at Evian declared: 'since we have no racial problem, we are not desirous of importing one'.

JEWISH REFUGEES FIND HAVENS IN EUROPE, 1933-1938

0 miles 200
0 kilometres 300

NORWAY
2,000

SWEDEN
3,200

North
Sea

Baltic Sea

DENMARK
2,000

HOLLAND
30,000

Berlin

GREATER GERMANY

POLAND
25,000

UNITED
KINGDOM
52,000

BELGIUM
12,000

Cologne
Aachen

Trier

CZECHOSLOVAKIA
5,000

St.Germain

Vienna

FRANCE
30,000

Dachau

AUSTRIA

HUNGARY
3,000

Bay
of
Biscay

Evian

SWITZERLAND
7,000

YUGOSLAVIA
7,000

ITALY
5,000

Adriatic
Sea

to
PORTUGAL
10,000

SPAIN
3,000

© Martin Gilbert 1982

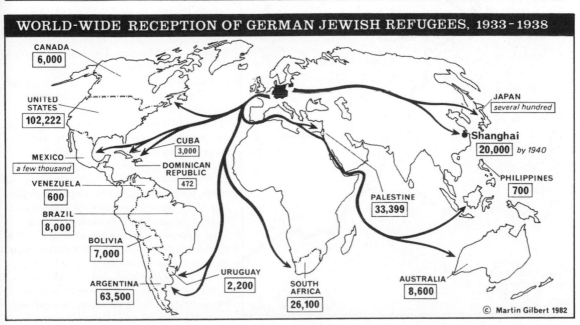

WORLD-WIDE RECEPTION OF GERMAN JEWISH REFUGEES, 1933-1938

CANADA
6,000

JAPAN
several hundred

UNITED
STATES
102,222

Shanghai
20,000 by 1940

CUBA
3,000

MEXICO
a few thousand

DOMINICAN
REPUBLIC
472

PHILIPPINES
700

VENEZUELA
600

BRAZIL
8,000

PALESTINE
33,399

BOLIVIA
7,000

URUGUAY
2,200

ARGENTINA
63,500

SOUTH
AFRICA
26,100

AUSTRALIA
8,600

© Martin Gilbert 1982

Map 17

JEWS IN THE WESTERN SUDETENLAND

GREATER GERMANY

SAXONY

Kraslice
66

Pernik
5

Abertamy
5

Nejdek
37

Ostrov
30

Chodov
54

Stara Role
19

Olovi
22

Rybare
292

As
51

Loket
55

Karlovy Vary
(Karlsbad)
2,120

Haslov
7

Lazne Frantiskovy
95

Cista
22

Cheb (Eger)
505

Becov
26

Okrouhlov
5

Mnichov
3

Marianske Lazne
(Marienbad)
495

CZECHOSLOVAKIA
SUDETENLAND

Broumov
68

Plana Chodova
13

Tachov
223

Cernosin
16

Tisova
10

Stribro
152

Flossenburg
concentration
camp

Rozvadov
17

Bor
35

Kladruby
21

Primda
3

Straz
45

GREATER

Velky Malahov
2

Bela
8

GERMANY

Blizejov
7

BOHEMIA

BAVARIA

Vseruby
44

0   miles   10

0   kilometres   20

© Martin Gilbert 1982

In October 1938, only six months after the German annexation of Austria, Germany annexed the Sudeten-German region of Czechoslovakia *(opposite)*. The area inside the broken line is shown in detail in the map on the left. Here, too, was a long-established Jewish community, whose origins went back in Cheb for example, to the thirteenth century.

Between the wars the Jews of the Sudetenland were protected by the democratic and egalitarian laws of Czechoslovakia, and were living in towns and villages throughout the region. The map on the left, based on the national census of 1930, shows the Jewish communities in the western areas. The largest of these towns, Karlsbad, known in Czech as Karlovy Vary, had long been a popular resort town and meeting place for Jews. Two Zionist Congresses had been held there in 1921 and 1923. At Marienbad, known in Czech as Marianske Lazne, Jewish doctors had contributed to the development of the spa, whose cures had been popular with Russian Jews during the nineteenth century. In 1937 the Great Assembly of the union of orthodox Jews had been held there.

Beginning in 1933, the Jews of the Sudetenland were increasingly harassed by local, German-speaking, Nazis. During the Sudeten crisis in the autumn of 1938, many synagogues were burned down, including the synagogues at both Cheb and Marienbad on September 23. As the Germans prepared to occupy the region, almost all the 20,000 Sudetenland Jews fled into the still independent Czechoslovak provinces of Bohemia and Moravia. Those who remained were arrested by the Nazis, and sent to concentration camps.

Following the German occupation of the Sudetenland in October 1938, the borders of Greater Germany, as shown opposite, were extended yet again. So too was the concentration camp system, with the opening of a new camp at Flossenbürg, and the enlargement of Dachau. Another new camp, Buchenwald, had been opened on 19 July 1937, for professional criminals. In June 1938 many political prisoners, including Jews, were sent there, followed shortly afterwards by a further 2,200 Austrian Jews.

The photograph shows a rollcall at Dachau in 1938. Often during such rollcalls the prisoners, Jews and non-Jews alike, were forced to stand for many hours, hungry and cold, and were savagely beaten if they fell.

Map 18

THE JEWS OF THE SUDETENLAND, OCTOBER 1938

Map 19

POLISH-BORN JEWS EXPELLED FROM GERMANY, 28 OCTOBER 1938

The next group of Jews to suffer under German policy were 15,000 Polish-born Jews who had been living and working in Germany for 10, 20 and even 30 years. Early in October 1938 the Polish Government announced that all Jews who had lived outside Poland for more than five years would have their passports revoked, and they would thereupon become 'stateless'. The Germans at once announced there would no longer be a place inside Germany for these 15,000 'stateless' Jews.

On October 18 these 15,000 Jews were forced to leave their homes throughout Germany, and to go, with only a single suitcase, to the nearest railway station. The rest of their belongings had to be left behind. Then they were taken through the night to the German-Polish border, and forced over the border at gun point.

At first the Polish Government was reluctant to take them in. Conditions, especially at the border town of Zbaszyn *(above)*, were appalling. Learning of this, a member of one of the families which had been expelled, a young man named Herszel Grynszpan, who was living in France, shot and killed a German diplomat in Paris.

Using the diplomat's death as their excuse, the Nazis launched a campaign of terror against all the Jews of Greater Germany. On 9 November 1938, in one night, the so-called 'night of broken glass', hundreds of synagogues were set on fire, Jewish shops looted, and Jews beaten up in the streets. By morning, 91 Jews had been killed. All the towns shown in the map opposite *(above)* were the scene of anti-Jewish violence, as were hundreds of smaller towns, villages and hamlets throughout Greater Germany.

The lower map shows the towns in one small region of Germany, with their Jewish populations of 1932. Each of these little communities was likewise attacked during the 'night of broken glass'.

The photograph shows the fire raging in the principal synagogue in Berlin.

DESTRUCTION OF THE SYNAGOGUES, 9 NOVEMBER 1938

North Sea

Baltic Sea

Kiel

Lübeck

Hamburg

Emden

Bremen

Stettin

Danzig

Königsberg

Allenstein

FREE CITY OF DANZIG

HOLLAND

Hanover

Brunswick

Berlin

Munster

Magdeburg

POLAND

Essen

GREATER GERMANY

Dusseldorf

Glogau

Cologne

Leipzig

Liegnitz

BELGIUM

Bonn

Dresden

Breslau

Oppeln

Coblenz

Chemnitz

Hindenburg

91
Jews killed

Plauen

SUDETENLAND

Gleiwitz

Frankfurt

Darmstadt

Wurzburg

Karlsbad

CZECHOSLOVAKIA

LUXEMBOURG

Mannheim

Furth

Saarbrücken

Karlsruhe

Nuremberg

FRANCE

Ulm

Augsburg

Freiburg

Constance

Munich

Linz

Baden

Salzburg

Bad Vöslau

Wiener Neustadt

Eisenstadt

Innsbruck

AUSTRIA

Graz

HUNGARY

SWITZERLAND

Klagenfurt

0   miles   100

0   kilometres   160

© Martin Gilbert 1982

JEWS OF THE DARMSTADT REGION

Gross-Gerau
200

Grafenhausen
44

Langen
80

Egelsbach
52

Babenhausen
52

Dieburg
271

Darmstadt
1,646

Gross-Umstadt
60

Pfungstadt

Gross-Bieberau
48

Ober-Ramstadt

Höchst

Wolfskehlen
3

Crumbach

Bad König

Reichelsheim
115

Michelstadt

Bensheim
180

Rimbach
85

Lorsch
70

Heppenheim

Birkenau
37

0   mile   10

0   kilometres   20

© Martin Gilbert 1982

14

Map 22

JEWS SENT TO CONCENTRATION CAMPS, 10 NOVEMBER 1938

Immediately following the 'night of broken glass', more than 35,000 Jews were seized throughout Germany, and sent to concentration camps, bringing to more than 60,000 the total number of Jews in the camps *(above)*. Hundreds died of ill-treatment, including 244 at Buchenwald alone in the first month of their imprisonment. Hundreds more committed suicide as a result of the harsh conditions and the brutality of the guards.

In March 1939 Hitler ordered his armies to enter the Bohemian and Moravian provinces of Czechoslovakia *(opposite, below)*. Tens of thousands of Jews were trapped, many of them refugees from Germany and Austria who had fled to Bohemia and Moravia a year before. Other Jews fled from Slovakia to Poland, as the Slovak province, where anti-semitic activities had been growing, declared its independence.

Jews had first been mentioned in Prague in AD 970, the first settled community in 1091. They survived repeated expulsions in the seventeenth century, to enjoy religious liberty and their own civil jurisdiction by 1700. Forbidden to follow many of the trades of the time, they had come to excel as

THE JEWS OF THE PRAGUE REGION

SUDETENLAND

Citov 9
Repin 3
Melnik 113
Spomysl 11
Bysice 4
Cernuc 1
Obristri 6
Nova Ves 37
Vstetaty 19
Zlonice 15
Velvary 57
Veltrusy 9
Tisice 5
Neratovice 12
Neumerice 6
Kralupy 52
Slany 111
Libcice 2
Klicany 12
Mratin 5
Brandysek 9
Velen 3
Brandys 69
Roztoky 7
Kladno 257
Bustehrad 10
Kysice 3
Hostoun 24
Prague 31,571
Unhost 24
Hostivice 6
Kolodeje 3
Mecholupy 18
Dubec 12
Ujezd Cerveny 8
Chodov 54
Chynava 4
Radotin 38
Ricany 41
Cernosice 6
Zbraslav 50
Beroun 133
Dobrihovice 12
Strancice 3
Revnice 24
Liten 11
Svinare 10
Davle 9
Vizina 4
Mnisek 15
Privoz 2
Kamenny 2
Pysely 12
Cisovice 4
Novaves 37
Tynec 3
Hostomice 68
Slapy 10

miles 10
kilometres 15

© Martin Gilbert 1982

BOHEMIA AND MORAVIA ANNEXED, 15 MARCH 1939

North Sea
Baltic Sea
MEMEL
DANZIG
EAST PRUSSIA
Berlin
RUHR
GREATER GERMANY
POLAND
SUDETENLAND
Prague
SAAR
SUDETENLAND
BOHEMIA
MORAVIA
RUTHENIA
SLOVAKIA
BAVARIA
Vienna
HUNGARY
AUSTRIA

miles 100
kilometres 200

© Martin Gilbert 1982

THE JEWS OF MEMEL, 21 MARCH 1939

miles 30
kilometres 40

Memel 2,470
LITHUANIA
7,000
Baltic Sea
MEMELLAND
River Nieman
River Nova
GREATER GERMANY
EAST PRUSSIA
Königsberg

© Martin Gilbert 1982

shoemakers, tailors, hatters, furriers and goldsmiths. Jewish musicians often played at banquets in the palaces of the nobility. Known as excellent fire-fighters, a group of 400 Jewish firemen were present at all festivities, and at coronations. But no Jew was allowed to call himself a citizen of Prague, and outside the Jewish quarter all Jews were compelled to wear yellow badges and peaked yellow hats.

Slowly, the situation improved: in 1677 a royal edict had been issued against throwing stones at Jews. By 1800 Prague had become a centre of Hebrew printing, learning and scholarship, and in the century before 1938 the Jews of Prague knew emancipation, cultural vitality, prosperity, and hope.

When German troops entered Prague on 15 March 1939, the city's 31,571 Jews, ten per cent of the total population, had been joined by a further 25,000 refugees from the towns and villages of Bohemia shown here *(above, left)*, whose Jewish populations are given according to the census of 1930.

Thousands of Czech Jews sought to escape, both by legal and illegal means. By the end of 1939 more than 19,000 had succeeded in leaving Europe altogether. But the rest were trapped.

Six days after the German occupation of Prague, Hitler sent his forces into Memel *(above, right)*. Here, the local Jewish community could trace its origins back to the sixteenth century. In 1924 Memel had become an autonomous region under Lithuanian sovereignty. Its minorities were protected by the League of Nations. By 1939, the 2,470 Jews of Memel had been joined by 7,000 Lithuanian Jews.

With the German occupation of Memel, most Jews fled into Lithuania.

Map 26

THE GERMAN INVASION OF POLAND, 1 SEPTEMBER - 5 OCTOBER 1939

17

Map 27

THE JEWS OF RURAL POLAND ON THE EVE OF WAR: A SAMPLE

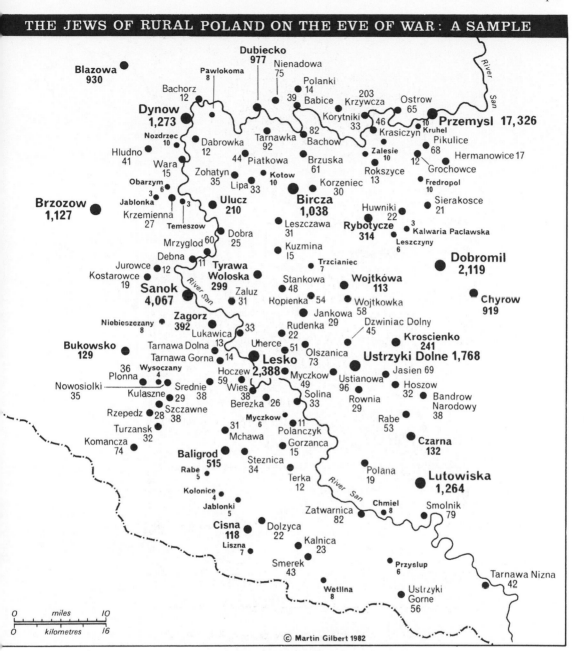

Blazowa 930

Dubiecko 977

Pawlokoma 8

Nienadowa 75

Bachorz 12

Polanki 14

Babice

Krzywcza 203

Ostrow 65

Dynow 1,273

Korytniki 33

Przemysl 17,326

Nozdrzec 10

Tarnawka 92

Bachow 82

Krasiczyn 46

Kruhel 10

Dabrowka 12

Piatkowa 44

Brzuska 61

Zalesie 10

Pikulice 68

Hludno 41

Wara 15

Zohatyn 35

Kotow 10

Rokszyce 13

12

Hermanowice 17

Grochowce

Obarzym 3 6

Lipa 33

Korzeniec 30

Fredropol 10

Brzozow 1,127

Jablonka

Krzemienna 27

Ulucz 210

Bircza 1,038

Huwniki 22

Sierakosce 21

3

Temeszow

Leszczawa 31

Rybotycze 314

Kalwaria Paclawska

Mrzyglod 60

Dobra 25

Kuzmina 15

Leszczyny 6

Debna

11

Trzciniec 7

Dobromil 2,119

Jurowce 12

Tyrawa Woloska 299

Stankowa 48

Wojtkowa 113

Kostarowce 19

Sanok 4,067

Zaluz 31

Ropienka 54

Wojtkowka

Chyrow 919

Zagorz 392

Jankowa 58

Dzwiniac Dolny 45

Niebieszczany 8

Lukawica 13

33

Rudenka 22

Kroscienko 241

Bukowsko 129

Tarnawa Dolna

Uherce 51

Olszanica 73

Ustrzyki Dolne 1,768

Tarnawa Gorna 14

Lesko 2,388

36

Wysoczany 4

Hoczew 59

Myczkow 49

Ustianowa 96

Jasien 69

Plonna

Wies 38

Solina 33

Hoszow 32

Bandrow Narodowy 38

Nowosiolki 35

Kulaszne 29

Srednie 38

Berezka 26

Rownia 29

Rzepedz 28

Szczawne 38

Myczkow 6

Polanczyk 11

Rabe 53

Turzansk 32

Mchawa 31

Gorzanca 15

Czarna 132

Komancza 74

Baligrod 515

Steznica 34

Polana 19

Lutowiska 1,264

Rabe 5

Terka 12

Kolonice 4

Jablonki 5

Zatwarnica 82

Chmiel 8

Smolnik 79

Cisna 118

Dolzyca 22

Kalnica 23

Liszna 7

Smerek 43

Przyslup 6

Tarnawa Nizna 42

Wetlina 8

Ustrzyki Gorne 56

0 miles 10

0 kilometres 16

© Martin Gilbert 1982

On 1 September 1939 the German army invaded Poland, advancing across a land where Jews had lived for over 800 years. The map above shows the number of Jews living in a small area of Poland, which in September 1939, was on one of the lines of advance of the German army as it drove through Poland.

The map on the left shows the main line of advance of the German army: the thicker arrows show the advance in the first five days of September, the thinner arrows, the advance in the next two weeks.

Rapid though the German advance was, the Polish forces fought with skill and bravery at many points, checking the German forces in a series of fierce battles. During the fighting, more than sixty thousand Polish soldiers were killed, of whom some 6,000 were Jews. In addition 3,000 Jewish civilians were among those killed during the bombing of Warsaw.

Map 28

POLAND'S LARGEST JEWISH COMMUNITIES ON THE EVE OF WAR

Baltic Sea

Vilna
55,006 *28%*
14th century

Bialystok
39,165 *45%*
18th century

Grodno
21,159 *42%*
14th century

Pinsk
20,220 *75%*
16th century

Lodz
202,497 *33%*
18th century

Warsaw
352,659 *29%*
15th century

Siedlce
14,685 *48%*
16th century

Brest-Litovsk
21,440 *52%*
14th century

Kalisz
16,220 *35%*
12th century

Miedzyrzec
12,000 *75%*
17th century

Kowel
12,785 *61%*
16th century

Radom
25,159 *23%*
17th century

Lublin
38,937 *35%*
14th century

Czestochowa
28,486 *30%*
18th century

Chelm
13,537 *47%*
15th century

Luck
17,366 *48%*
10th century

Rowne
22,737 *71%*
16th century

Kielce
18,083 *40%*
16th century

Bedzin
21,625 *45%*
17th century

Przemysl
17,326 *34%*
14th century

Lvov
99,595 *33%*
14th century

Sosnowiec
20,805 *22%*
19th century

Tarnopol
14,000 *44%*
16th century

Tarnow
19,330 *44%*
15th century

Cracow
56,515 *26%*
14th century

Drohobycz
17,000 *44%*
15th century

Kolomyja
15,000 *33%*
16th century

Rzeszow
14,000 *36%*
15th century

Stanislawow
24,823 *41%*
17th century

0   miles   100

0   kilometres 100

© Martin Gilbert 1982

The map above shows those Polish cities with 12,000 or more Jewish inhabitants at the time of the census of 1931. Also given is the percentage of Jews among the total population of the town.

On the map opposite are some of the towns in which, from the first days of the German occupation, Jews were singled out for abuse, violence, and death. The figures show only some of those killed, mostly in savage attacks on Jews at prayer, or in random shootings. Thousands of Jews, and thousands of non-Jews, were killed during these early days of German rule. Jews, who formed a tenth of the Polish population, accounted for nearly a third of those killed. The photograph, taken by a German soldier shows a typical incident, 'mocking a Jew'.

Map 29

GERMAN ATROCITIES AGAINST JEWS, 2 SEPTEMBER-13 NOVEMBER 1939

Bydgoszcz

Aleksandrow
60
September 7
16
September 16

Nowe-Miasto
7
September 14

Pultusk
14
September 14

Wloclawek

River Vistula

River Bug

Ostrow **30**
September 8
560
September 11

Wyszkow
65
September 11

Wegrow
Siedlce
20
September 20

Minsk
Mazowiecki

Of **16,336** *Polish civilians executed in 714 localities, in the first six weeks of the war, at least* **5,000** *were Jews*

Ozorkow
24
September 5
Zgierz
7
September 7

Warsaw
53
November 13

Rawa
Mazowiecka
23 *September 10*

Lukow
100
September 19

Laskarzew
20
September 17

Turek
15

Zloczew **80** *September 4*

Sieradz
33 *September 20*

Zdunska Wola
3 *September 3*

P O L A N D

Wieruszow
17
September 3

Kruszyna
12 *September 4*
Lelow
4 *September 3*
Czermno **3** *September 12*

Konskie
20 *September 4*
20 *September 12*

**GREATER
GERMANY**

SILESIA

Czestochowa **180**
September 3

Zarki **90** *September 4*

Bedzin

Wolbrom

Tarnobrzeg
5

River Vistula

River San

Mielec
35
September 13

Strzyzow
4 *September 15*

0 miles 40
0 kilometres 60

© Martin Gilbert 1982

Sosnowiec
13
September 4

Trzebinia
37
September 8

Karwodrza
12 *September 11*

14 *September 15*

Map 30

THE JEWS OF DANZIG, 1-17 SEPTEMBER 1939

Following the German invasion of Poland, and even while that invasion was in progress, German troops entered the Free City of Danzig, which was immediately annexed to the German Reich. With the dominance of the local Nazi Party in Danzig in 1937, many of Danzig's 9,000 Jews had managed to emigrate to western Europe, Britain, the United States and Palestine. But more than 5,000 Jews, many of them old people, were trapped in the city as the German army entered on 1 September 1939 (above).

On September 2, as German control was imposed throughout the Danzig territory, a concentration camp was opened at Stutthof, and two weeks later several hundred leading Danzig Jews, including the writer and journalist, Jacob Lange, and the cantor of the Danzig synagogue, Leopold Shufflan, were deported there. Within a week most of them had died as a result of deliberate brutality.

On September 9, while German troops still battled with Polish forces, all Jewish men in the small Ruhr town of Gelsenkirchen (opposite, above) were deported to the concentration camp of Sachsenhausen, near Berlin. Of the original Jewish community of 1,400 in 1933, nearly 700 had managed to emigrate by 1939. Now, scarcely a week after the outbreak of war, the men were sent eastwards, and the women and children left to fend for themselves.

By the end of the German-Polish campaign, 6,000 Jewish soldiers had been killed and as many as 400,000 Polish soldiers had been captured, of whom some 61,000 were Jews. The Jews were at once separated from the Poles: thousands were sent to prisoner-of-war camps inside Germany, where they were denied the basic rights of prisoners-of-war and treated instead as if they were concentration camp inmates, with less rations than other prisoners, forced to do especially heavy work. At Lamsdorf 5,000 Jewish prisoners were housed in barns, 700 or 800 to each barn, without any floor covering, and one loaf of bread had to be shared by six or eight men. At Rathorn the two days' ration for five men was one loaf of bread and half a jar of soup. At Stablack, as a result of savage beatings by the German overseers at the various construction works to which they

THE GELSENKIRCHEN DEPORTATION, 9 SEPTEMBER 1939

North Sea

Baltic Sea

Danzig

EAST PRUSSIA

HOLLAND

Sachsenhausen
concentration camp

Berlin

Warsaw

Gelsenkirchen

300

Lodz

RUHR

BELGIUM

RHINELAND

G R E A T E R
G E R M A N Y

Breslau

POLAND

SILESIA

BOHEMIA

Prague

Cracow

MORAVIA

0 miles 100
0 kilometres 160

© Martin Gilbert 1982

JEWISH PRISONERS-OF-WAR IN GERMANY, 1939–1940

North Sea

Baltic Sea

EAST PRUSSIA
Stablack

Hammerstein

Danzig

Neubrandenberg

Stargard

Insterburg

Berlin

River Vistula

Alten Grabow

Gelsenkirchen
Dortmund
Rathorn

Luckenwalde

POLAND
conquered 1 September – 5 October 1939

River Elbe

River Oder

River Rhine

Hammer
Limburg

6,000
Jewish soldiers killed

Frankenthal

61,000
Jewish soldiers taken prisoner

Lamsdorf

and many of these prisoners-of-war deported

Nuremberg

Moosburg

0 miles 80
0 kilometres 10

© Martin Gilbert 1982

were sent, 10 to 15 Jews died each day. At Neubrandenburg the German commander issued instructions in October 1939 to the effect that all 'Aryan' prisoners-of-war were entitled to the uniforms and personal effects of their fellow Jewish prisoners. As a result, the Jews were sent to work half-naked and barefoot, and many of them froze to death.

These Jewish prisoners-of-war were among the first victims of a Nazi policy that, while severe at all times against conquered peoples, singled out Jews for particularly savage treatment. For the fate of some surviving Jewish prisoners-of-war in 1944 and 1945, see pages 191, 198 and 204.

Map 33

THE GERMAN-SOVIET PARTITION OF POLAND, 28 SEPTEMBER 1939

SWEDEN

Baltic Sea

Memel

LATVIA

LITHUANIA
annexed by
Lithuania

Swieciany

Vilna

2,400

Königsberg

Danzig

EAST
PRUSSIA

S

Lida

Grodno

Bydgoszcz

Poznan

Pultusk

Lomza

Wolkowysk

Bialystok

Baranowicze

annexed by
Germany
678,000

Warsaw

Brest-
Litovsk

Pinsk

SOVIET
UNION

Kalisz

Lodz

Siedlce

250,000
escape
eastward

annexed by
the Soviet Union
1,309,000

GREATER
GERMANY

Wielun

Radom

Lublin

VOLHYNIA

Luck

Rowne

GENERAL
GOVERNMENT
1,139,000

Chelm

Zamosc

UPPER
SILESIA

20,000
escape
southward

Bielsko

Cracow

Tarnow

Lvov

Brody

S = Suwalki region
of Poland.
2,400 Jews
expelled to
Lithuania

PROTECTORATE OF
BOHEMIA & MORAVIA

Dynow

Przemysl

Tarnopol

AUSTRIA

SLOVAKIA

EASTERN
GALICIA

Stanislawow

RUTHENIA

Kolomyja

RUMANIA

- - - The frontiers of Poland
between 1918 and 1939

HUNGARY

0   miles   50

——— The eastern frontier of Greater
Germany from October 1939

0   kilometres   75
© Martin Gilbert 1982

On 28 September 1939 Poland was partitioned between Nazi Germany and the Soviet Union, while Lithuania annexed the Vilna region. In the following two months, before the border was sealed, more than a quarter of a million Jews escaped from the German to the Soviet side. These Jews were to constitute the majority of the survivors of Polish Jewry by the end of the war *(page 229)*.

The map above shows the number of Jews living in the three principal divisions of Poland at the time of the German invasion. With the eastward extension of the frontiers of Greater Germany, nearly two million more Jews were brought under German rule: four times the number of Jews who had been living in Germany when Hitler came to power in January 1933.

The first German acts of terror in Poland had been the September murders *(page 20)*. Now a new policy was put briefly and brutally into operation: expulsion. The figures shown on the map opposite give some of the main expulsions eastward, where figures are available. By the end of 1939, tens of thousands of Jews had been driven to the border rivers and forced to swim them. Hundreds had been drowned as they tried to cross. Others had been shot and killed as they swam.

Of the 1,800 Jews driven from Chelm, only 400 survived the perils of expulsion. Hundreds of others were denied refuge at the last moment when Soviet soldiers refused to allow them to cross into Soviet territory.

Map 34

JEWS MURDERED, OR DRIVEN EASTWARD DURING OCTOBER 1939

Ostrolenka

Przasnysz

Bialystok

River Narew

7,000

Ostrow

Pultusk

8,300

Wyszkow

Kaluszyn

Warsaw

Brest-Litovsk

River Vistula

*annexed by
Germany*

*annexed by
the Soviet Union*

Kowel

River Bug

Chelm

1,800

of whom 1,400

*were murdered
on the march*

Hrubieszow

Luck

Tarnobrzeg

3,800

Rozwadow

Sokal

River Vistula

Lezajsk

2,000

Lancut

10,000   Jaroslaw

River San

Przemysl

Lvov

over 500 *murdered
between 14 and 28 September
before the Germans handed the
city to the Russians.
Among the dead*

Dr. Asscher Gitter

and other leading citizens

Rymanow

1,000

Sanok

| 0 | *miles* | 40 |
| 0 | *kilometres* | 60 |

S L O V A K I A

HUNGARY

© Martin Gilbert 1982

Map 35

JEWISH PRISONERS-OF-WAR AND NON-JEWISH CIVILIANS MURDERED, 1939-1940

GREATER
EAST
PRUSSIA

BIALYSTOK
REGION

River Narew

Lomza
assembly point

Zambrow
assembly point
250

950

annexed by
the

Soviet

Union

Wegrow

Bielany
25

Wawer
107

Warsaw
233

Krosniewice
transit camp

Siedlce

Biala Podlaska
200

River Bug

116

Zyrardow
transit camp

annexed by
Germany

Okrzeja
300

GENERAL

Bronislawow
70

GOVERNMENT

Parczew
480

Krolowiec
133

Lubartow

Wlodawa
320

Radom
transit camp

Skloby
360

Chlewiska
40

Lublin
880

Szalas
300

Skarzysko-Kamienna
300

Jozefow
44

© Martin Gilbert 1982

WARTHEGAU

River Vistula

In the opening months of the Second World War the Germans particularly ill-treated Jewish soldiers who had been taken prisoner while fighting with the Polish army. Some were sent to Germany *(page 22)*. Others, kept in Poland, were also treated savagely from the first days of their capture. Those at the assembly points of Lomza and Zambrow *(above)* were to be transferred under German escort to the German side of the partition line. But of the 1,200 assembled at Zambrow, 250 were murdered on the spot.

At the transit camp at Zyrardow, the Jewish prisoners-of-war were kept in the local stadium for 10 days without food, surviving only because local Poles managed to throw food in to them. On the Day of Atonement, 24 September 1939, these Jewish prisoners-of-war were forced to clean the latrines with their bare hands, and treated with particular brutality.

Another group that suffered terribly were the Jewish soldiers whom the Germans took prisoner during the Polish campaign, whose birthplaces were in those parts of eastern Poland which had just been annexed by the Soviet Union. One train load was brought to Wlodawa, to be sent eastward across the border; 200 had died of hunger or had frozen to death during the journey from central Poland. Near Wlodawa, the survivors were made to take the corpses out of the train. The SS guards then opened fire, killing 120 more of the prisoners.

A further group of Polish Jewish prisoners-of-war was brought to Lublin. They were told that they were to be sent to Soviet Russia. On the march northwards, ostensibly towards the border, almost all of them were killed. The survivors were held in the prisoner-of-war camp at Biala Podlaska, where another 200, denied medical attention, died of typhus. Extreme brutality against Jewish prisoners-of-war was also

Map 36

recorded at transit camps set up at Krosniewice, Zyrardow and Radom.

Thousands of non-Jews, as well as Jews, suffered cruelty during these early days of the German occupation of western Poland. Between September 1939 and June 1940, in each of the towns and villages shown in small type *(left)*, Polish civilians were shot, some at random, some because they were the political, religious, or intellectual leaders of their community: as many as 360 at Skloby. As with the killing of Jews, the method was barbaric. At Szalas, for example, all 300 males over the age of 15 were seized, many machine-gunned, and the rest locked in a school which was then set on fire. The list, even for the region shown here, is incomplete. Elsewhere in the occupied regions, the scale of killing of non-Jews was similar; more than 16,000 in the first month and a half of the occupation *(page 20)*, and continually increasing during 1940. At Torun *(right)*, twelve young boys aged 11 to 16 were shot as a reprisal for the breaking of a window in the local police station.

On 12 December 1939 two years' forced labour was made compulsory for all Jewish males between the ages of 14 and 60. Labour camps were set up throughout the General Government and in the Warthegau *(right)*. At first Jews were seized in the streets in order to fill the camps. Later, organized conscription took place. Many died in the camps of brutality, and exhaustion. The photograph shows part of the barracks of one such labour camp, near Dabrowa.

EASTERN LABOUR CAMPS BY JANUARY 1940

Baltic Sea

LITHUANIA

0 miles 60
0 kilometres 100

Danzig
1 camp
GREATER DANZIG AND WEST PRUSSIA

GREATER EAST PRUSSIA

THE SOVIET UNION

Bydgoszcz
4 camps
Torun

Poznan
25 camps

WARTHEGAU

Lodz
6 camps

Warsaw
14 camps

THE GENERAL GOVERNMENT

VOLHYNIA

GREATER   GERMANY

SILESIA

Lublin
28 camps

Kielce
21 camps

Dabrowa Gornicza
6 camps

EAST UPPER SILESIA

BOHEMIA & MORAVIA

Cracow
12 camps

Rzeszow
10 camps

EASTERN GALICIA

SLOVAKIA

RUTHENIA

HUNGARY

© Martin Gilbert 1982

Map 37

'LUBLINLAND' DEPORTATIONS, OCTOBER 1939 – APRIL 1940

North Sea

Baltic Sea

Stralsund
15 February 1940

Hamburg
21 October 1939

Schneidemühl [160]
12 March 1940

Stettin
15 February 1940
[1,000]

THE
SOVIET
UNION

Ciechocinek
Inowroclaw • Nieszawa
Poznan • Gniezno
Lipno
Warsaw
Konin

GREATER
GERMANY

Kalisz

Lodz

Lublin
Piaski
Belzyce • Glusk
Zarzecze

Moravska
Ostrava
17 October 1939

Nisko

[95,000]
in Lublinland
in April 1940

Prague
26 October 1939

Brno
26 October
1939

SLOVAKIA

0 miles 80
0 kilometres 140

© Martin Gilbert 1982

Vienna
20 October 1939

Even before the new German-Soviet border had been fixed, the Germans were planning to drive the Jews from hundreds of towns and villages in the nearly annexed territories. As Hitler himself declared: 'Out with them from all the professions and into the ghetto with them: fence them in somewhere, where they can perish as they deserve.'

On 21 September 1939 it was decreed that all communities with less than 500 Jews were to be dissolved, and that the Jews were hereafter to live in certain restricted areas in the larger cities, or in a special area set aside for them in the poor village region between Lublin and Nisko, the so-called 'Lublinland reservation' *(above)*.

Even Jews waiting at Hamburg for the next ship to the United States, then neutral, were deported eastwards, as shown here. Also deported were Jews from Vienna, from three former Czechoslovak towns, Prague, Brno and Moravska Ostrava, as well as from the Baltic ports of Stralsund and Stettin.

By the end of the winter, lacking proper housing, food or medical help, hundreds, if not thousands of these deportees to Lublinland had died. Others worked in harsh conditions, savagely beaten by guards, in a forced labour camp set up near Zarzecze, and many died. Some, who managed to escape eastwards into the Soviet Union, were immediately deported to labour camps in Siberia, where many of them also died.

Meanwhile, on 30 October 1939, the

JEWS WEST OF OZORKOW

0 miles 7
0 kilometres 12

Drzewce 3
Besiekiery 12
Zalesie 3
Grabow 31
Chelmno 33
Siedlec 4
Chorki 6
Blonie 13
Leczyca 4,051
Dabie 1,163
Wilczkowice 5
Topola 14
Stawiszyn 672
Jankow 5
Ozorkow 4,949
Uniejow 1,100
Niewiesz 10
Parzeczew 174
River Warta
Druzbin 4
Poddebice 1,333
Bratkow 16
River Ner

© Martin Gilbert 1982

RURAL JEWS EXPELLED, OCTOBER 1939

0 miles 15
0 kilometres 20

Wloclawek 4,000

River Vistula

Kutno 7,000

Dabie

W A R T H E G A U

Leczyca

Uniejow

Ozorkow 4,700

River Warta

Poddebice

Lodz 162,000

Pabianice 8,500

Zdunska Wola 10,000

Zelow 4,500

Belchatow 5,500

Wielun 4,000

GENERAL GOVERNMENT

© Martin Gilbert 1982

head of the SS, Heinrich Himmler, had fixed the following three months as the period during which all Jews had to be cleared out of the rural areas of western Poland. In the Poznan region, 50 communities were at once uprooted: seven of them are named opposite.

From Lodz, hundreds of women, children and old people were deported eastward by train in sealed freight-cars, mostly to the Lublin region. At the same time, Jews living in the rural areas of western Poland were forced to leave their homes, taking with them only what they could carry in sacks or bundles, and to go to the towns and cities shown on the right-hand map. An idea of the numbers of those uprooted can be seen in the boxes: 4,700 Jews, for example, were forced into the city of Ozorkow, bringing the total population to more than 9,000. Hundreds of communities were involved: those from the region west of Ozorkow are shown above. In some of the smaller villages, such as Drzewce, there was only a single Jewish family. They too were driven out. In one of these villages, Chelmno, lived a total of 33 Jews, all of whom were forced to leave. Just over a year later, their village became the site of the first death camp (page 69).

In the cities to which Jews were driven, overcrowding was severe. Poverty followed swiftly for tens of thousands of families, already stripped of their possessions, and now without a livelihood. The photograph (left) is of one such deportee, a Jewish boy in Lublin.

POLISH JEWS EXPELLED FROM WESTERN POLAND, SEPTEMBER - NOVEMBER 1939

Baltic   Sea

Strzelno
1

Puck
31

Wejherowo
62

Chylonia
5

Gulf
of
Danzig

Borders of 1919
to 1939

POMERANIA

THE POLISH CORRIDOR

Kartuzy
35

Danzig

Skarszewy
40

Tczew
93

EAST
PRUSSIA

Koscierzyna

Zblewo
12

Starogard
125

Brusy
24

Karsin
3

Gniew
20

Czersk
5

Skorcz
19

Chojnice
110

POLAND

Nowe
31

Lubawa
26

Kamien
12

Osie
26

Tuchola
118

Grudziadz
297

Lasin
23

Nowe
Miasto
61

Sepolno
183

Bukowiec
12

Swiecie
171

Radzyn
12

Sypniewo
3

Chelmno
74

Lisewo
9

Brodnica
56

Dziadlowo
35

Wiebork
64

Wabrzezno
92

Lidzbark
60

Chelmza
72

Gorzno
1

Golub
104

Torun
354

Mlyniec
3

0 miles 5
0 kilometres 40

© Martin Gilbert 1982

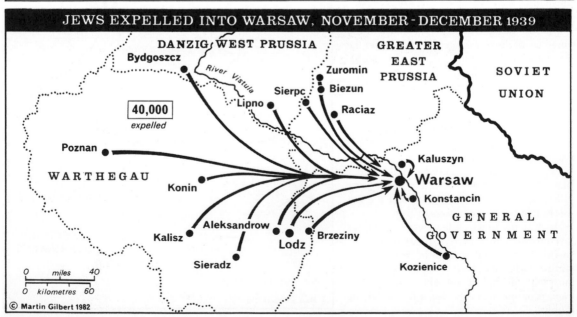

JEWS EXPELLED INTO WARSAW, NOVEMBER - DECEMBER 1939

DANZIG-WEST PRUSSIA

GREATER
EAST
PRUSSIA

SOVIET
UNION

Bydgoszcz

River Vistula

Zuromin

Sierpc

Biezun

Lipno

Raciaz

40,000
expelled

Poznan

Kaluszyn

WARTHEGAU

Konin

Warsaw

Konstancin

Kalisz

Aleksandrow

Brzeziny

GENERAL
GOVERNMENT

Lodz

Sieradz

Kozienice

0 miles 40
0 kilometres 60

© Martin Gilbert 1982

As the eastward expulsion of Jews continued, incredible distress was caused, both in the uprooting of settled communities, and in the disruption of life in the towns to which they were sent. The German plan was carefully prepared and ruthlessly pursued. As Hitler had made clear to the Reichstag on 6 October 1939, strict measures were needed for what he described as 'adapting and regulating the Jewish problem'. By the end of January 1940 some 78,000 Polish Jews had been driven out of their homes.

The map on the right shows the new German administrative division, and the first three provinces – Greater Danzig and West Prussia, Greater East Prussia, and the Warthegau – from which Jews were expelled during the first few months of the German conquest of Poland. The map below, with figures for the number of inhabitants at the time of the 1931 census, shows how Jews from the city of Poznan, and from several of the villages around it, were first driven westwards to a central collecting point, then eastwards into the General Government, and then dispersed. Also dispersed were the Polish Jews of the new Greater Danzig region *(opposite, above)*. This region had been part of the German Empire before 1914.

But the largest single destination for those who had been uprooted was Warsaw *(opposite, below)*, a city that was already the home of more than 350,000 Jews.

DEPORTATION REGIONS

© Martin Gilbert 1982

THE FIRST WARTHEGAU EXPULSIONS, 7 NOVEMBER 1939

Szubin 77
Wagrowiec 206
Budzyn 21
Znin 134
Wronki 187
Inowroclaw 252
Buk 70
Poznan 2,088
Grodzisk 61
Sochaczew
Warsaw
WARTHEGAU
GENERAL GOVERNMENT
Lodz
Piotrkow
Radom
SILESIA
Kielce

© Martin Gilbert 1982

As the Polish expulsions continued, ancient communities were dispersed. The map above shows the first expulsions from Kalisz, where Jews had first come from the Rhineland more than seven centuries before. In 1919, at the beginning of Polish rule, two Kalisz Jews had been killed by local anti-semites (page 2). At the outbreak of the Second World War, 20,000 Jews in the town made up almost half the population. Of those expelled, some 7,000 Kalisz Jews reached Warsaw by the end of the year. But more than 1,000 able-bodied men were sent to a nearby labour camp at Kozminek.

In April 1940 the German army moved again, northwards into Denmark and Norway (left). In Denmark, 6,000 Jews were left unmolested at the insistence of the Danish authorities, as were the 1,400 Jewish refugees who had reached Denmark from Germany, Austria and Czechoslovakia, in 1938 and 1939. In Norway (right), some 1,400 Norwegian Jews, and about 300 refugees, were likewise unmolested, but only for six months. In October 1940 they were forbidden to continue in all academic or other professions. There were, however, none of the killings, beatings, forced labour and expulsion which had become daily events in German-occupied Poland.

Map 46

THE JEWS OF NORWAY AT THE TIME OF THE GERMAN INVASION

Arctic Ocean

FINNMARK 7

TROMS 22

NORDLAND 13

North Atlantic Ocean

NORWAY

SWEDEN
neutral

NORD-TRÖNDELAG 1

SOR TRÖNDELAG 227

MORE 34

HEDMARK

OPLAND 3

14

Gulf of Bothnia

Bergen 27

BUSKERUD 25

Oslo 749

AKERSHUS 134

TELEMARK 5

OSTFOLD 38

Baltic Sea

ROGALAND 10

AUST-AGDER 1

VESTFOLD 50

VEST-AGDER 4

© Martin Gilbert 1982

0 miles 80
0 kilometres 100

32

Map 47

THE FIRST DEPORTATION TO AUSCHWITZ, 14 JUNE 1940

Lines of German advance
4-14 June 1940

Areas conquered by
Germany by 14 June 1940

© Martin Gilbert 1982

On 10 May 1940 the German army invaded Holland, Belgium, Luxembourg and France *(above)*. Within five weeks, on June 14, as German forces approached Paris, yet another concentration camp was being set up in German-occupied Poland. Situated just outside the town of Auschwitz, it was intended as a punishment camp for Polish political prisoners, not as a concentration camp for Jews. But in order to prepare the old barracks, 300 Jewish forced labourers had been brought from Auschwitz town.

The first inmates were mostly non-Jewish Poles, 728 in all, from a prison in Tarnow. Many of them had been caught at the eastern border trying to get to France through Hungary. Other Poles taken in that first train to Auschwitz were schoolteachers and priests. Three Jews were also among these first inmates: Emil Wieder and Isaac Holzer, both lawyers, and Maximilian Rosenbusch,

the Director of the Hebrew school in Tarnow. As the deportees' train was passing through Cracow, they heard the station announcer report the fall of Paris.

Like all concentration camp inmates, these first Auschwitz prisoners were put to forced labour, often doing heavy work that was not needed, such as digging ditches. At times they were tormented by having to queue on their knees for their daily bowl of soup. After the first successful escape, on July 6, there was a punitive 20-hour rollcall. After a second escape on October 28, a rollcall was held in bitter weather from 12 noon to 9 p.m., during which 200 prisoners died.

Elsewhere in Poland, thousands of Jews were being sent to forced labour camps, mostly to build fortifications along the new Soviet frontier *(opposite)*. Thousands of other Jews were brought from Slovakia to these labour camp regions.

Map 48

SLAVE LABOUR ON THE GERMAN BORDER, MAY–DECEMBER 1940

Baltic Sea

Danzig

EAST PRUSSIA

SOVIET-OCCUPIED POLAND

Mlawa

Rypin

River Vistula

Pultusk

Nasielsk

Serock

POLESIA

Warsaw
May 1940

Miedzyrzec

border fortifications

GERMAN-OCCUPIED POLAND

Radom
May 1940

2,000

almost none survived

Lublin
May 1940

VOLHYNIA

River Bug

Czestochowa
August 1940

1,000

almost none survived

SILESIA

Zamosc

River Vistula

Belzec

Cieszanow

the 'Otto line'

Cracow

Mielec

Tarnow

Auschwitz

PROTECTORATE OF BOHEMIA & MORAVIA

EASTERN GALICIA

Zilina

Ruzomberok

Presov

Humenne

S L O V A K I A

Banska Bystrica

Kosice

HUNGARIAN-OCCUPIED RUTHENIA

HUNGARY

© Martin Gilbert 1982

JEWS DEPORTED FROM GERMANY TO THE PYRENEES, 22 OCTOBER 1940

North Sea

Baltic Sea

Danzig

Hamburg

Stettin

Torun

POLAND

Berlin

Poznan

Warsaw

River Vistula

Leipzig

GREATER

Aachen

Cologne

RHINELAND

Erfurt

Chemnitz

Breslau

Coblenz

GERMANY

Cracow

Auschwitz

15,000 *deported*

GERMAN-OCCUPIED FRANCE

River Seine

River Rhine

BAVARIA

Nuremberg

Lieba Lust *born Auschwitz 26 December 1875 died Gurs 3 December 1940*

Augsburg

SWITZ.

Munich

Salzburg

Vienna

AUSTRIA

Budapest

HUNGARY

Graz

'VICHY' FRANCE

ITALY

YUGOSLAVIA

River Danube

Zagreb

Gurs 1,260

Récébédou

Noé 200

302

Pyrenees

Rivesaltes 102

SPAIN *neutral*

0 miles 100

0 kilometres 200

© Martin Gilbert 1982

On 22 October 1940 the German Government deported more than 15,000 German Jews from the Rhineland to internment camps in France, at the foothills of the Pyrenees. As a result of the conditions in the camps, nearly 2,000 of the deportees died. The towns shown on the map above are the birthplaces of some of the deportees, including Danzig, Warsaw, and even Auschwitz.

The small map *(right)* shows the numbers deported to Gurs from part of the upper Rhine. These Jews had been German patriots. From Mannheim alone, 126 Jews had died fighting for Germany in the First World War: among them five soldiers with the common Jewish surname Mayer.

The map on the far right gives the birthplaces, names and ages of deportees with the surname Mayer who died while in Gurs internment camp.

JEWS DEPORTED TO GURS, 22 OCTOBER 1940

PALATINATE

Weinheim 40

Speyer 55

Mannheim 2,000

Mosbach 51

SAAR

Landau 89

Bruchsal 79

Saarbrücken 177

Pforzheim 183

Ettlingen 9

BADEN

River Rhine

ALSACE

Offenburg 91

Alt Breisach 34

0 miles 40

0 kilometres 60

© Martin Gilbert 1982

Map 51

TWENTY JEWS WITH THE SURNAME MAYER WHO DIED IN GURS

Rimbach
Mina Mayer, aged 75

Frankfurt-am-Main
Julius Mayer, aged 54

Mühlheim
Marie Mayer, aged 78

Osthofen
Emanuel Mayer, aged 68

Grossbockenheim
Max Mayer, aged 63

Grünstadt
Johanna Mayer, aged 84

Mannheim
Julius Mayer, aged 56

Mergentheim
Meta Mayer, aged 53

Ulmet
Salo Mayer, died before
his first birthday

Neidenstein
Lehmann Mayer, aged 86

Niederhochstadt
Laura Mayer, aged 63

Germersheim
Selma Mayer, aged 71

Bruchsal
Rosalie Mayer, aged 80

Iggelheim
Michel Mayer, aged 82

Malsch
Frieda Mayer, aged 77

Rastatt
Cecile Mayer, aged 75

Julius Mayer, aged 27

Nonnenweier
Maier Mayer, aged 74

Ichenhausen
Eva Mayer, aged 79

Freiburg
Joseph Mayer, aged 59

River Rhine

River Main

River Rhine

River Danube

0   miles   20
0 kilometres 20

© Martin Gilbert 1982

Map 52

JEWS FORCED INTO GHETTOS, OCTOBER 1939 TO DECEMBER 1940

Plonsk
August 1940

Wloclawek
November 1940

River

River Bug

WARTHEGAU

Zychlin
19 July 1940

Wolomin
15 November 1940

Kutno
16 June 1940

Vistula

Warsaw
15 November 1940

Siedlce
6 May 1940

Tuliszkow
January 1940

Kolo
December 1940

Bolimow
11 June 1940

Chocz
March 1940

Glowno
29 December 1940

Lodz
1 May 1940

Kozminek
January 1940

Deblin
April 1940

Lutomiersk
July 1940

Tomaszow
1 June 1940

Zdunska Wola
September 1940

Piotrkow
28 October 1939

THE

GENERAL

Radomsko
20 December 1939

GOVERNMENT

Czestochowa
March 1940

Chmielnik
March 1940

Jedrzejow
January 1940

Pinczow
February 1940

River Vistula

```
0        miles        40
0      kilometres      60
```

© Martin Gilbert 1982

Starting with the town of Piotrkow on 28 October 1939, the Germans began to confine the Jews in Poland to a particular area of each town in which they lived. Sometimes this area was the already predominantly Jewish quarter. But often it was a poor or neglected part of the town, away from the centre. Jews from the rest of the town were then forced to leave their homes, and to move into this other, often much smaller area, in which even the basic amenities were not available.

Not only the Jews of each of the towns shown in the map on the left, but also deportees from the Warthegau, and from the surrounding rural communities, were forced to move into these new ghetto confines; at Piotrkow 8,000 local Jews were joined by a further 8,000 deportees.

In each ghetto food supplies and medical provisions were restricted. Intense overcrowding, hunger and disease led to widespread suffering, and death. The photograph was taken in the Lodz ghetto, where 5,000 were to die from starvation in the first six months of 1941 (page 41).

Meanwhile, in Germany itself, experiments had been tried on non-Jewish, and also on some Jewish patients from mental homes and old people's homes. The aim of the experiments was to kill all whom the Nazis judged unfit to live. The victims, including the children, were killed by gas in the euthanasia centres shown here.

After the German conquest of Poland more than 1,000 Poles were taken from nearby psychiatric clinics to a wood outside the Polish village of Piasnica Wielki, where they were shot. In October 1940, 290 Jews, old people, cripples, and the mentally ill from the Old Age Home in Kalisz, were put in a lorry to be taken to the town of 'Padernice' (below). No such town existed. Just outside Kalisz, in the woods at Winiary, all 290 were gassed inside the lorry by exhaust fumes, and buried in the woods.

GERMAN EUTHANASIA CENTRES, 1940

Baltic Sea

North Sea

Piasnica Wielki **1,200** October-December 1939

Brandenberg
Bernberg

Kalisz

Sonnenstein

Hadamar
over **10,000**

total killed **70,273**
by November 1941

Grafeneck

Schloss Hartheim
13,000

0   miles   200
0   kilometres   300

© Martin Gilbert 1982

THE JOURNEY TO 'PADERNICE', 27 OCTOBER 1940

0   miles   2
0   kilometres   2

River Prosna

Kalisz

Winiary
290

to 'Padernice'

© Martin Gilbert 1982

Map 55

WARSAW JEWS EXPELLED INTO THE WARSAW GHETTO, NOVEMBER 1940

River Vistula

to Danzig

Bielany

Marymont
2,313

Zoliborz

Brodno
523

Goledzinow
1,160

Targowek
1,043

to Moscow

Powazki

Praga Polnoc
8,758

Praga

to Lublin

WARSAW GHETTO
280,024

20,968
13,160
2,791
3,189

Praga-Poludnie
13,698

Grochow
1,408

Kolo
and Wola
2,317

Towarowy
23,255

Solec
5,357

Koszyki
5,471

Ujazdowski
2,075

to Berlin

Ochota
3,040

Sielce - Czerniakow
2,433

Warsaw municipal boundary

Mokotow
2,888

to Cracow

© Martin Gilbert 1982

0   mile   1
0   kilometres   2

Just over a year after the establishment of the first ghetto, at Piotrkow *(page 37),* orders were given to confine all the Jews of Warsaw, as well as all the Jews who had already been deported to Warsaw, inside one section of the city. The Warsaw ghetto was to become the largest of all the ghettos established by the Germans in Poland. The section of the city chosen for it was one in which more than 280,000 Jews were already living.

In October 1940 a wall was built around the area designated for the ghetto. Jews were made both to build the wall and to pay for it. As soon as it was built, the thousands of Jews who lived elsewhere in Warsaw were

forced to leave their homes, to abandon most of their possessions, and to move into the new ghetto area *(above)*. One Warsaw Jew, Chaim Kaplan, wrote in his diary of the expulsion from the Praga suburbs: 'By the thirty-first of October, Praga must be empty of its Jewish inhabitants, who were rooted to its soil for hundreds of years. Most of them are poor. They have no money to move their belongings. And where would they move them to?' Many Poles, Kaplan added, 'drove the Praga Jews from their apartments in advance, before the fixed date'.

Early in 1941, 72,000 Jews were expelled from towns throughout the Warsaw region

Map 56

JEWS DEPORTED INTO THE WARSAW GHETTO, FEBRUARY - MARCH 1941

Warsaw

GHETTO

Bledow

Sochaczew

Blonie

Pruszkow

72,000
deported
into Warsaw

Bolimow

Zyrardow

Piaseczno

Jeziorna

Karczew

Mszczonow

River Vistula

0 miles 5
0 kilometres 8

© Martin Gilbert 1982

(above), and driven into the ghetto, bringing the total number of refugees to 150,000. Conditions inside the ghetto were appalling: terrible overcrowding, minimum rations, and almost no contact with the outside world for 400,000 people.

Under the ration scales imposed by the Germans, all Germans in Warsaw were entitled to 2,310 calories a day, foreigners to 1,790 calories, Poles to 934 calories, and Jews to a mere 183 calories. Yet Jews had to pay twice as much as Poles, and nearly 20 times as much as Germans, for each calory. Inside the ghetto, food distribution was organized by the Jews themselves. The photograph, one of more than 300

photographs taken by a member of the Warsaw photographic studio, Studio Forbert, was entitled simply 'meal time'. More than 13,000 Jews died of starvation in Warsaw between January and June 1941 *(page 41)*.

Attempts to make conditions as bearable as possible were made by a special Jewish Council, set up by the Germans. The Council provided what relief it could, and arranged cultural activities, concerts, and education. There were many orphanages in the ghetto, their difficult work inspired by the leadership of their directors, including Janusz Korczak. On 12 August 1942 he was to insist on accompanying his children in one of the Warsaw deportations *(page 99)*.

Map 57

THE SPREAD OF TERROR AND DEATH, JANUARY TO JUNE 1941

North Sea

Baltic Sea

Warsaw
13,000
died of starvation and disease
January – June 1941

Amsterdam
400
22 February 1941

Biala Podlaska
12
prisoners of war
15 May 1941

Bremen
hundreds
early 1941

BELGIUM

Kalisz
439
gassed
1 January 1941

Lublin

Lodz
5,000
died of starvation and disease
January – June 1941

Paris
3,600
interned
14 May 1941

Suresnes
GERMAN-OCCUPIED FRANCE

GREATER GERMANY

Kielce   Opole
Lagow
Modliborzyce

Cracow

Mauthausen

VICHY FRANCE

Vienna
5,004
15 February – 12 March 1941

RUMANIA
Bucharest
120
murdered in the streets
22-23 January 1941

Zagreb
6
April 1941

Black Sea

Noé
Le Vernet
Les Milles

Gurs
Rivesaltes
internment camps
Argelés

Adriatic Sea

SPAIN
neutral

TURKEY
neutral

Mediterranean Sea

791
on board the "Darien"
reached Palestine
by sea 9 March 1941

| 0 | miles | 200 |
| 0 | kilometres | 300 |

several thousand deported to the Sahara, for slave labour see page 56

© Martin Gilbert 1982

Map 58

BIRTHPLACES OF JEWS EXECUTED IN FRANCE FOR RESISTANCE, 1941

Plungian · Polotsk

· Mogilev

· Slonim

Siedlce

Warsaw · Brest-Litovsk

Grodzisk ·

Lodz · Lukow · Piaski

Dzialoszyn → Opole Lublin · Busk

Bedzin · Przemysl

Darmstadt

Nikolaiev

Suresnes · Paris · Kishinev

133

FRANCE

GREATER

GERMANY

North Sea

Baltic Sea

BRITAIN

Black Sea

0 miles 200

0 kilometres 300

© Martin Gilbert 1982

During the first six months of 1941, the rigour of Germany's policy towards the Jews was constant and severe. On 1 January 1941 a further 439 old and sick Jews were taken from the Old People's Home at Kalisz, and gassed by exhaust fumes in a nearby wood (*see also page 38*). At Biala Podlaska, 12 more defenceless Jewish prisoners-of-war were savagely murdered. In each of the ghettos shown on page 37, death from starvation and disease was a daily occurrence, with more than 18,000 dead in Warsaw and Lodz. From 22 February 1941 any Pole selling food to a Jew outside the Warsaw ghetto was automatically sentenced to three months' hard labour, and the ghetto ration was reduced to three ounces of bread a day. 'Although the ghetto of Lodz was intended as a mere trial,' the Cologne *Zeitung* reported on 5 April 1941, 'a mere prelude to the solution of the Jewish question, it has turned out to be the best and most perfect temporary solution of the Jewish problem.' Nine days later, any Jew leaving the Lodz ghetto was ordered to be shot on sight.

More than 40,000 German and Belgian Jews were deported into the Warsaw ghetto. New ghettos were also set up in Cracow, Lublin and Kielce. From Vienna, more than 5,000 Jews were deported to these eastern ghettos and labour camps, while from Amsterdam, more than 400 Jews were seized as hostages and deported to the stone quarries of Mauthausen concentration camp; the events leading to this deportation are described on pages 65–6.

In Paris, several thousand foreign-born Jews were seized and interned in May 1941. At the same time, thousands of Polish- and German-born Jews, who had fought in the French Foreign Legion against Germany in 1940, were deported to slave labour camps in the Sahara. Outside Paris, at Suresnes, 133 Jews were shot for resistance during 1941, the first executions taking place on 16 April 1941. The map above shows the birthplaces of some of those shot, as recorded by the Gestapo: 10 had been born in Warsaw, and almost all had been born within the borders (shown here dotted) of the former Russian Empire. Many, like Charles Weinberg from Kishinev, were in their fifties. One of those shot, Antoine Hajje, had been born in Cyprus; another, Elias Salomon, in Beirut.

Outside Greater Germany, anti-semitic violence in Bucharest left 120 Jews dead in the streets (*left*): men, women and children who had been hunted down by armed gangs. A few survivors managed to reach Palestine by sea.

The photograph shows work on the Sahara railroad (*see also page 43*).

Map 59

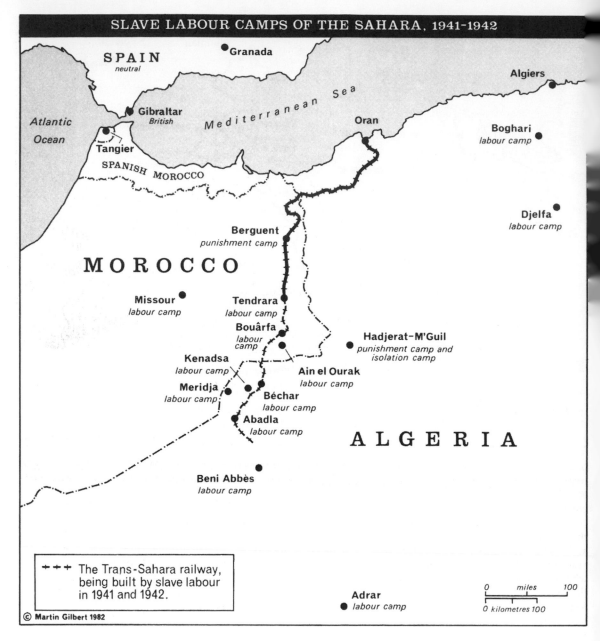

SLAVE LABOUR CAMPS OF THE SAHARA, 1941-1942

SPAIN
neutral

Granada

Algiers

Atlantic
Ocean

Gibraltar
British

Mediterranean Sea

Oran

Boghari
labour camp

Tangier

SPANISH MOROCCO

Djelfa
labour camp

Berguent
punishment camp

MOROCCO

Missour
labour camp

Tendrara
labour camp

Bouârfa
labour camp

Hadjerat-M'Guil
punishment camp and isolation camp

Kenadsa
labour camp

Ain el Ourak
labour camp

Meridja
labour camp

Béchar
labour camp

Abadla
labour camp

ALGERIA

Beni Abbès
labour camp

+ + + The Trans-Sahara railway, being built by slave labour in 1941 and 1942.

Adrar
labour camp

0 miles 100
0 kilometres 100

© Martin Gilbert 1982

In April 1940 more than 1,500 Jews were serving in the French Foreign Legion, hoping to fight against Nazi Germany. But with the German conquest of France in June 1940 they were first 'demobilized', then interned, and finally sent to labour camps in French North Africa *(above)*. Many of these Jews were refugees from Germany and Austria who had been in France at the outbreak of war.

A law of 4 October 1940 gave Vichy France the power to intern Jews even inside the Unoccupied Zone, and on 22 March 1941 a law signed by Marshal Pétain authorized the construction of a Trans-Sahara railway. The work was done, in harsh conditions, by all who had been interned: former Spanish Republican soldiers, Poles, Czechs, Greeks and Jews.

The camp at Hadjerat-M'Guil was opened on 1 November 1941, as a punishment and isolation camp. It contained 170 prisoners, nine of whom were tortured and murdered in conditions of the worst brutality. Two of those murdered were Jews, one of whom had earlier been in a concentration camp in Germany but had been released in 1939 and

SLAVE LABOUR CAMPS ON THE RIVER BUG, FEBRUARY 1941

had fled to France. This young man's parents had become refugees in London. On learning of their son's murder in the Sahara, they committed suicide.

Shown above is the deportation of more than 5,000 Jews from Vienna to the Kielce and Lublin ghettos, and to the labour camps along the River Bug (above). There, together with Jews deported from Warsaw and Lodz, they were forced to drain marshes and build fortifications on the Soviet border, the 'Otto Line', intended to act as a barrier against Soviet tanks. One of the main labour camps, at Belzec, was later to become one of the four eastern death camps (page 77).

Another group of Jews who were sent to forced labour were skilled workers living in the region of the Upper Silesian coalfields. There were 93,628 Jews living in this region, in 32 communities, the six largest of which, among them the town of Auschwitz, are shown here (right). Thousands of able-bodied Jews were rounded up in these towns and sent to work in German mining, metallurgy and textile plants and factories in the region, as many as 5,000 men from Bedzin.

SLAVE LABOUR GANGS, MARCH 1941

Map 62

THE GERMAN CONQUEST OF YUGOSLAVIA AND GREECE, APRIL 1941

GREATER **Graz**
GERMANY

HUNGARY

TRANS | YLVANIA

Subotica
250

BA CSKA

BANAT

Timisoara

RUMANIA

ITALY

Zagreb

Fiume

Y U G O S L A V I A

Novi Sad
250

Belgrade

Bucharest

Zara
(Italian)

Adriatic Sea

Sarajevo

Nis

BULGARIA

Dubrovnik

70,000 *Jews in 1940*

Sofia

ITALY

Skopje

ALBANIA
*occupied by Italy
from April 1939*

Bari

Valona

Salonica

Aegean Sea

TURKEY
neutral

CORFU

G R E E C E

Ionian Sea

ZANTE

Athens

75,000
Jews

Mediterranean Sea

O miles 100

O kilometres 150

© **Martin Gilbert 1982**

CRETE

On 6 April 1941 the German armies invaded Yugoslavia and Greece, and by the end of the month a further 145,000 Jews had been brought under Nazi tyranny *(above)*. Those of the Banat, shown opposite according to the Yugoslav census of 31 March 1931, lived in small and scattered communities north of Belgrade, between the River Tisa and the Rumanian border. Numbering over 3,000 people, they were all driven from their homes by the Germans in August 1941, within four months of the German conquest of Yugoslavia. Taken to Tasmajdan camp, near Belgrade, they were shot in the camp itself, and on the banks of the Danube, in daily executions: on 20 August 1941 the whole Banat region was declared *Judenrein*, 'purged of Jews'.

Map 63

THE JEWS OF THE BANAT

HUNGARY

Krstr 11

Arandelovo 39

Nova Kanjiza 46

Coka 49

Mokrin 38

Kikinda 100

Sajan 9

Padej 28

RUMANIA

Novi Becej 167

Torda 10

Jasa Tomic 56

Kumani 14

Melenci 32

Veliki Beckerek 1,352

Boka 3

BACSKA

Aradac 4

Ecka 33

Jarkovac 5

BANAT

Vrsac 404

Perlez 18

Seleus 5

River Danube

Kovacica 37

Padina 33

Alibunar 31

Bela Crkva 67

YUGOSLAVIA

Novo Selo 1

Delibiato 10

Gaj 6

SREM

Pancevo 507

River Danube

Kovin 75

Tasmajdan concentration camp 3,000

Belgrade Sajmiste concentration camp

SERBIA

© Martin Gilbert 1982

River Tisa

0 miles 10
0 kilometres 20

By the end of October 1941 almost no Banat Jews were left alive in Tasmajdan: the life, the culture and the achievements of more than 30 communities had been destroyed for all time.

West of the Banat, the towns of Sobotica and Novi Sad were occupied by Hungarian forces on 11 April 1941. In Subotica the Germans executed 250 members of a Jewish youth movement who had carried out the first acts of sabotage against the occupation forces. In Novi Sad, Hungarian troops and local Germans murdered at random 250 Jews and 250 Serbs.

From the outset of the war, Jews were active in the Yugoslav resistance. The first secret radio in Zagreb was operated by two Jewish brothers. More than 2,000 Yugoslav Jews later fought with Tito's partisans, and a specifically Jewish unit of 250 men, formed in 1943, lost more than 200 fighting against the Germans. One leading resistance fighter, Moša Pijade, a Jew, later became a Vice-President of Yugoslavia.

THE JEWS OF WESTERN CROATIA ON THE EVE OF WAR

Cakovec 533

Varazdin 486

Ludbrijeg 74

HUNGARY

Koprivnica 339

Krapina

Virje 15

Djurdjevac 29

River

Donji Miholjac 119

Zlata 13

Klanjec

Zabok 6

Krizevci 126

Drava

River Danube

Loka 1

Sevnica 4

Zagreb 8,702

Bjelovar 360

Virovitica 233

Slatina 174

Osijek

Samobor 8

Dugo Selo 23

Klostar Ivanic 5

Daruvar 136

Nasice 161

see map 66

Jastrebarsko

Ivanic 16

Lekenik 11

CROATIA

Pakrac 209

Pisarovina 15

Sisak 230

Pozega 248

Petrinja 14

Jasenovac 2

Vinica 23

Karlovac 347

Sunja 9

Slavonski Brod 462

Kostajnica

River Sava

Leskovac 93

Nova Gradiska 207

Ogulin 21

BOSNIA

Dvor 1

see page 75

Cazin 1

Bihac 149

0 miles 30
0 kilometres 40

© Martin Gilbert 1982

RABBIS AND CANTORS MURDERED BY CROAT 'USTACHI'

Murska Sobota
M. Roth, aged 70

Cakovec
Elia Gruenwald
chief rabbi aged about 55

Ludbrijeg
(Ludberg)
Dr. Deutsham
aged about 70

River Danube

0 miles 30
0 kilometres 50

Varazdin
Dr. Rudolf Guech
aged about 70
Jakob Kohn

Koprivnica
Leo Wolfenzon, aged about 55
Dr. N. Kohn, aged about 58

N. Schwartz aged
about 45

Krizevci
Lavoslav Buchsbaum
aged 72

Virovitica
Adolf Springer,
chief cantor aged 45

**Donji
Miholjac**

Paul Froehlich, aged 28
Isidor Guren, aged about 60
Dr. Simon Ungar, aged
about 60

Bjelovar
Izidor Dolf
aged about 45

Slatina
Hinko Gruenwald, aged
about 95

Osijek

Vijoslav Mandel, aged
about 32

Zagreb

Daruvar
Josip Gilman aged about 65
Leopold Katz, aged 65

Nasice
Jakov Schmelzer
aged 35

Vucovar

Pakrac
Izak Freides,
aged about 55

Pozega
Mordeschil Rikow
aged about 70

Dakovo
Alexander Roth,
cantor

Vincovci
Izidor Hersmovic aged about 60
Mijo Propper, aged about 60

Karlovac
David Meissl,
cantor aged about 45
killed with his son,
his three daughters
were saved

Sisak
Dr. M. Heisz, chief rabbi
aged about 60
Jakov Klinkovstein
chief cantor, aged
about 65

Nova Gradiska
Andrija Trilnik aged
about 30

Brcko
Leon Katan,
aged 66

Zagreb
David Atijas, cantor
Arnold Basch, cantor
Miroslav Freiberger, chief rabbi
Lavoslav Kahn, cantor, 45
M. Loewy, Dean of the Rabbanical School, 70
Eugen Mandel, cantor, 35
Samuel Singer, cantor 65
Dragutin Vogel, cantor, 27
Josip Weissmann, retired chief cantor, 73

Banja Luka
N. Kohn,
rabbi and cantor

Travnik
Izak Baruch

© Martin Gilbert 1982

THE JEWS OF EASTERN CROATIA AND THE SREM ON THE EVE OF WAR

HUNGARY

Popovac 11

Knezevi Vinograd 25

Belisce 96

Darda 23

Koska 15

Valpovo 30

Osijek 2,600

EASTERN CROATIA

Cepin 9

Dalj 16

Podgorac 9

Ernestinova 3

Bobuta 7

Vukovar 306

Semeljci 10

Vinkovci 647

River Danube

Dakovo 254

Ivankovo 15

Sarengrad 4

Cerevic 7

Beocin 37

Sremski Karlovci 2

Indija 39

Andrijevci 10

Slakovci 8

SREM

Maradik 3

Babina Greda 5

Sid 59

Erdevik 27

Ruma 215

Stara Pazova 68

Zupanja 75

Vrbanja 10

Sremska Mitrovica 115

Nikinci 4

Zemun 523

Belgrade

Rajevo Selo 6

Drenovci 5

Brcko 112

Racinovci 2

River Sava

© Martin Gilbert 1982

for Bosnia, see page 75

Following the German conquest of Yugoslavia on 17 April 1941, Croatia became an independent State, ruled by the pro-Nazi 'Ustachi'. The top maps show the Jewish communities of Croatia and the Srem according to the Yugoslavia census of 1931. The areas plotted are shown on the small map *(right)*.

Persecution of the Jews began at once. In Ruma, the synagogue was demolished. In Vukovar, the community leaders were arrested, and then 'ransomed' back to the community. In Osijek, German soldiers, local Germans and Croat 'Ustachi' burned the main synagogue, destroyed the Jewish cemetery, looted Jewish property, and imposed a crippling 'fine' on the Jewish community.

The map opposite *(below)* gives the names of some rabbis and cantors who were murdered during the late spring and early summer: some were venerable rabbis, scholars and teachers; others were young men embarking upon their careers. Doctors, nurses, midwives, chemists, dentists and vets, whose work had been for the whole Croatian community, were also killed. Many young Croat Jews were to fight with Tito's partisans.

GERMANY AND CROATIA

Baltic Sea

Berlin

GREATER GERMANY

Warsaw

Prague

Lvov

SLOVAKIA

Vienna

Budapest

HUNGARY

CROATIA

RUMANIA

YUGOSLAVIA

Banja Luka

Travnik

Belgrade

DALMATIA

BOSNIA

SERBIA

Adriatic Sea

ITALY

© Martin Gilbert 1982

Map 68

THE JEWISH COMMUNITIES OF SERBIA

CROATIA

BANAT

River Danube

Zemun
concentration camp
established April 1941

Veliko
Gradiste
9

Belgrade
7,906

Pozarevac
62

Zabrezje
1

River Sava

Umka
3

122 shot
29 July 1941

Smederovo
78

Sabac
89

Obrenovac
10

Ripanj
3

Mladenovac
2

Loznica
3

Palanka
8

Arandelovac
3

Lapovo
4

Kamenica
2

Valjevo
25

Jagodina
24

Cuprija
1

River Drina

Kragujevac
95

Paracin
6

Rogacica
47

Cacak
7

Uzice
21

Kraljevo
9

Aleksinac
6

Pozega
248

Krusevac
12

S E R B I A

Priboj
1

Raska
2

Sjenica
19

Duja
Poljana
9

Novi Pazar
249

0   miles   25

0   kilometres   40

Tutin
6

© Martin Gilbert 1982

After 500 years of struggle, persecution and expulsion, the Jews of Belgrade achieved full civil rights in 1878 in the newly independent Serbia. Between the wars they were active in Serbian professional and business life. Smaller Jewish communities settled throughout Serbia, as in the region south of Belgrade (above).

On 14 April 1941, within a few hours of the German occupation of Belgrade, Jewish shops were looted, and within a few weeks all Jewish communal activity was forbidden.

On 29 July 1941 the Germans executed 122 'Communists and Jews' for resistance.

Undeterred, Jews from the youth movement joined the resistance, sabotaging German military installations.

By November 1941 more than 15,000 Jews had been deported from throughout Serbia to the concentration camp at Zemun, where by June 1942 they had been killed in mobile gas units, disguised as Red Cross vans.

On 29 August 1942 Berlin was informed officially that the Jewish problem was 'totally solved' in Serbia, 'the only community', the report boasted, 'in which this has been achieved'. Of Serbia's 23,000 Jews, 20,000 had been murdered.

Map 69

EASTERN ESCAPE ROUTES OF POLISH JEWS, MAY 1940 - MAY 1941

Arctic Ocean

SOVIET
UNION

SWEDEN

Moscow

Trans-Siberian railway

Lake
Baikal

Kovno

Warsaw

Odessa

Belgrade

Caspian
Sea

Vladivostok

JAPAN

Istanbul

IRAN

CHINA

Tokyo

to San Francisco
and Vancouver

Jerusalem

Shanghai

INDIA

Hong Kong

Pacific

Ocean

DUTCH

Batavia EAST INDIES

Indian

Ocean

AUSTRALIA

Sydney

© Martin Gilbert 1982

In the year before the German invasion of
the Soviet Union, hundreds of Jews living in
the Soviet-annexed regions of Poland and the
Baltic States, as well as refugees from
German-occupied Poland, tried to escape to
potentially safer regions. In the Lithuanian
city of Kovno, the British Consul, Thomas
Preston, helped provide 400 'illegal'
Palestine certificates for Jews who were then
able to make their way through Istanbul to
Jerusalem, while a further 800 received legal
certificates. A few hundred Jews were able to
cross the Baltic Sea to Sweden. The leaders
of several Jewish youth movements,

however, decided to return to Warsaw, to
help organize resistance there.

Several hundred Polish and Lithuanian
Jews managed to get permission to enter
Japan. A few others received transit visas,
issued between 20 and 31 August 1940 by
Sugehara, the Japanese Consul in Kovno,
enabling them to cross the Trans-Siberian
railway to Japan, ostensibly for the Dutch
East Indies. They were then able to move on
to Australia, the United States and Canada.

But those who managed to escape were
only a fragment of those trapped in eastern
Poland, the Baltic States and western Russia.

Map 70

RUSSIAN JEWRY, A SAMPLE

0 miles 40
0 kilometres 60

Orel 3,597
Kromy 56
Starodub 3,317
Dimitrovsk 21
Novozybkov 4,825
Maloarchangelsk 28
Dimitriev 186
Gluchov 2,551
Kursk 4,154
Berezna 697
Sosnitsa 1,141
Korop 787
Lgov 183
Myena 1,321
Borzna 697
Oboyan 118
Konotop 5,763
Sudzha 53
Nezhin 6,131
Sumy 2,627
Romny 8,593
Priluki 11,163
Lubny 6,039
Mirgorod 1,994
Kharkov 81,138
River Donetz
Cherkassy 10,886
Poltava 18,474
Chigirin 408
Kobelyaki 1,400
Izium 268
Kremenchug 28,969
River Dnieper
Aleksandrija 4,395
Novomoskovsk 1,421
Elizavetgrad 18,358
Ekaterinoslav 62,073
Pavlograd 3,921
Chaplino 59
Bobrinets 2,265
Krivoi Rog 6,430
Zaporozhe 11,319
UKRAINE
Nikopol 2,699
Tokmak 1,898
Mariupol 7,332
Nikolaiev 21,787
Melitopol 11,438
Nogaisk 186
Berislav 395
Berdiansk 2,138
Cherson 14,837
Genichesk 1,776
Sea of Azov
Dzhankoi 3,294
CRIMEA
Kerch 3,067
Eupatoria 2,409
Saki 53
Karasubazar 190
Feodosia 3,248
Bakchisarai 275
Sevastopol 5,204
Simferopol 21,500
Black Sea
Balaklava 70
Yalta 2,353
© Martin Gilbert 1982

On 22 June 1941 German forces invaded the Soviet Union. As they advanced they moved through areas of dense Jewish settlement, in which lived more than 2,700,000 Jews as well as several hundred thousand Jewish refugees from western Poland.

The figures shown here (left) of the number of Jews in some of the cities, towns and villages of western Russia are taken from the Soviet census of 1926. In cities such as Kharkov Jews constituted more than 20 per cent of the total population, and between 1926 and the outbreak of war, the Jewish population of most of the towns shown here had increased. Some had almost doubled: there were as many as 150,000 Jews in Kharkov on the eve of the German invasion. In the Crimea, ancient Jewish communities dating back to Greek and Roman times, and Jewish collective farms set up in the 1920s, existed side by side.

The Jews of several towns shown on the left-hand map had lived through the pogroms in Tsarist times (page 1). Many more had been the victims of the massacres of 1918 and 1919, which had claimed 85,000 lives (page 2). Some of the towns, such as Starodub, had taken a lead in organizing Jewish self-defence during that period. Others, a few years later, had been at the centre of the famine region, when millions of Soviet citizens had perished.

During the early 1920s tens of thousands of Russian Jews had emigrated, some to avoid Communist persecution, others to escape the all-pervading poverty. But the majority had no choice but to remain in their homes and with their families, working in shops and offices, tilling the fields, and simply trying to exist in the harsh world of Stalinism.

Hitler had other plans for these millions of Jews. He wanted them neither as subjects, nor as slaves. He had made his plans before the German invasion: in May 1941, at Pretzsch, in Saxony, special mobile killing squads, the 'Einsatzgruppen', were set up. Each squad had been allocated a particular area of the Soviet Union for its future activities. Thus Einsatzgruppe A was to be responsible for the murder of Jews in the Baltic States, while Einsatzgruppe D was to work in the Ukraine and the Crimea.

Just as the German army was confident that it could defeat the Soviet Union, and conquer all of western Russia, so the SS was convinced that it could, by mass executions on the spot, 'solve' the Jewish question in

Map 71

THE GERMAN INVASION OF RUSSIA, AND MASS MURDER PLANS, 22 JUNE 1941

Russia, by murdering all the Jews it could catch. No family was to be spared. Nor were any resources to be wasted in setting up ghettos, nor in the deportation of Jews to distant camps or murder sites. The killing was to be done in the towns and villages, at the moment of military victory.

When the German army invaded Russia in June 1941, its advance was so rapid that less than 300,000 Jews were able to escape eastward, to safety beyond the Volga.

The photograph, taken from the personal album of one of the officers in the picture, shows the arrival of a detachment of Einsatzgruppe D in the town of Drohobycz, in the Polish province of Eastern Galicia, which Russia had annexed in October 1939. part of the task of these killing squads was to recruit local anti-semites, whether Ukrainians, Lithuanians, or Latvians, who could help them to round up, terrorize and destroy each Jewish community, however small. For the work of this particular detachment in Drohobycz itself, see page 54.

The map above shows the regions allocated to the different killing squads, and the initial points of attack of the German army and its Rumanian ally on 22 June 1941.

Map 72

SOME JEWISH COMMUNITIES IN THE VOLHYNIA ON THE EVE OF WAR

Pohost
894

Serniki
1,073

Lubieszow
17

0   miles   16

0   kilometres   24

Wysock
1,060

Kamen Kashirski
750

P O L E S I A

Dabrowica
3,225

Wlodzimierzec
1,500

Bereznica
1,372

Rafalowka
651

Tomaszgrod
193

Maniewicze
549

Trojanowka
212

Antonowka
578

Klesow
90

Poworsk
37

Sarny
4,950

Rokitr
788

Mielnica
1,040

Stepan
1,588

Holoby
209

Sokul
167

Kolki
860

Osowa
832

Berezne
2,818

Rozyszcze
4,070

V O L H Y N I A

Derazno
741

Kostopol
3,920

Ludwipo
1,088

Torczyn
1,758

Zofjowka
1,825

Siedliszcze
788

Luck
15,879

Klewan
1,814

Aleksandrja
1,536

Miedzyrzecz
2,330

Olyka
2,479

Tuczyn
2,622

Nieswicz
30

Ostrozec
751

Rowne
25,000

Korzec
4,895

Hoszcza
963

Targowica
784

Mlynow
731

Zdolbunow
1,500

1921 – 1939

Boreml
1,018

Warkowicze
1,053

Ozieriany
946

Demidowka
707

Dubno
7,000

Mizocz
1,048

Ostrog
9,240

Bereteczko
2,625

Kozin
653

EASTERN
GALICIA

Rachmanow
62

WESTERN
UKRAINE

Polish- Soviet border

Radzwillow
3,120

Krzemieniec
6,240

Szumsk
2,040

© Martin Gilbert 19

In the first three weeks of their invasion of the Soviet Union, the German forces made rapid advances. In their wake, the specially trained mobile killing squads began the systematic murder of Jews, in every city, town and village of western Russia. The ma above shows the number of Jews living in the larger towns and villages of part of the Volhynia, an area inside the Russian Empir until 1914, and within the independent

Map 73

JEWS MASSACRED BETWEEN 22 JUNE AND 16 JULY 1941

Baltic Sea

Gulf of Riga

Riga
400

Moscow

Jelgava
2,000

Jekabpils
700

Siauliai
3,000

Rietavas
500

Vandziogala
34

Widze
200

Virbalis
500

Kovno
3,000

Swieciany
100

Vilna
5,000
4-20 July

Wilejka
150

Marijampole
70

T H E

R=Radzilow **1,500**

Grodno
80

Lida
200

Minsk
2,000

J = Jedwabne **1,000**

S=Szczuczyn **1,900**

Augustow
1,000

S
W
R

Krynki
30

Nowogrodek
50

German forces advancing

W=Wasosz
1,185

J

Bialystok
5,200

Baranowicze
400

Warsaw

Kobryn **70**

Brest-Litovsk
5,000

Janow
400

S O V I E T

G R E A T E R
G E R M A N Y

David Grodek
1,000

see map 72

Tuczyn **70**

Sokal
200

Toporow **180**

German forces advancing

Lvov
3,000

Kamionka Strumilowa
200

Zloczow **3,500**

Kiev

Sambor
100

Drohobycz
400

Jezierno
180

Tarnopol **5,000**

U N I O N

SLOVAKIA

Boryslaw
200

Skalat
560

Stryj
300

Czortkow
200

H U N G A R Y

Czernowitz
2,400

Hotin
2,000

Novoselitsa
800

Marculesti
1,000

Jassy
2,421
in two death trains organized by Rumanian fascists

Odessa

0   miles   100
0   kilometres   150

© Martin Gilbert 1982

R U M A N I A

Polish state between the wars. The Volhynia was annexed by Russia at the time of the Nazi-Soviet partition of Poland in October 1939. In the area shown here, there were also more than 100 smaller Jewish communities.

In all, more than a quarter of a million Jews were living in the Volhynia in 1939. The figures above show some of the German killing squad massacres during the first three weeks following the invasion.

Map 74

JEWS MASSACRED BETWEEN 17 JULY AND 31 AUGUST 1941

Gulf of Riga

Baltic Sea

ESTONIA

LATVIA

Liepaja **3,000**

LITHUANIA

Dvinsk

EAST PRUSSIA

Volkavyskis **900**

see map 75

Kovno

Augustow **1,500**

Moscow

Stawiski **2,000**

Wolozyn **1,000**

Iwje **225**

Oszmiana **700**

GREATER

Tykocin **2,100**

Korelicze **105**

Stolpce **80**

Lubotyn **228**

Zdzieciol **120**

Zambrow **1,100**

Warsaw

Slonim **1,200**

THE   SOVIET   UNION

GERMANY

Czyzew **3,500**

POLAND

Pinsk **11,000**

Pripet marshes

Kamen Kashirsky **88**

Pohost **150**

Sarniki **150**

Korzec **312**

Dubno **80**

Kiev

Beresteczko **300**

Zborow **850**

Lvov

see map 76

Zhitomir **2,530**

Stanislawow

UKRAINE

RUTHENIA

Kamenets Podolsk 14,000

German forces advancing

Hotin **3,000**

mostly deportees from Hungarian-occupied Ruthenia (see page 184)

Kirovo **6,000**

HUNGARY

Czernowitz **4,000**

Kalinindorf **1,875**

Orgeev **200**

Nikolaiev **5,000**

Jassy **4,000**

RUMANIA

Kishinev **12,287**

Black Sea

Sea of Azov

Kilia **2,000**

CRIMEA

miles 0 — 100
kilometres 0 — 150

© Martin Gilbert 1982

During the second six weeks of the German advance into Russia, the work of the killing squads continued without respite. This map, like the previous map and the maps on the right, shows only a small percentage of the total killings. For many places, particularly the smaller villages and hamlets, no record survives. Nor was the killing confined to SS units. In Lithuania local non-Jews were among the most savage killers, while in the south, Rumanian troops and militia murdered thousands of Jews in the area of

MORE JEWS MASSACRED, 17 JULY – 31 AUGUST 1941

Joniskis
355

Pasvalys
1,349

LATVIA

Rokishkis
4,188

Dvinsk
21

Dagda
216

Seduva
664

Aglona Mental Home
544

Panevezhys
8,837

Zarasai
2,569

Raseiniai
3,043

LITHUANIA

Kedainai
2,201

Utena
1,038

Agriogala
38

Ukmerge (Vilkomir)
1,647

POLAND

Wilkia
402

River Niemen

Jonava
552

Kovno
2,581

Kaisiadorys
1,911

Vilna
1,000

Wilejka
250

Prienai
1,078

Ponary
20 July – 8 August
444
12 – 31 August

Marijampole
156

Alytus
952

0 miles 40
0 kilometres 60

© Martin Gilbert 1982

EASTERN GALICIAN KILLINGS, SUMMER 1941

Mosty Wielkie
119

River Bug

Krzemieniec
800

Brody
250

VOLHYNIA

UKRAINE

Busk
30

Lvov
2,000

Zloczow
300

Tarnopol
3,000

Bobrka
63

Jezierno
180

Mikulince
30

Podwoloczyska
70

Trembowla
40

EASTERN GALICIA

Stryj
10

Husiatyn
200

Buczacz
350

Czortkow
400

Stanislawow
1,000

Zaleszczyki
800

0 miles 30
0 kilometres 40

© Martin Gilbert 1982

Rumanian military advance. Throughout Eastern Galicia *(right)* Ukrainian peasants frequently set upon the Jews, murdering hundreds before the German killing squads arrived. But it was the German squads whose work was on the larger scale, including the first 'five figure' massacre of Jews by Einsatzgruppe D in Kishinev between 17 and 31 July 1941 *(page 58)*. A second 'five figure' massacre took place on August 27 and 28, of Jews who had earlier been deported to Kamenets Podolsk from Hungary. These were not Hungarian citizens but Jewish refugees who had fled to Hungary and Ruthenia in 1938 and 1939 from Germany, Austria, Slovakia and Poland. Some had lived in Hungary as 'Aryans', on false identity papers. Others had obtained the right to live in Hungary as 'transients' on their way to Palestine. Rounded up and deported eastward during July, over 18,000 had been sent to camps in and around Kamenets Podolsk. On 27 August 1941 heavily armed SS units, with Ukrainian militia support, marched 14,000 of these refugees some 10 miles to a series of bomb craters, ordered them to undress, and opened fire with machine-guns. Many of those who died had been buried alive.

Map 77

THE JEWS OF BESSARABIA ON THE EVE OF WAR

Hotin
5,786

Romancauti
180

Secureni
4,216

Otaci
2,785

Zgurita
2,541

Noua Sulita
4,154

Briceni
5,354

River Dniester

Soroca 5,452

Lipcani
4,698

Edineti
5,349

Liublin 274

Chetrosu
140

Vascaut
34

Vartujeni
1,834

Rascani
2,060

Dumbraveni
1,198

Vadu Rascu
1,970

Marculesti
2,237

Alexandreni
1,018

Floresti
529

Cotiugeni
367

Glodeni
214

Balti
14,259

Capresti
1,815

Raspopeni
158

Rezina
2,889

Limbeni
39

Sangerei
167

Chiperceni
208

Falesti
3,258

Telenesti
2,811

Bravicea
413

Susleni
110

Valea
lui-Vlad
1,281

Sculeni
1,207

Cornesti
338

Orhei
6,408

Parlita
1,064

Calarasi
3,662

Peresecina
241

Criuleni
240

Ungheni
1,390

Varzaresti
205

Vadu lui-Voda
9

Nisiporeni
380

Ciuciuleni
291

Kishinev
41,405

Tighina (Bendery)
8,294

Lapusna
165

Hancesti
1,523

River Pruth

Carpineni
271

Gura Galbena
111

Taraclia
151

Causani
1,870

Olanesti
110

Palanca
24

Leova
2,326

Cimislia
925

BESSARABIA

Romanesti
1,995

Volintiri
420

Cazaci
136

Comrat
392

Borodino
50

Cetatea Alba
(Akkerman)
4,239

Baimaclia
509

Berezina
125

Saba
159

Gotesti
35

Tarutino
1,546

Sarata
316

Cahul
803

Arciz
842

Taraclia
46

Tatar Bunar
1,202

Tuzla
118

Colibasi
2

Bolgrad
1,222

Kilia
1,969

Reni
1,201

Ismail
1,680

Black Sea

0   miles   30

0   kilometres   50

© Martin Gilbert 1982

Until 1941 Bessarabia was part of the Tsarist Empire. The murder of 49 Jews during the Kishinev pogrom in 1903 *(page 1)* had led to protest demonstrations in London, Paris and New York, and a letter of rebuke from Theodore Roosevelt to the Tsar. In 1918 the region became part of Rumania but remained strongly anti-semitic. The city of Kishinev was a focal point of Jewish culture and political life, while Jewish agricultural communities thrived throughout the province.

With the return of Soviet rule to Bessarabia in June 1940, all Jewish

Map 78

MASSACRES, DEPORTATIONS AND DEATH MARCHES FROM BESSARABIA, from July 1941

Zhmerinka 3,274 *in ghetto*

REICHSKOMMISSARIAT UKRAINE

Bar *camp under German control*

PODOLIA

Copai Gorod 2,200 *in ghetto*

Murafa 4,500 *in ghetto*

Shargorod 5,300 *in ghetto*

Lucenets 2,897 *in ghetto*

Djurin 3,500 *in ghetto*

River Bug

Manicovca

Mogilev-Podolsk 15,000 *in ghetto*

Crijopol

Balanowka

Obadowka

Secureni

Briceni

Otaci

Tibulovca

camp under German control from 1942

Bershad 9,200 *in ghetto*

Jampol

T R A N S N I S T R I A *under Rumanian administration*

Olgopol *see page 87*

Lipcani 800 *8 July* 1,200 *on death march 20 July - 6 Aug*

Soroca

Edineti 1,000 *5-7 July*

Zgurita

River Dniester

Vascaut

Cotiugeni

Balta 2,723 *in ghetto*

Birzula

B E S S A R A B I A *under Rumanian control from July 1941*

Vartujeni

Cusminca

Ramnita

Marculesti

Rezina

148,000

Jews from Bessarabia perished in Transnistria

Limbeni

Parlita

Rautel forest **many thousands**

Balti 50 *8 July* 44 *9 July*

Falesti

Orhei 200 *6 August*

several hundred escape to Soviet central Asia June - July

RUMANIA

MOLDAVIA

Dubossary

Criuleni

Jassy

Kishinev

10,000 *17-31 July*
1,411 *1 August*
551 *7 August*
325 *8 August*
41,000 *after deportation*

Tiraspol

Tighina

River Pruth

0	miles	50
0	kilometres	80

© Martin Gilbert 1982

institutions were closed and on 13 June 1941 many of the Jewish leaders, as well as wealthy Jews, were exiled to Siberia, where many died. But with the arrival of the Nazi killing squads in July 1941, the scale of murder, as indicated above, exceeded anything previously known.

Following the initial killings, internment camps were set up throughout the province. At the camp in Edineti, after the initial slaughter, 70 to 100 people died every day in July and August 1941, mostly of starvation.

Then in September the Jews of Bessarabia were forced out of the province in hundreds of death marches, some of which are shown above. In all, more than 148,000 Bessarabian Jews perished in the ghettos and camps of Transnistria. During these marches more than half of the victims died: of exposure, disease, hunger, thirst and the savage brutality of the Rumanian and German guards, who would often pick a group of marchers at random, order them aside, and shoot them.

Map 79

THE JEWS OF THE BUKOVINA ON THE EVE OF WAR

miles 10

kilometres 20

Kolomyja

GREATER GERMANY
(EASTERN GALICIA)

Sniatyn

Kuty

Cincau
57

Dorosauti
58

Ocna
115

Zastavna
635

Davidesti
48

Cozmeni
640

Lujeni
381

Sadagura
1,488

RUMANIA
(BESSARABIA)

Banila pe Ceremus
517

Milie
197

Ispas
143

Vijnita
2,666

Berhomet
979

Stanestii
622

Broscauti
115

Costesti
274

Cabesti
120

Jadova
50

Panca
25

Czernowitz
(Cernauti)
42,932

River

Pruth

Nova
Jadova
325

Mihova
243

Storojinet
2,482

Rastoace
71

Mareniceni
25

Gura Putilei
115

Dintinet
56

Banila
688

Cires
100

Iordanesti
99

Budinet
8

River

Ciudeiu
570

Petrauti
138

Siret

RUMANIA
(MOLDAVIA)

Toraceni
58

Putila
382

Crasna Putnei
169

Crasna Iliesti
97

Igesti
100

Fradautii
Noui
104

Siret
2,121

Sarghieni
204

Straja
134

Vicovul de Sus
334

Bainet
23

Zamostea
129

Plosca
99

Seletin
737

Brodina
234

Putna
214

Dornesti
84

Zvorastea
28

River Ceremos

BUKOVINA

Argel
11

Sucevita
10

Marginea
23

Radauti
5,647

Serbauti
14

Granicesti
9

Clit
4

Darmanesti
92

Moldovita
452

Poiana
11

Moldova Sulita
55

River

Vatra
136

Frumosul
88

Ilisesti
131

Suceava
3,533

Liteni
11

HUNGARY
(TRANSYLVANIA)

Breaza
94

Carlibaba
154

Moldova

Vama
392

Paltinoasa
14

Campulung-Moldovenesc
1,488

Frasin
156

Gura
Humoruliu
1,951

Ciocanesti
7

Stulpicani
151

Iacobeni
228

Ostra
10

RUMANIA

Vatra Dornei
1,750

© Martin Gilbert 1982

DEPORTATIONS AND DEATH MARCHES FROM THE BUKOVINA, JUNE-NOVEMBER 1941

Bar
concentration camp

PODOLIA

Zhmerinka
ghetto

Copai Gorod
ghetto

Murafa
ghetto

Shargorod
ghetto

Djurin
ghetto

Lucenets
ghetto

TRANSNISTRIA

| **124,632** | *perished in deportation from Bukovina* |

Mogilev-Podolsk
ghetto

Otaci

River Dniester

| **3,106** | *murdered 8 July to 29 August 1941* |

Czernowitz

| **30,000** | *deported 1-15 November 1941* |

16 September 1941

Broscauti

Costesti

Jadova

Panca

Nova Jadova

Cires

Storojinet

Budinet **2,482**

Banila

Igesti

Petrauti

Lipcani

**Noua Sulita
DOROHOI REGION**

| **3,000** |

Edineti

| **12,000** | *in camp* |

| **70-100 a day** | *mid-July to mid-September* |

BESSARABIA

River Pruth

**Dorohoi
5,384**

deported 12-14 November 1941

BUKOVINA

| **144,197** | *in 1930* |

© Martin Gilbert 1982

THE BUKOVINA

Oslo

Stockholm

Leningrad

Moscow

North Sea

Warsaw

Kiev

Berlin

**GREATER
GERMANY**

Lvov

BUKOVINA

Paris

Vienna

HUNGARY

RUMANIA

Black Sea

Rome

Belgrade

Istanbul

Athens

© Martin Gilbert 1982

CRETE

The Jews of the Bukovina, like those of
Bessarabia, were driven eastwards to ghettos
in Transnistria. Uprooted from more than
100 communities, they too were marched
away, interned, and then marched off again.
Within a year more than 120,000 had died
(page 74). The photograph was taken at the
start of a Bukovina death march.

THE JEWS OF ESTONIA ON THE EVE OF WAR

FINLAND

Helsinki

Gulf of Finland

Baltic Sea

Leningrad

German front line 1 September 1941

Tallin 4,213

Paldiski 1

Nomme 109

Keila 1

Rakvere 100

Johvi 8

Narva 370

ESTONIA

Tapa 16

Haapsalu 11

Türi 2

Paide 31

Mustvee 6

DAGO 10

Karuse 37

Poltsamaa 2

Jogeva 5

Lake Peipus

SOVIET UNION

OSEL

Pärnu 500

Viljandi 226

Kuressaare 37

Moisaküla 1

Tartu 1,766

Lake Pskov

Kilingi-Nomme 1

Torva 1

Voru 199

Pskov

Valga 521

Anstla 3

Petseri 5

Gulf of Riga

LATVIA

0 miles 40
0 kilometres 60

© Martin Gilbert 1982

ESTONIA CONQUERED. 3 SEPTEMBER 1941

Oslo

Helsinki

Stockholm

Leningrad

North Sea

Baltic Sea

Pskov

ESTONIA

Moscow

Vilna

Berlin

Warsaw

GREATER GERMANY

Vienna

Czernowitz

Budapest

Loborgrad

BOSNIA

Belgrade

Bucharest

Black Sea

Sarajevo

Sofia

Rome

Adriatic Sea

Ankara

0 miles 200
0 kilometres 400

© Martin Gilbert 1982

The Jewish community of Estonia owed its origins to the Cantonists: Jewish boy soldiers conscripted for the army of Tsar Nicholas I at the age of 12, and sometimes even at eight or nine. These boys served a compulsory 25 years, a system which had started in 1827 and which continued for more than 20 years. On demobilization, many Cantonists settled in Tallin, known in Russian as Reval. A further 2,000 Russian Jews came in Tsarist times to live in the university town of Tartu, known to the Jews by its German name, Dorpat.

In the inter-war years Estonia was the only country in eastern Europe to adhere to the minority treaties of the League of Nations. Jewish autonomous institutions, set up in 1926, were controlled by a Jewish Cultural Council. For ten years Jewish life flourished. But from 1934, a local fascist movement encouraged anti-semitism.

In 1940 Estonia was annexed by the Soviet Union. Five hundred Jewish communal leaders, as well as many 'capitalist' Jews, were then deported to Siberia, where many died. But following the German invasion of Russia in June 1941, some 3,000 Estonian

JEWISH COMMUNITIES IN BOSNIA ON THE EVE OF WAR

Jasenovac

C R O A T I A

River Sava

Bosanska
Dubica
7

Stara
Gradiska
concentration camp
set up in April 1941

Bosanska
Gradiska
28

Bosanski
Brod
79

Odzak
3

Bosanski
Samac
29

Derventa
143

Modrica
13

Brcko
112

Bijeljina
321

Prijedor
45

Gradacac
45

Janja
4

Ljubija
6

Doboj
54

Gracanica
22

Dubrava
20

Banja Luka
368

Tesanj
18

Tuzla
314

Teslic
16

Zvornik
75

B   O   S   N   I   A

Zivinice
7

Kljuc
4

Zepce
71

Vlasenica
60

Ljubovija

Kladanj
12

Srebrenica
4

Jajce
31

Travnik
364

Zenica
234

Olovo
30

Donji Vakuf
3

Kruscica
concentration camp
set up in April 1941

Visoko
113

Visegrad
107

Fojnica
3

Kiseljak
17

Sarajevo
8,196

miles 25

kilometres 40

© Martin Gilbert 1982

Jews found refuge in the Soviet Union. After the German occupation of Tallin in September, the remaining 1,000 Jews were murdered by the SS killing squads.

After the German invasion of Bosnia, a few Jews managed to flee over the mountains into Italian-occupied territory, but the majority were deported to concentration camps controlled by the Croat fascist 'Ustachi'. The majority died in the camps.

The Jewish community of Sarajevo had been built up during the sixteenth century by Jewish refugees from Spain. These 'Sephardi' Jews spoke their own language, Ladino, and helped, as merchants and traders, to link Bosnia with the outside world. After the Austrian annexation of Bosnia in 1878, hundreds of Ashkenazi Jews, from Vienna, Prague and Budapest, joined the local communities. Between the wars, during the 'Yugoslav era', the Jews of Bosnia enjoyed full civil liberties. But disaster struck from the first days of the German occupation, with the burning down of the synagogue by German troops and local Muslims.

By November 1941 a total of 14,000 Bosnian Jews had been deported to the camps shown here *(right)*. Less than 1,000 survived the war.

THE JEWS OF BOSNIA MURDERED

miles 40

kilometres 60

Loborgrad
4,000
women

C R O A T I A

Jasenovac
4,000
men

Stara Gradiska
6,000
children

children

women

men

Tuzla

B O S N I A

Travnik

Kruscica

Sarajevo

Italian
zone

D A L M A T I A

Mostar
1,600

Adriatic
Sea

© Martin Gilbert 1982

Map 86

MASSACRE AND REVOLT IN SEPTEMBER AND OCTOBER 1941

Zagare
2,236 *murdered*
150 *shot*

Nevel
710

Moscow

Yanovichi
1,180

Krasnopole
1,940

Vitebsk
3,000

Krupki
1,500

Rudnya
6,200

Shklov
3,000

Borisov
8,000

Mogilev
2,760

Tatarsk
resistance
25 October 1941

Lomza
3,500

Zambrow
1,000

see map 88

Bobruisk
380

Parichi
1,700

Starodub **270**
resistance
25 October 1941

see map 87

Vilna

Lida

Pripet marshes

Lelchitsy
1,400

Chernigov
280

Ostrog

Ovruch
30

Korosten
340

Radomyshl
13,020

Toporow **120**
Przemyslany
500

Komarno
300

Kozowa **300**
Buczacz
400

Bolechow
1,000

Zhitomir
7,500

Babi Yar

Kiev
33,771
29-30 September

Voronezh

Stanislawow
10,000

Litin
2,000

Skvira
1,000

Sniatyn
400

Vinnitsa
28,000

Uman
24,000

Kremenchug
7,000

Dnepropetrovsk
15,000

Kosow
2,200

Zbaraz
70

Berdichev
14,803

Ananayev
300

Kirovograd
5,000

Delatyn
1,950

Dubossary
6,000

Nikolaiev
5,000

Melitopol
2,000

Mariupol
8,500

Taganrog
3,000

Odessa
48,000

Kherson
410

Belgrade
449
11 October

Sea of Azov

Kakhovka
740

Black Sea

0   miles   100
0   kilometres   150

© Martin Gilbert 1982

Baltic Sea

GREATER GERMANY

HUNGARY

RUMANIA

SERBIA

German front line, October, 1941

As the German armies approached Moscow, the killing squads continued their work behind the lines. The map above shows some of the main killings. The map opposite *(above)* shows the details in the Vilna region of Lithuania, where a German lieutenant carefully recorded for his superiors the precise number of those killed on each day of his squad's activities, dividing his statistics into men, women and children.

The killing squads were heavily armed and had strong local support. The Jews were unarmed, and surrounded by an extremely hostile peasantry, who sometimes attacked them even before the killing squads had arrived. In some cases this random butchery of so many Jews led the SS to order the locals to stop the killing, in order to put it on a 'systematic' basis, according to the killing squad schedules. Despite the overwhelming odds against them the Jews rose in revolt wherever they could. The first revolts, as shown above, were at Tatarsk and Starodub. To crush this resistance, German regular

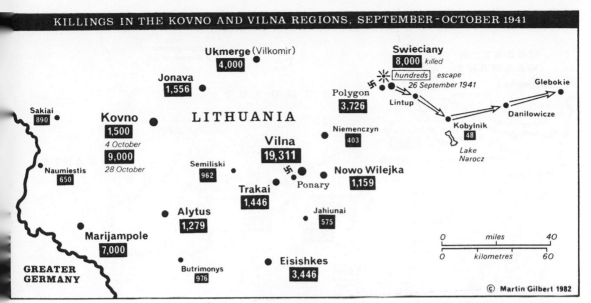

KILLINGS IN THE KOVNO AND VILNA REGIONS, SEPTEMBER-OCTOBER 1941

Ukmerge (Vilkomir)
4,000

Swieciany
8,000 *killed*

hundreds *escape*
26 September 1941

Glebokie

Jonava
1,556

Polygon
3,726

Lintup

Danilowicze

Sakiai
890

Kovno
1,500
4 October
9,000
28 October

LITHUANIA

Niemenczyn
403

Kobylnik
48

*Lake
Narocz*

Vilna
19,311

Naumiestis
650

Semiliski
962

Nowo Wilejka
1,159

Trakai
1,446

Ponary

Alytus
1,279

Jahiunai
575

Marijampole
7,000

GREATER
GERMANY

Butrimonys
976

Eisishkes
3,446

0 *miles* 40
0 *kilometres* 60

© Martin Gilbert 1982

army units were brought in. Where necessary, as resistance spread, the Germans used artillery fire, and even air support.

At Kiev the Jews were driven into Babi Yar, a ravine in the suburbs, and then machine-gunned by an SS killing squad, helped by Ukrainian militiamen.

At Vilna the Jews were confined to a ghetto inside the city, where hundreds were murdered. Others were taken away in batches of a thousand and more to pits eight miles away, at the village of Ponary. Here too, they were shot.

Any Jews who managed to escape from their executioners at the pits were killed by a special unit of Germans and Lithuanians. Hundreds of other Jews were murdered inside Vilna itself, and in the notorious Lukiszki prison. In two months, throughout the former eastern provinces of Poland *(right, below)*, more than 20,000 Jews were murdered.

On 26 September 1941 the Jews of Swieciany were rounded up and taken to a former army camp in the nearby Polygon woods, where they were massacred. On the evening before, several hundred young men and women had managed to break through the Lithuanian police cordon and escape eastwards, to towns not yet reached by the killing squads. These Jewish communities were liable at any moment to be subjected to the activities of the killing squads, for, as the map opposite shows, the front line, with its chaos and confusion had long since moved much further east.

FURTHER KILLINGS, SEPTEMBER-OCTOBER 1941

LITHUANIA

Olkieniki
1,000
25 September

WHITE
RUSSIA

Lida
2,000
28 October

Koidanov
1,500

Szczuczyn
50

Nieswiez
5,000
30 October

Kleck
4,000
31 October

Slutsk
300

Lachowicze
2,000
28 October

POLESIA

Hancewicze
3,000
13-15 September

Antopol
150
October

*Pripet
marshes*

1921 to 1939

River Bug

VOLHYNIA

Kostopol
1,400
*women and children
October*

GREATER
GERMANY

Miedzyrzec
1,500
October

Poland's eastern border with Russia

Ostrog
2,500
September

EASTERN
GALICIA

0 *miles* 50
0 *kilometres* 80

© Martin Gilbert 1982

64

Map 89

THE DESTRUCTION OF THE JEWS OF CROATIA, 1941-1944

GREATER
GERMANY
Klagenfurt

AUSTRIA

annexed by Germany, April 1941

SLOVENIA
annexed by
Italy
April
1941

Trieste

ISTRIA

HUNGARY

Danica
2,000

Zagreb

CROATIA

Karlovac

Loborgrad
hundreds

Osijek

BACSKA
annexed by
Hungary

Jasenovac
20,000

Dakovo
2,000

Gradiska
2,000

Jadovno
2,000

under
Croat
control
April-September
1941

3,000
escape

BANAT

RUMANIA

Belgrade

Zara
Italian

Adriatic

DALMATIA

under Italian control, 1941-1943

BOSNIA

Split

Sea

ITALY

SERBIA
under German occupation
from April 1941

© Martin Gilbert 1982

miles 60
kilometres 80

Following the German army's conquest of Yugoslavia, a pro-German regime was established in Croatia, with its capital at Zagreb *(above)*. On 30 April 1941 this new Croat State introduced its first racial laws, removing Jews from public office and ordering all Jews to wear a yellow badge. Within a few weeks, several wealthy Jews had been seized in Zagreb and held as hostages until local Jews could provide 100 kilogrammes of gold for their release, thus impoverishing the community. By the end of May all Jewish cultural institutions had been closed, synagogues ransacked, and cemeteries destroyed.

In May 1941 the first Croat concentration camp was set up, at Danica. It was quickly followed by four more camps, at Jadovno, Gradiska, Loborgrad, and Dakovo. More than 6,000 Croat Jews were deported to these camps, and during July and August almost all of them were murdered. On 1 October 1941 a further camp was established at Jasenovac.

By the end of 1942 the remaining 20,000 Croat Jews had been rounded up and sent to Jasenovac, where most of them were starved to death, beaten to death or shot. By the spring of 1945, as the Soviet army and Yugoslav partisan forces approached the camp, only a few hundred were still alive *(page 207)*.

Between April 1941 and April 1942 more than 3,000 Croatian Jews escaped over the mountains to Italy and the Italian-controlled coastal zone. But by a law of 30 April 1941, people with only one Jewish parent were 'protected' from deportation.

Because of the successful intervention by the Catholic Church and the Papal Nuncio to save the Jewish partners in mixed marriages, 1,000 Croat Jews survived the war.

In Holland the Jews had been confined to special parts of the towns, denied the right to teach or to remain in the civil service, and ordered to wear a yellow star. Nazi agitators repeatedly raided the Jewish quarter of

DUTCH JEWS DEPORTED TO MAUTHAUSEN

425 deported

25

400

MAUTHAUSEN AND ITS SUB-CAMPS

© Martin Gilbert 1982

Amsterdam, beating up Jews in the streets. At the beginning of February 1941 a Dutch Nazi had been killed when the Jews resisted one such attack. At the same time the Germans accused a Jewish tavern owner, Ernst Cahn, of daring to resist a German patrol. Cahn was shot, the first Dutch citizen to die in front of a German firing-squad. A few days later, on 22 February 1941, the SS raided the Jewish quarter of Amsterdam as a reprisal for the earlier resistance: 425 Jews were arrested, beaten, and deported to Buchenwald *(above, right)*. Some died there. The rest, among them the distinguished Czech pharmacologist, Emil Starckenstein, were transferred shortly afterwards to Mauthausen. Within three days of their arrival, they were killed in the stone quarry, the centre of Mauthausen's forced labour network *(right)*.

The photograph is of the gallows at Mauthausen, photographed at liberation *(pages 221–2)*.

Map 92

TWELVE EASTWARD DEPORTATIONS, 16 OCTOBER – 29 NOVEMBER 1941

Riga
LATVIA

REICHSKOMMISSARIAT OSTLAND

North Sea

Baltic Sea

Minsk

WHITE RUSSIA

Hamburg
1,034

Emden

Berlin
4,187

GREATER GERMANY

Lodz

Warsaw

RUHR
Düsseldorf
984

Cologne
2,007

Würzburg
202

BOHEMIA

Prague
5,000

Frankfurt
1,113

Luxembourg
512

Nuremberg
618

Brno
3,000

Vienna
5,000

Munich
1,000

A U S T R I A

Lublin

GENERAL GOVERNMENT

EASTERN GALICIA

0   miles   150
0   kilometres   200

© Martin Gilbert 1982

In the autumn of 1941 the SS decided to deport more than 22,000 Jews to the ghettos of Lodz, Warsaw and Lublin, and to the former Soviet cities of Riga and Minsk *(above)*. The first of these deportation trains left on 16 October 1941. On reaching the ghettos, the Jews were faced with starvation. On reaching Riga and Minsk, many were taken to nearby woods and shot.

Meanwhile, beginning on 10 October 1941, thousands of Slovak Jews were sent to labour camps at Sered, Vyhne and Novaky, while the remaining Jews living in what had once been Czechoslovakia were ordered out of their homes and sent to specially designated 'ghetto areas' in 14 selected towns *(opposite, above)*. Already, on 1 September 1941, these Jews had been

ordered to wear the yellow star, and to cease all business activity. In Slovakia alone more than 10,000 Jewish shops and businesses had been closed down.

The largest of the new ghettos was established on 24 November 1941 in the small fortress town of Theresienstadt, known in Czech as Terezin. By the end of the war, 73,614 Jews had been deported to Theresienstadt from Bohemia and Moravia, and thousands more from elsewhere in Greater Germany.

In November the eastward deportations continued, as did the work of the mobile killing squads *(right)*. At the same time, as an experiment, 1,200 prisoners at Buchenwald were taken to the euthanasia institute at Bernberg, and gassed.

BOHEMIAN, MORAVIAN AND SLOVAK JEWS FORCED INTO GHETTOS, 10 OCTOBER 1941

SUDETENLAND

GERMANY

GREATER

MORAVIA

BOHEMIA

SLOVAKIA

FELVIDEK
annexed by Hungary

Cheb · Karlovy Vary · Marianske Lazne · Plana · Plzen · Teplice · Usti · Theresienstadt · Mlada Boleslav · Brandys · Prague · Kolin · Hradec Kralove · Pardubice · Klatovy · Trebic · Boskovice · Olomouc · Unicov · Moravska Ostrava · Lipnik · Holesov · Kromeriz · Brno · Uhersky Brod · Ivancice · Mikulov · Breclav · Zilina · Ruzomberok · Poprad · Bardejov · Presov · Trencin · Novaky · Vyhne · Kosice · Trnava · Sered · Nitra · Bratislava · Galanta · Dunajska Streda · Komarno · Levice

0   miles   60
0   kilometres   80

© Martin Gilbert 1982

MASSACRE AND DEPORTATION, NOVEMBER 1941

North Sea

Baltic Sea

GERMAN-OCCUPIED-RUSSIA

RUHR

RHINELAND

BAVARIA

TRANSNISTRIA

UKRAINE

Black Sea

Borisov 7,000
Monastyrshchina 1,010
Riga 10,000
Rumbuli forest
Vitebsk 4,090
Lyubavichi 700
Kovno 5,000
Berezino 1,000
Vilna 1,341
Mogilev 3,730
Ponary
Minsk 12,000
Nowogrodek 400
Rogachev 3,500
Wolozyn 300
Swierzen 500
Bobruisk 20,000
Mir 1,500
Gomel 4,000
Slonim 9,000
Rowne 15,000
Kremenchug 8,000
Kamionka Strumilowa 500
Berdichev 2,000
Boryslaw 1,500
Czernowitz 30,000
Lvov 3,000
Stryj 1,200
Nadworna 2,500
Odessa 25,000
Przemyslany 400
Kolomyja 1,000
Belgrade

Berlin · Bernberg · Lodz · Düsseldorf 489 · Buchenwald 1,200 · Bayreuth 50 · Theresienstadt · Essen 252

0   miles   100
0   kilometres   200

© Martin Gilbert 1982

Map 95

CHELMNO DEATH CAMP, THE FIRST VICTIMS, 8-14 DECEMBER 1941

River Warta

Kolo 2,300 *8 December*
Kolo station
Powierce station
Zawadki mill
Chelmno wood
Chelmno
River Ner

Wladyslawow 115
Brudzew 20
River Warta
Tuliszkow 232
Dabie 975
14 December

Turek 1,757

Uniejow 492

| 0 | miles | 2 |

| 0 | kilometres | 4 |

Kowale Panskie 4,000 *interned* 1,100 *deported* *10 December*

Dobra 350

© Martin Gilbert 1982

Map 96

DEPORTATION, MASSACRE AND THE FIRST DEATH CAMP, DECEMBER 1941

North Sea

Baltic Sea

Riga 15,000

Liepaja 3,500

Nevel 43

Rzhev 840

Moscow

German military advance by December 1941

Jody 700

Polotsk 7,000

Mekhov 200

Vilna 385

Mogilev 315

Nowogrodek 400

Parichi 1,500

Bobruisk 5,280

Koryukovka 90

Munster 403

Warendorf 6

Chelmno

Warsaw 29,538 died of starvation July–December 1941

GREATER GERMANY

Brzezany 1,000

Horodenka 500

Slaviansk 1,000

Artemovsk 90

Fulda 131

Karasubazar 2,500

Feodosia 2,000

Zabie 500

Zablotow 1,000

CRIMEA

Zemun 15,000 December 1941–January 1942

Belgrade

miles 0 200

kilometres 0 300

Black Sea

© Martin Gilbert 1982

The successful gassing of 1,200 Jews from Buchenwald in November 1941 was followed two weeks later by a second gassing experiment. The place chosen was a wood near the Polish village of Chelmno; the victims were Jewish villagers from several nearby communities *(opposite)*. The method chosen was to bring the Jews by narrow guage railway from Kolo to Powierce, drive them with whips to the river, lock them overnight, without food or water, in the mill at the hamlet of Zawadki (seen here in a photograph taken in 1980), and then, in the morning, drive them in lorries to the woods near Chelmno, gassing them by exhaust fumes during the journey. The bodies were then thrown into deep pits, while the lorries returned to the mill for more victims. In all, five lorries were used, three of which held up to 150 people, and two up to 100. By noon, the whole trainload had usually been destroyed.

The first gassing at Chelmno took place on 8 December 1941. It was judged a success, and was continued on an ever widening scale. The next 1,000 victims had already been taken by truck from six villages to Kowale Panskie, and were held there until the journey to Chelmno on 10 December 1941.

Even as the gassings at Chelmno began, the deportations from Germany to Riga continued, as did the mass murder of deportees almost immediately after their arrival *(above)*. Thus on 13 December 1941 the last six Jews living in Warendorf were deported to Riga and killed: their small community dated back to 1387, and had been 41 strong in 1933. Most had managed to emigrate by 1939. In the south-east, German forces had conquered the Crimea. Here too, community after community was being wiped out by the killing squads.

It was not only at Chelmno that mobile gas vans were being used. At the concentration camp at Zemun, just outside Belgrade, some 15,000 Jews from all over Serbia were gradually but systematically being gassed in vans disguised as Red Cross vehicles. By June 1942 all had been killed: an average of 120 every day. No sooner had the vans completed their task at Zemun than they were transferred to Riga *(page 91)*.

GLOBAL WAR: THE U.S.A., THE AXIS POWERS, AND JAPAN

© Martin Gilbert 1982

THE KILLING OF JEWS CONTINUES: THE BALTIC STATES

© Martin Gilbert 1982

Map 99

JEWS MARKED OUT FOR DEATH, 20 JANUARY 1942

USSR 5 million

ESTONIA "Free of Jews"

NORWAY 1,300

LATVIA 3,500

DENMARK 5,600

LITHUANIA 34,000

HOLLAND 160,800

BIALYSTOK DISTRICT 400,000

WHITE RUSSIA 446,484

BELGIUM 43,000

BALTIC STATES

EASTERN TERRITORIES

Berlin
Wannsee

GERMANY 131,800

GENERAL GOVERNMT 2,284,000

420,000

UKRAINE 2,994,684

FRANCE OCCUPIED ZONE 165,000

BOHEMIA & MORAVIA 74,200

88,000

SLOVAKIA

FRANCE UNOCCUPIED ZONE 700,000 including French North Africa

AUSTRIA

HUNGARY 742,800

43,700

10,000

RUMANIA 342,000

CROATIA 40,000

SERBIA

ITALY 58,000

BULGARIA 48,000

ALBANIA 200

GREECE 69,600

KOS

MOROCCO

ALGERIA French North Africa

TUNISIA

RHODES

0 miles 200
0 kilometres 300

CRETE

© Martin Gilbert 1982

By December 1941 the German armies were masters of Europe, and on 7 December 1941 the Japanese entered the war against the United States and Britain (opposite, above).

From Estonia the killing squads reported to Berlin with their usual precision the murder over the previous six months of 229,052 Jews in Latvia and Lithuania (opposite, below). All 1,000 Jews caught in Estonia had also been killed.

At the Wannsee suburb of Berlin, German officials gathered on 20 January 1942 to discuss the final destruction of European Jewry. They also noted, as seen on the map above, what they believed to be the precise number of Jews still to be killed. The 'low' figures for the Baltic States indicate their knowledge that so many thousands had been killed already. At the Wannsee Conference plans were made for what was called the 'Final Solution', to be carried out by means of slave labour for all able-bodied Jews, the separation of men from women, and mass deportation.

Map 100

JEWS MARKED OUT FOR DEATH, JANUARY 1942, BUT BEYOND NAZI RULE

Arctic
Ocean

North
Atlantic
Ocean

GREAT BRITAIN
330,000

REPUBLIC OF IRELAND
4,000

PORTUGAL
3,000

SPAIN
6,000

SWEDEN
8,000

FINLAND
2,300

North
Sea

Baltic Sea

Riga
Minsk

Moscow

German front line, January 1942

Wannsee · Berlin
· Chelmno

SWITZERLAND
18,000

Bogdanovka · ⚡ Atmicetka

⚡ Jasenovac

Gurs

TURKEY-IN -EUROPE
55,000

Yalta
Black Sea

0   miles   300
0 kilometres 400

Mediterranean   Sea

© Martin Gilbert 1982

Among the statistics presented by the SS to the Wannsee Conference were the number of Jews in Britain and Finland, as well as in all the neutral countries of Europe, whom the Gestapo hoped eventually to bring within the scope of the 'Final Solution'.

In 1942 the Finns agreed to deport 11 Jewish refugees. But when these 11 were murdered by the Gestapo, the Finnish Government refused to allow any further deportations (page 231).

Meanwhile, the gassings at Chelmno, and the killing squad slaughter in Russia, continued, as did the deaths from starvation in the Warsaw ghetto, and the death marches from the Bukovina (opposite, above). Those

Jews in Odessa who had not been murdered earlier were deported to concentration camps, where thousands died of brutality, starvation and disease. At Novi Sad, on 23 January 1942, Hungarian fascists drove 550 Jews and 292 Serbs to the river and on to the ice, and, after firing on the ice to break it up, shot all those who managed to stay afloat. In Titel 35 of the 36 Jews of the town were shot.

In the Crimea (opposite, below) ancient communities and modern collective farms were being wiped out so thoroughly that on 16 April 1942 Berlin was officially informed by the local SS: 'the Crimea is purged of Jews' (page 84).

DEPORTATION AND MASSACRE, JANUARY 1942

WHITE RUSSIA

German front line, January 1942

0 miles 150
0 kilometres 200

Izbica Kujawska **1,000** 14 January

Brdow **600** 12 January

Bugaj **600** 12 January

Mozyr **1,500**

Kiev **8,000**

Kharkov **14,000**

Drobitzky Yar

Artemovsk **3,000**

Chelmno

Klodawa **1,140** 9 January

Lodz **3,000** 16 January

Warsaw

Pripet marshes

Brzezany **400**

Khmelnik **6,800**

Vinnitsa **5,000**

Novomoskovsk **140**

River Dnieper

Pavlovgrad **3,670**

Sea of Azov

River Vistula

5,123 deaths from starvation

Northern Bug

River Dniester

Southern Bug

TRANSNISTRIA

Dumanovka **18,000**
Bogdanovka **48,000**
Atmicetka **5,000**
Vertugen **23,000**

1942 to 1943

Mielec **500**

Dolina **2,000**

BUKOVINA deportations continue

BESSARABIA deportations continue

CRIMEA

HUNGARY

in all **2,550** Serbs and **700** Jews

killed by Hungarian fascists in occupied Yugoslavia

Titel

Novi Sad

Odessa **19,852** 12 January to 23 February

Black Sea

© Martin Gilbert 1982

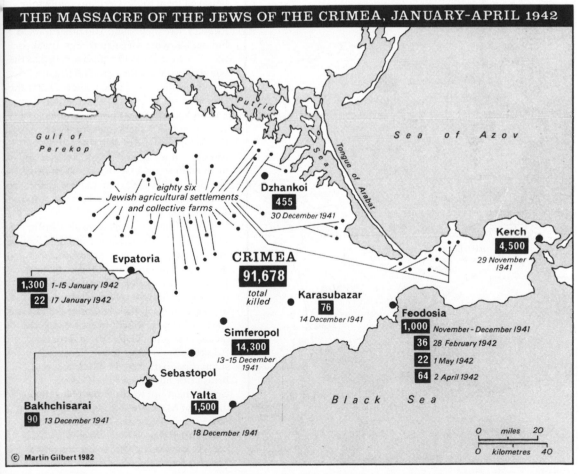

THE MASSACRE OF THE JEWS OF THE CRIMEA, JANUARY–APRIL 1942

Putrid

Gulf of Perekop

Sea of Azov

Sivash Sea

Tongue of Arabat

eighty six Jewish agricultural settlements and collective farms

Dzhankoi **455** 30 December 1941

Kerch **4,500** 29 November 1941

Evpatoria

CRIMEA **91,678** total killed

Karasubazar **76** 14 December 1941

1,300 1–15 January 1942
22 17 January 1942

Simferopol **14,300** 13–15 December 1941

Feodosia **1,000** November–December 1941
36 28 February 1942
22 1 May 1942
64 2 April 1942

Sebastopol

Bakhchisarai **90** 13 December 1941

Yalta **1,500** 18 December 1941

Black Sea

0 miles 20
0 kilometres 40

© Martin Gilbert 1982

Map 103

EASTERN KILLINGS, AND THE 'STRUMA'

WHITE RUSSIA

Lepel `1,000` *28 February*

SOVIET UNION

Cherven `1,800` *I February*

Pyshno `26`

Kursk `100` *I February*

VOLHYNIA

under German occupation

Shamovo `500` *2 February*

UKRAINE

Brailov `3,000` *12 February*

Hulievca `650` *13 March*

Czernowitz

Cihrin `722` *9 March*

Taganrog

Jassy

Sea of Azov

RUMANIA

CRIMEA

Caucasus

Bucharest

Constanta *12 December 1941*

B l a c k   S e a

Simferopol `300`

BULGARIA

sunk 24 February 1942

Istanbul *arrived 15 December 1941*

Sile

`709` *drowned*

`1` *saved*

Sea of Marmara

T U R K E Y

neutral

KOS *under German occupation*

RHODES *under German occupation*

SYRIA

CRETE *under German occupation*

CYPRUS

intended route

M e d i t e r r a n e a n
S e a

Haifa

Tel Aviv

PALESTINE

British Mandate

Alexandria

E G Y P T

TRANS-JORDAN

SAUDI ARABIA

`0` miles `150`
`0` kilometres `300`

© Martin Gilbert 1982

German front line: January 1942

The eastern killings continued during February 1942, with shootings such as those at Radom, and the deportation by lorry from Sierpc to Mlawa, when hundreds were murdered on the journey itself.

Hundreds of Jews were also deported to slave labour camps, such as the one at Cieszanow *(right)*, where conditions were so harsh that almost no one survived.

Jewish resistance also grew. A group of Jews from Tomaszow Lubelski *(right)* organized a partisan unit which fought the Germans for some months, until it was betrayed by local Poles. Elsewhere, small groups of Jews still managed to escape, and to maintain themselves in the woods. Thus the four Jewish families living in the village of Hola *(opposite, below)*, who were about to be deported to the ghetto in Wlodawa, escaped to the woods east of Zamolodycze, where they found several families already in hiding. Within a short time, armed Ukrainian peasants forced the families out of the forest, locked them into a barn, and then betrayed them to the Germans. Only four Jews managed to escape, to the Skorodnica forest. There they found 100 other Jews in hiding, but when German troops attacked them 75 were shot. The survivors fled to the woods near Maryanka, and managed to acquire a rifle from Lubien village. Later they helped smuggle 75 Jews from the Wlodawa ghetto, and a further 46 men, women and girls from the village of Adampol. The group then set up its base deep in the Skorodnica forest, built up an armoury of 15 rifles and, in an ambush on a German truck, killed 10 Germans. Later the group joined other Jewish partisans in the Parczew forest *(pages 109 to 110)*.

The SS killing squads were also still at work *(left)*, in White Russia and the Ukraine in February, and in the Transnistrian deportee camps in March. Meanwhile, the Jews of neighbouring Rumania, as well as thousands of Jewish refugees who had managed to reach Rumania from Poland and Czechoslovakia, sought boats in which to escape across the Black Sea, and on to Palestine. Boats were scarce, German submarines patrolled the Black Sea, and British officials pressed the Turkish Government not to allow the boats through the Sea of Marmara, hoping thereby not to offend Arab opinion in Palestine.

One such ship was the 'Struma', which had left Rumania on 12 December 1941. The ship was flying the neutral Panamanian

DEPORTATION, MASSACRE AND REVOLT, FEBRUARY 1942

Sompolno **1,000**

Mlawa
death march

Sierpc **500** 6 February

River Vistula

River Bug

Warsaw **4,618** *deaths from starvation in February*

Chelmno

WARTHELAND

G R E A T E R

POLAND

Radom **40** *'Bloody Thursday' 19 February*

see below

Wlodawa
resistance led by Mendel Heler *and* Meir Lalimacher

Pripet marshes

U K R A I N E

G E R M A N Y

Tomaszow Lubelski **1,500** 25 February

Belz **1,000**

Cieszanow *slave labour camp*

Brailov

E A S T E R N

G A L I C I A

SLOVAKIA

© Martin Gilbert 1982

0 miles 50
0 kilometres 80

ESCAPE, BETRAYAL, MASSACRE AND SURVIVAL WEST OF WLODAWA

Krywowierba

woods

Lubien

Wola

Adampol **46** *escape*

Adampol estate

River Bug

Zamolodycze

Hola **21** *killed* **4** *survived*

25 *in hiding*

woods

100 *in hiding*

75 *shot*

Wlodawa

Maryanka

25 *in hiding*

Skorodinica

75 *escape*

Suchawa

© Martin Gilbert 1982

0 miles 2
0 kilometres 4

flag, but while it was still in the Black Sea, Germany and Italy declared war on Panama, following the United States' entry into the war a week earlier. As a result, the ship was flying, in German eyes, an 'enemy' flag. After four days in the Black Sea, it reached Istanbul. But under British pressure, the Turks ordered the ship back into the Black Sea, where it was sunk, probably by the Germans, on 24 February 1942. All but one

refugee was drowned. 'Palestine', commented the British High Commissioner in Jerusalem, 'was under no obligation to them', and he went on to explain, that he was acting in accordance with the 'basic principle that enemy nationals from enemy or enemy-controlled territory should not be admitted to this country during the war', a principle, he insisted, that applied even to refugees from enemy territory.

Map 106

FOUR DEATH CAMPS AND THE ACCELERATION OF MURDER

The death camp at Chelmno had been in operation for more than six weeks by the time of the Wannsee Conference of 20 January 1942 (page 72). In March 1942 the town-by-town killings in the east continued (above), while at the same time (also above), three new death camps were being prepared, at Belzec, Treblinka and Sobibor, where, as at Chelmno, no-one was kept alive for slave labour. These four camps had a single purpose: to kill every Jew within a few hours of arrival.

As soon as these four 'death' camps were in operation, thousands of Jewish communities were marked out for deportation, first from German-occupied Poland, then from elsewhere in Greater Germany, and finally, from western and southern Europe. The deportees were told they were going to Poland to be 'resettled' in farms and labour camps. In fact, their only destination was a death camp and immediate death.

Between 8 December 1941 and 28 February 1942, more than 13,000 Jews had been deported to Chelmno and gassed. Adolf Eichmann himself had witnessed this process. Then, on 17 March 1942 the first deportations took place to the second of the death camps, just south of the village of Belzec. The deportees came from as far west

as Mielec (opposite above), as well as from Lublin, and from the village of Belzec itself. In all, 6,786 Jews were murdered in this first set of deportations. A group of a dozen or so Jews from the nearby village of Lubycza Krolewska, who had been at work for more than a month finishing construction in the camp, were also killed.

The gas chambers at Belzec operated for more than nine months, the killing process being supervised by SS men, assisted by Ukrainian and Estonian guards. A special rail spur from the main line to the unloading ramp could take 20 goods wagons at a time: these wagons were shunted on, leaving the rest of each train to wait its turn.

Hardly had the first Jews been gassed at Belzec, than the German authorities began a search throughout the western provinces of Germany for those Jews, often only a single family, living in isolated communities in remote country regions. From one such region, in the hills above Bad Kissingen (opposite, below), 83 Jews were seized, as well as 23 in Bad Kissingen itself. Deported eastward across Germany, Bohemia and Poland to Belzec, they were first held in two nearby internment camps, Izbica Lubelska and Piaski, and then sent on to Belzec, where they were gassed (pages 79 and 80). Not a single one of these deportees survived.

FIRST DEPORTATIONS TO BELZEC, 17 MARCH 1942

miles 25
kilometres 40

Lublin
1,600

Trawniki

Piaski

Dubienka
843

River Bug

VOLHYNIA

Krasnystaw

Izbica
Lubelska

Hrubieszow
1,343

LUBLIN
REGION

Szczebrzeszyn

Zamosc

GENERAL
GOVERNMENT

Zwierzyniec

Tomaszow
Lubelski

Belzec village 500

Belzec
camp

Lubycza
Krolewska

Mielec
4,500

WESTERN GALICIA

Lubaczow

EASTERN
GALICIA

Debica

Rzeszow

Jaroslaw

© Martin Gilbert 1982

GERMAN JEWS SEARCHED OUT FOR DEPORTATION TO BELZEC, 24 MARCH 1942

Höchheim
9

Bad Neustadt
3

River Saale

Brückenau
4

Kleineibstadt
6

Geroda
6

Steinach
4

Platz
2

Kleinbardorf
3

Schondra
6

Poppenlauer
14

Völkersleier
4

Bad Kissingen
23

Massbach
3

miles 5
kilometres 10

Lendershausen
2

Pfaffenhausen **13**

Kleinsteinach
4

© Martin Gilbert 1982

78

THE JEWS OF THE WURZBURG REGION ROUNDED UP FOR DEPORTATION

Laudenbach **11**

Thungen **3**

River Main

Schwanfeld **8**

River Main

Theilheim **31**

Zeilitzheim **7**

Gerolzhofen **19**

Lülsfeld **3**

Veitshochheim **4**

Rimpar **6**

Estenfeld **4**

Nordheim **4**

Altenschönbach **5**

Prichsenstadt **7**

Würzburg

320 deported
24 March

Höchberg **4**

Grosslangenheim **2**

Wiesenbronn **3**

Kitzingen **76**

Oberalterheim **4**

Reichenberg **12**

Mainbernheim **2**

Geroldshausen **2**

Gossmannsdorf **3**

Marktbreit **23**

Giebelstadt **5**

Acholshausen **2**

Huttenheim **3**

Allersheim **2**

Gaukönigshofen **25**

Obernbreit **5**

0   miles   5
0   kilometres   10

© Martin Gilbert 1982

THREE DEPORTATIONS FROM GERMANY TO BELZEC, 24 MARCH 1942

Jülich **42** 24 March

Görlitz

Radom

Piaski

Bad Kissingen **106** map 108

Dresden

Breslau

Izbica Lubelska

Chemnitz

Kielce

map 109

Gleiwitz

Würzburg **320** 24 March

Fürth **224** 24 March

Belzec

0   miles   80
0   kilometres   125

© Martin Gilbert 1982

The search for the remaining Jews of Germany continued during the last week of March 1942 and the first three weeks of April. Throughout the Würzburg region *(top)* single families and small communities were seized and taken to Würzburg, from where, on 24 March 1942 the first of three deportations took place, with 320 deportees. Together with the Jews collected at Bad Kissingen, Jülich and Fürth, all were deported eastwards *(above)*, held for a few days in the village of Piaski, and then taken to Belzec *(opposite)*; not one survived.

Throughout March Jews were also deported to Belzec from Eastern Galicia and the Lublin region. From Lublin itself almost all the city's large Jewish community was deported within two weeks.

The deportation of Jews to Chelmno also continued *(opposite)*. In the deportations from Opole were many Austrian-born Jews who had been deported from Vienna to Poland two years before *(page 27)*.

In Warsaw thousands of Jews continued to die of starvation. In other towns, such as Rohatyn and Tarnopol, the Jews were driven to nearby woods, and murdered. Near Ilja, on March 14, Jews who had been sent to

Map 111

MASS MURDER, DEPORTATION AND REVOLT, MARCH 1942

Baltic Sea

REICHSKOMMISSARIAT OSTLAND

resistance led by Josef Rodblat and David Rubin — Ilja 900 — 17 March

resistance led by R.M.Bromberg, M.P.Malkevich and Hersh Smolar — Minsk 5,000 — 2 March

GREATER GERMANY

Baranowicze 3,000 — 4 March

WARTHEGAU

Krosniewice 900 — 2 March

Kutno 7,000

Chelmno

Zychlin 3,200 — 3 March

Warsaw at least 4,000 deaths from starvation in March

Radoszkowicze 850 — 11 March

Ozorkow 500

Kazimierz Dolny 2,000

Lublin 10,000 — 18-25 March

REICHSKOMMISSARIAT UKRAINE

Poddebice 2,000

Wawolnica 1,500

Piaski 3,400

Kozminek 1,000

Opole Lubelskie 3,000 — 31 March

Izbica Lubelska 2,200 — 24 March

Siennica Rozana 272

Rawa Ruska 1,500 — 20 March

Zamosc hundreds

GENERAL GOVERNMENT

Bilgoraj 2,500

Belzec

Zolkiew 700 — 15 March

Tomaszow Lubelski hundreds

Lvov 15,000

Drohobycz 1,500

Rohatyn 2,000 — 20 March

Tarnopol 1,000 — 25 March

EASTERN GALICIA

Stanislawow 6,000 — 31 March

```
0      miles      40
0      kilometres      80
```

© Martin Gilbert 1982

work on a farm joined a group of Soviet partisans, and went into hiding in the forest. Three days later two Jewish leaders at Ilja, who had refused to hand over partisan sympathizers to the SS, themselves escaped to the forest to join the partisans. As a reprisal, the Germans shot all old and sick Jews in the street, then forced 900 more into a building, locked it, and set it on fire. All 900 perished.

In Minsk 5,000 Jews were taken from the ghetto to a newly dug pit on the outskirts of the town and machine-gunned. No ammunition was wasted on the hundreds of Jewish children seized that day: they were thrown into the pit alive to die of suffocation. The Jews of Minsk tried to organize a resistance group. But on 31 March 1942 the Gestapo raided the ghetto, capturing several of the resistance leaders.

FIRST DEPORTATIONS TO AUSCHWITZ, 26-27 MARCH 1942

GREATER GERMANY

Majdanek

Belzec

Auschwitz

Compiègne

Drancy

Zilina

Nitra

Paris
1,112
*27 March
to Auschwitz*

Trnava

Komarno

SLOVAKIA

Bratislava
2,000
*26-27 March
to Auschwitz*

FRANCE

© Martin Gilbert 1982

BIRTHPLACES OF SOME OF THE FIRST PARIS DEPORTEES

North Sea

Copenhagen

Dvinsk

Kovno

Smolensk

London

Grodno

Minsk

Atlantic Ocean

Berlin

Tatarsk
Zhitomir

Warsaw

Kiev

Line of German advance

Saar

Leipzig

Rouen

Drancy
Paris

Nancy

Prague

Auschwitz

Lvov

Zloczow
Zablotow

Nikolaeiv

Nuremberg

Skole

Kishinev

Odessa

Budapest

Ismail

Simferopol

Perpignan

Black Sea

Constantinople

Salonica

Bursa

*Salomon Benatore
aged 39*

Bergama

Smyrna
*Moreno Cohen
aged 41*

Bizerta

Oran
*Robert Cohen
aged 21*

Algiers

Bône
*Jacob Aziz
aged 32*

Tunis

Marrakech
*Aron Cohen
aged 46*

Mediterranean Sea

German forces

Haifa
*Ignatz
Baum
aged 41*

*Mardoche Douani
aged 40*

Alexandria

0 miles 200
0 kilometres 400

© Martin Gilbert 1982

Map 114

BIRTHPLACES OF POLISH JEWS IN THE FIRST PARIS DEPORTATION

The first deportations from western Europe to Belzec had taken place on 24 March 1942 *(page 78)*. Two days later, the first deportations of Jews to Auschwitz began, first from Slovakia, and on the following day from France *(opposite)*. At Auschwitz, all were sent to the barracks. No gassings took place there until 4 May 1942 *(page 87)*.

The first Jews deported to Auschwitz from France on 27 March 1942 were all foreign-born Jews who had been rounded up in Paris seven months earlier, and interned. Their birthplaces ranged from Marrakech to Haifa, and from London to Simferopol *(opposite, below)*. Many had left their birthplaces between the wars, to seek a new livelihood in France. Others had reached France as refugees. The majority had been born in Poland *(above)*, within the area that had now become a part of Greater Germany. One of these first Paris deportees, Israel Chlebowski, had been born in the village of

Przytyk, scene of the pogrom of 1936 in which three Jews had died *(page 8)*. Another, Henry Eckstein, had been born in London 26 years before. Lazarc Mnouchine had been born in Tatarsk, one of the first towns in which the Jews had challenged SS killing squads in the autumn of 1941 *(page 63)*. The 41-year-old Moses Schneider had been born in Auschwitz itself, then a market town in the Austro-Hungarian Empire.

The Paris deportation of 27 March 1942 was timed by the SS with precision. The train left Paris at 17.00 hours, reaching the border of Greater Germany at 13.59 on the following day, and arriving at Auschwitz at 5.33 in the morning of March 31.

Even French-born Jews were now subjected to the full rigours of anti-Jewish legislation. On 29 May 1942 all Jews were forbidden access to all public places, squares, restaurants, cafés, libraries, public baths, gardens and sports grounds.

MASS MURDER AND DEATH CAMP DEPORTATIONS, APRIL 1942

Wloclawek

see facing page

Chelmno

Warsaw
at least **4,432** *deaths from starvation in April*

Leczna
200 *to Sobibor*
2,225 *to Belzec*

Lubartow
800 *9-10 April*

Sobibor

Piaski
4,200 *to Belzec*

Radom **70** *shot*
hundreds deported 28 April

Tomaszow Mazowiecki
100
27 April

Krasnik
2,000
12 April

Uchanie
1,650 *10 April*

Zamosc
3,000
11 April

Krasniczyn
1,000

Radomysl nad Sanem
384

Krasnystaw
1,000

Belzec

Sokal
35 *shot*

Auschwitz

Biecz
70
30 April

Cieszanow
5,000

Lubaczow
2,000

Grybow
300
30 April

Przemysl
several hundred shot 28-30 April

Sniatyn
1,000

Horodenka
1,500
4 April

Tlumacz
1,200
3 April

Kolomyja
1,000
2 April

Peczenizyn
1,000

Zablotow
400

Kuty
950

0 ____ miles ____ 50
0 ____ kilometres ____ 80

© Martin Gilbert 1982

FURTHER DEPORTATIONS TO IZBICA AND BELZEC, APRIL 1942

GREATER GERMANY

Poppenlauer
14

Schweinfurt
30

Bad Kissingen
23

Coburg
27

Bamberg
105 *25 April*

Piaski

Nuremberg
650 *24 April*

Izbica Lubelska

Hammelberg
13

Karlbach
27

Hassfurt
16

BOHEMIA

Belzec

Nordlingen
25

BAVARIA

EASTERN GALICIA

Krumbach
16

Landshut
11 *2 April*

Ceske Budejovice
909
18 April

SLOVAKIA

Lindau
3

Fischach
56

Augsburg
129
3 April

Memmingen
22

SWITZERLAND
neutral

0 ____ miles ____ 150
0 ____ kilometres ____ 200

© Martin Gilbert 1982

TEN DEPORTATIONS TO CHELMNO, APRIL 1942

Radzejow 600
Brzesc Kujawski 200 · 30 April
Wloclawek 3,000 · 22 April
Piotrkow Kujawski 550
Lubraniec 100
Gostynin 2,000 · 16 April
Gabin 2,000
Sanniki 250 · 17 April
WARTHEGAU
narrow gauge railways
standard gauge railway
River Vistula
River Warta
Kolo
Powierce station
Zawadki mill
Chelmno death camp
Chelmno village
River Ner
Grabow 1,240
Leczyca 1,700 · 10 April
River Bzura

0 miles 20
0 kilometres 30

© Martin Gilbert 1982

NAZI-DOMINATED EUROPE, APRIL - MAY 1942

Parafianowo 600
Krzywicze 350
Dokszyce 600
Dolhinow 1,000
Zdzieciol 1,200
Dobrush 70
Slavuta 12,000
Brailov 300
Piryatin 1,530
Berdichev 70
women and children of mixed marriages 27 April
North Sea · Baltic Sea
Danzig
Berlin
Warsaw
Chelmno
Auschwitz · Belzec · Kuty
Augsburg
SWITZ
Budapest
Bucharest
Rome
Adriatic Sea
Salonica
Black Sea
CRIMEA declared 'purged of Jews', 16 April
Athens
RHODES
CRETE
Tunis
Malta
Mediterranean Sea
Derna · Tobruk
Homs · Benghazi
Tripoli
Giado 562
LIBYA
El Alamein
Cairo EGYPT
German front line
0 miles 200
0 kilometres 400
5,000 slave labourers
© Martin Gilbert 1982

Throughout April 1942 the eastern killings continued (right), as did the deportations to the death camps of Belzec (opposite, above), Chelmno (above), and Auschwitz.

From Bavaria and Bohemia, the remnants of once flourishing communities were sent to be 'resettled' in the east (opposite, below). Their destination was not, however, an eastern labour camp or ghetto, but two transit camps, Izbica and Piaski, from where they were sent the few further miles to Belzec, and its gas chamber. With the deportation of 3 April 1942, the once 1,000-strong Jewish community of Augsburg ceased to exist. Jews had lived in the town since AD 1212, and in the fifteenth century it had been a centre of Jewish culture.

In Warsaw, thousands more Jews died of starvation during April (opposite, above).

Two thousand miles to the south (right), the 38,000 Jews of Libya, having been briefly under British control at the end of 1941, had come once more under Italian rule in February 1942. Jewish shops were at once plundered, and 2,600 Jews deported to a camp at Giado, for forced labour, building military roads. The death toll was high: in 14 months 562 died of starvation and typhus.

In April 1942 a further 1,750 Jews were taken from Tripoli to forced labour sites at Homs, Benghazi and Derna. Hundreds perished from hunger and the heat. Others, forbidden to use the air-raid shelters, were killed during Allied bombing raids.

DEPORTATION, MASSACRE AND REVOLT, MAY 1942

Werenow
3,000
11 May

Radun
2,000 *10 May*

Wolozyn
1,000
10 May

Iwje
2,500 *8 May*

WHITE

RUSSIA

Wasiliszki
2,000 *10 May*

Lida
12,000
8 May

youths escape to the woods

youths escape to the woods

Stolpce

Szczuczyn
2,060 *9 May*

Zoludek
1,400
8 May

Wolkowysk
2,000

Dereczyn
250

BIALYSTOK
REGION

REICHSKOMMISSARIAT OSTLAND

● **Warsaw**
at least **3,636**
deaths from starvation in May

0   miles   40
0 kilometres 60

Sobibor

GREATER
GERMANY

VOLHYNIA

Tyszowce
1,000
22 May

Kozin
450
30 May

Miedzyrzecz
1,600 *22 May*

Komarow Osada
1,500
23 May

Laszczow
350
27 May

Korzec
2,200
21 May

Szczebrzeszyn
280
8 May

Hoszcza
670
20 May

Belz
1,500

Belzec

Dubno
5,000
27 May

Radziwillow
1,500 *29 May*
resistance led by
Asher Czerkaski

Lvov
over **1,000** *shot*
5 May

Przemyslany
all inmates of the Jewish hospital murdered

REICHSKOMMISSARIAT

UKRAINE

GENERAL

GOVERNMENT

SLOVAKIA

Dunajevtsi
3,000
10 May

Tlumacz
180
18 May

© Martin Gilbert 1982

NEWS OF MASS MURDER REACHES THE WEST, MAY 1942

BRITAIN
London

700,000
total

May 1942

Berlin

Chelmno

Warsaw

Sobibor

Radom

Rowne
15,000

GREATER GERMANY

Lublin

Belzec

Majdanek

Auschwitz

Tarnow

Lvov
30,000

SOVIET UNION

Cracow
50

Stanislawow
15,000

Tarnopol
5,000

German front line in May 1942

0   miles   200
0 kilometres 300

© Martin Gilbert 1982

Map 121

NINETEEN DEPORTATIONS TO SOBIBOR, MAY 1942

Baranow
1,500
8 May

Ryki
2,500
7 May

Lysobyki
500

Parczew forest

Wlodawa
2,000
23 May

Michow
2,500
10 May

Deblin
2,500
6 May

Konskowola
3,500
8 May

Lubartow
800
9 May

Sobibor

Pulawy
3,500

Markuszow
1,500
9 May

Siedliszcze
1,000
18 May

Wawolnica
500

Lublin

Chelm
4,300
21 May

Opole
3,000

Jozefow
1,000
7 May

Gorzkow
1,200
14 May

Wysokie
1,000

Zolkiewka
1,000
12 May

Turobin
2,750
12 May

River Vistula

River Bug

0 miles 15
0 kilometres 20

© Martin Gilbert 1982

Throughout May 1942 the killings east of the General Government continued *(opposite, above)*. So also did the deportations to Sobibor *(above)*, Belzec, Chelmno and Auschwitz *(pages 87–8)*. In Przemyslany all the inmates of the Jewish hospital were dragged from their beds and shot. At Dubno 5,000 Jews, judged 'non-productive' for the German war effort, were taken outside the town and killed. At Chelm local Jews, and Slovakian Jews who had been deported there two years before, were deported to Sobibor and gassed.

At that very moment, the first news had reached London *(opposite, below)*, smuggled out of Poland by the underground Jewish Socialist Party in Warsaw, telling of the mass murder of 700,000 Jews in Eastern Galicia and the east. Specific figures were given of mass killings in four towns, as well as of other killings in Radom, Lublin, Cracow and Tarnow. Throughout Eastern Galicia, the report stated, 'men, fourteen to sixty years old, were driven to a single place, a square or a cemetery, where they were

slaughtered or shot by machine-guns or killed by hand grenades. They had to dig their own graves. Children in orphanages, inmates in old-age homes, the sick in hospitals were shot, women were killed in the streets. In many towns the Jews were carried off to "an unknown destination" or killed in adjacent woods.'

Only one death camp, Belzec, was named in the report. But it warned that mass killings were still in progress.

Although the victims were weak from hunger and privation, always unarmed against machine-guns and grenades, alone among hostile local populations, and facing vicious torture if they challenged Nazi power, many Jews attempted nevertheless to break out of the SS and local police cordons. In the three examples shown opposite *(above)*, some young men and women did succeed in reaching the woods, and in forming, or joining, partisan groups. Some record survives of these particular acts of resistance. Many other such acts went unrecorded.

Map 122

TEN FURTHER DEPORTATIONS. MAY 1942

Gabin
2,150
12 May

Chelmno

Brzeziny
1,700
14 May

Ozorkow
2,000
21 May

Lodz

Brzeziny Lodzkie
5,000
10 May

Pabianice
8,000 *deported 16 May*
150 *murdered on the spot*

WARTHELAND

Zloczew
280

GREATER   GERMANY

GENERAL

GOVERNMENT

Dabrowa Gornicza
630
5 May

Zawierce
2,000

Bedzin
2,000

Sosnowiec
1,500
12 May

Gleiwitz
586

Birkenau ● Monowitz
Auschwitz

SILESIA

0   miles   20
0   kilometres   30

SLOVAKIA

© Martin Gilbert 1982

The gassing of more than two million Jews at Auschwitz began on 4 May 1942, first at Auschwitz itself, then at the nearby camp of Birkenau, where four gas chambers and crematoria were built during 1942 and early 1943 for the purpose of mass murder. A few Jews from each deportation were selected to 'live' as slave labourers, some in barracks at Birkenau itself, others at nearby factories, including a synthetic oil and rubber plant later built at Monowitz. While at Birkenau, many Jews, and in particular Jewish women were selected by SS doctors for medical experiments.

Because Birkenau became known during the war as Auschwitz II, and the slave labour camp in Monowitz as Auschwitz III, most accounts of the deportation of Jews to Birkenau name 'Auschwitz' as the destination, rather than Birkenau, to which they were in fact deported. For nearly two years, all deportees to Birkenau were brought to the railway sidings just outside Auschwitz station, and marched or taken by truck to Birkenau. In April 1944 a direct rail spur was built to Birkenau, almost to the gates of two of the four gas chambers there.

Throughout May 1942 the deportations to Chelmno continued unabated. The map on the left shows six communities destroyed there in one month. Of the Jews of Ozorkow, 2,000 were gassed, while 800 able-bodied men and women were sent to factories in the Lodz ghetto. At Pabianice all 150 patients in the Jewish hospital were murdered on the spot, before the rest of the community was sent to death at Chelmno.

Jewish resistance continued. But the chances of success were remote, as heavily armed SS units moved from town to town. Each Jewish community was unarmed and isolated; forbidden contact with all neighbouring communities, cut off from every normal means of communication, terrified by rumours of slaughter, but having no real knowledge of the fate of the Jews elsewhere.

Sometimes whole villages were able to escape *(opposite, above)*. But once they had reached the immediate safety of nearby woods, the families and their leaders had to begin the desperate search for food. Often they were refused food by villagers who were themselves hungry, or even hostile. Then, in their own time, the Germans were able to launch full-scale military attacks: those shown here by heavy black arrows, the first

JEWISH VILLAGERS RESIST DEPORTATION, 9 MAY 1942

DISTANT DEPORTATIONS AND AN ACT OF DEFIANCE, MAY 1942

in October 1942, the second in December 1942, were on three separate fronts, supported by artillery, armoured vehicles, grenades, machine-guns, and carried out by armed men who had been trained for military combat and were now being sent to destroy small groups of isolated Jewish families on the verge of starvation.

There was also Jewish defiance in Berlin (*above*). A public display of anti-Nazi posters by a student group led to the capture of one group; all 152 were shot.

As a reprisal for the shooting of the SS chief, Reinhardt Heydrich, in Prague, on May 27, the SS launched 'Operation Reinhardt' against both Czechs and Jews. Some 2,000 Czechs were killed in Prague as well as in the village of Lidice. From the Theresienstadt ghetto, 3,000 Jews were deported to Auschwitz and gassed.

Map 125

ESCAPE, RESISTANCE, DESTRUCTION, MAY - OCTOBER 1942

As the SS continued its drive to deport Jews to death camps and labour camps, the Jews themselves continued to try to escape to the woods and forests *(above)*. These were not escapes of the young and strong, leaving behind the women, children, the old and the sick. Rather, many of the escape leaders sought to save whole families. Once in the woods, survival for more than a few months was virtually impossible. Those who did manage to escape faced full-scale German military campaigns, local peasant hostility and betrayal. The terrible privations of forest life took their toll: no medical help, hardly any food, brackish water, and the ravages of extremes of climate – summer heat and insects, followed by autumn storms and sub-zero winter temperatures. Of more than 100 Jews who escaped from Janow to the Puszcza Solska, for example, no more than ten survived the war.

Nevertheless, the spirit of resistance was strong. These were not 'sheep to the slaughter', but brave men and women, willing, unarmed, to challenge the armed strength of a victorious army. No outside State supported them, while only a few local villagers were prepared to give them haven.

The photographs *(right)*, taken by the author in 1980, show one such forest area: the Parczew forest, the story of which is told on pages 109–10.

June 1942 saw no relaxation in the SS deportation plan, or in the executions in the east. Hardly had the German army reached the Russian cities of Smolensk and Priluki, than more than 3,000 Jews were murdered. From Czernowitz, in the Bukovina (pages 59–60), a further 4,000 were deported eastwards to Transnistria (above, top), of

whom less than half survived the war. The deportations to Auschwitz continued without pause, with four from Paris, 50 from Slovakia in four months, and five from the Auschwitz region (opposite). In Warsaw a further 4,000 Jews died of starvation during June. At Belzec and Sobibor more than 23,000 Jews were gassed.

Among those deported to Belzec, from Cracow, was the 65-year-old Mordechai Gebirtig, a carpenter whose Yiddish songs and melodies were sung throughout Poland. His best known, 'Our town is burning', was written after the Przytyk pogrom (page 8). Gebirtig was deported and killed with his wife and two daughters. Another distinguished Cracow Jew, the writer Abraham Naumann, aged 70, was shot in the street during the round-up.

On 9 June 1942 a special gas van, used earlier at Zemun for the murder of Serbian Jews (page 70), was sent to Riga (left), for the continuing killing not only of Riga's Jews, but of tens of thousands of Jews deported to Riga from Greater Germany six months before. So heavy was its task, that on 15 June 1942 the SS in Riga ordered a second van.

As the killings continued, so did the attempts at resistance: at Dzisna (opposite) 2,000 Jews managed to break out of the ghetto. Many were caught, but some reached Russian partisan units, and fought with the Red Army against the Germans.

Map 128

DEPORTATION, MASS MURDER AND REVOLT, JUNE 1942

O miles 60
O kilometres 80

Baltic Sea

EAST PRUSSIA

REICHSKOMMISSARIAT OSTLAND

Miory **1,000** 2 June

Druja 1,000 ✷ revolt

Braslaw **3,000** ✷ revolt 3 June

✷ revolt

Dzisna **4,000** 14 June

Glebokie ✷ revolt **2,500** 19 June

Oszmiana **300** 16 June

Ilja *several hundred* 7 June

Grodek **1,700** 22 June

Augustow

Bogusze *slave labour camp* **1,750**

BIALYSTOK REGION

Lida **1,200** 10 June **5,000** 25 June

Molczadz **200** 3 June

Slonim ✷ *armed resistance* 29 June **10,000**

Dereczyn **100**

Lachowicze **1,200** 10 June

THE GERMAN REICH

Treblinka *camp in preparation* ✷

Warsaw *at least* **4,000** *deaths from starvation in June*

Biala Podlaska **3,000** 10 June

Kobryn **4,000** 6 June

Slawatycze **1,000**

Wlodawa *several hundred children under ten years old*

Sobibor

REICHSKOMMISSARIAT UKRAINE

VOLHYNIA

Krzepice **1,000**

Pilica **3,000** *to Belzec but several hundred escape*

THE GENERAL GOVERNMENT

Cycow **500**

Krasniczyn **1,000** 6 June

Uchanie **1,650** 10 June

Dubienka **2,670**

Luck **2,000** June

Chrzanow **4,000**

Olkusz **3,000**

Dabrowa Tarnowska **500**

Grabowiec **1,200** 8 June

Hrubieszow **3,049** 2 June

✷ *resistance led by* Joel Szczerbat

Sosnowiec **2,000**

Tarnow **11,000**

Belzec

Belz **100** 2 June

Bielsko Biala **5,000**

Auschwitz

Cracow **2,000** 1 June **5,000** 6 June

WESTERN GALICIA

EASTERN GALICIA

Namestovo **300**

1,000

Lutowiska **800** *murdered in the market place*

Cadca **500**

Liptovsky Svaty Mikulas

Poprad **1,000**

Presov **4,600**

Humenne **2,000**

Zilina **2,500**

Ruzomberok **950**

Vranov **1,600**

Medzilaborce **1,500**

Kolomyja **3,000**

Senica **800**

Handlova **80**

Brezno **250**

Sabinov **1,200**

Michalovce **4,500**

Banska Bystrica **1,200**

Roznava **1,000**

Kassa (Kosice)

Bansка Stiavnica **400**

Revuca **500**

Trebisov **2,500**

Nitra **4,500**

Krupina **1,250**

Levice

© Martin Gilbert 1982

92

Map 129

THE JEWS OF HOLLAND ON THE EVE OF DEPORTATION

North Sea

GRONINGEN
4,708
Leeuwarden
● Groningen
● Winschoten

FRIESLAND
852
● Assen

Westerbork

DRENTE
2,498
Meppel ●
● Hoogeveen

NORTH
HOLLAND
87,566
● Alkmaar

● Zwolle

OVERIJSSEL
4,385
● Almelo

Zaandam
Bloemendaal
Zandvoort ●
Haarlem
● Heemstede
● **Amsterdam**
● Naarden
Bussum ● ● Laren
Hilversum
Apeldoorn
● Deventer
Hengelo ●
Enschede ●

Voorburg
Leiden ●
de Bilt
● Amersfoort
● Zutphen
Lochem ●

The Hague
SOUTH
HOLLAND
25,648
Rijswijk ●
● **Utrecht** Zeist ●
GELDERLAND
6,642
Winterswijk ●

Gouda ●
UTRECHT
3,802
Arnhem
Nijmegen ●

Schiedam ● **Rotterdam**
Dordrecht ●
● Oss
● Hertogenbosch

NORTH BRABANT
2,281
● Tilburg

ZEELAND
174
● Eindhoven

GREATER GERMANY

LIMBURG
1,441

BELGIUM

● Maastricht

0 miles 30
0 kilometres 50

The figures show the
number of Jews in the
Dutch Provinces in 1941

● Towns with **300** to **700** Jewish inhabitants
● Towns with **1,000** to **3,000** Jewish inhabitants
● Towns with **8,000** to **14,000** Jewish inhabitants
● Amsterdam: **80,000** Jewish inhabitants

© Martin Gilbert 1982

Since May 1940 the 140,000 Jews of Holland *(above)* had been deliberately cut off from the community around them. On 9 May 1942 the yellow star was made compulsory.

On 14 July 1942 thousands of Dutch Jews were arrested in Amsterdam, and on the following day the first train, with 1,135 Dutch Jews on board, left Holland for an 'unknown destination' *(opposite)*. By the end of the month, nearly 6,000 had, in fact, reached Auschwitz, where the majority were gassed.

The photograph shows the special railway spur being built from the internment camp at Westerbork to the main railway line.

From Germany, hundreds of Jews were deported to the Theresienstadt ghetto, and kept there, isolated and starving.

Map 130

DISTANT DEPORTATIONS, JULY 1942

Westerbork

1,135 *15 July*

7 trains left Holland in July

586 *16 July*

309 *16 July*

1,000 *24 July*

1,010 *27 July*

1,007 *31 July*

931 *21 July*

North Sea

Baltic Sea

Danzig

0 — miles — 100
0 — kilometres — 150

Padderborn
all Jewish
orphans deported

G R E A T E R   G E R M A N Y

Düsseldorf
260
22 July

Boppard
10
27 July

Bacharach
5
26 July

Kempten
200
25 July

Theresienstadt

Auschwitz
*the first 100 women handed
over for sterilization and
other medical experiments,
10 July 1942*

© Martin Gilbert 1982

HOLLAND

Map 131

DEPORTATION, MASSACRE AND REVOLT, JULY 1942

Danzig

miles 60

kilometres 80

GREATER GERMANY

Szarkowszczyzna
revolt 600 *killed 18 July*
900 *escape*

Minsk
25,000
28-30 July

Molczadz
1,000
15 July

Nieswiez
600
22 July

revolt led by
Shalom Cholawsky

Dereczyn
3,000 *24 July*

ghetto revolt 15 July

Bialystok

Kosow
1,200 *25 July*

Kleck
1,000
21 July

revolt

Treblinka

Antopol
1,100

Bereza Kartuska
1,000
15 July

Byten
840
25 July

Chelmno

Warsaw
66,701 *deported*
and at least
4,000
died of starvation in July

GENERAL GOVERNMENT

Kobryn
2,000
25 July

Drohiczyn
1,700
26 June

Pinsk
*all patients in the
Jewish hospital murdered*

REICHSKOMMISSARIAT
UKRAINE

Lutomiersk
700

Kowale
Panskie
3,000
20 July

Sobibor

Kowel
24,000
mid July

Luck
4,000
4 July

Chelm 300

Czestochowa

Jozefow
1,500 *shot
13 July*

Olyka
5,673
27-28 July

Rowne
5,000
14-15 July

Pilica

12,000
21-25 July
Tarnobrzeg

Rozwadow

Brody

Bedzin

Baranow

Sokolow

Belzec

Uhnow
1,000

Cracow

Radomysl

Ropczyce

Debica

Rawa
Ruska
2,000 *27 July*

Bochnia

Pilzno

Wielopole

Strzyzow

Rzeszow
22,000
7-13 July

Niemirow
500

Sasow
1,000
15 July

Zimgrod
1,000 *murdered in nearby
woods*

Sambor
50 *shot*

*murdered at an
'unknown
destination'
possibly Belzec,
or a nearby
wood*

SLOVAKIA

Stanislawow
1,000 *shot*

Tluste
200
mid July

© Martin Gilbert 1982

On 22 July 1942 the Germans embarked upon their most ambitious project: the deportation of more than half a million Jews from the Warsaw ghetto. The death camp prepared for them was at Treblinka, scarcely more than 40 miles from the ghetto. In one month alone, 66,701 Jews were deported from Warsaw to Treblinka, and gassed on arrival.

In an attempt to warn of what was happening, to organize armed resistance, and to link the scattered and isolated ghettos, a Jewish Fighters' Organization, known by its Polish initials ZOB, was set up in Warsaw. Bialystok, Brody, and in five of the ghettos south-west of Warsaw (*above*).

The deportations to Chelmno and Belzec continued (*above*). Further east, as the killing squads continued their executions, the last Jews alive in Nieswiez, 600 artisans,

fought with sticks and clubs to resist their killers. Most were murdered. At Kleck a few dozen, fortunate to possess a pistol or two, broke away from the ghetto and were able to join the partisans in the forests.

During August 1942 the Dutch and French deportations continued (*opposite, below*). Now, for the first time, Jews from Luxembourg and Belgium were deported to Auschwitz.

To prevent the Swedish Government from giving its protection to Dutch Jews, the Germans had decided, on 17 July 1942, to deprive all Jews in Holland of their Dutch citizenship. Two weeks later, to forestall a further Swedish effort to help the Jews of Holland, the Germans decided not to disclose the whereabouts of the deportees. Thus Auschwitz remained an 'unknown destination', 'somewhere in the east'.

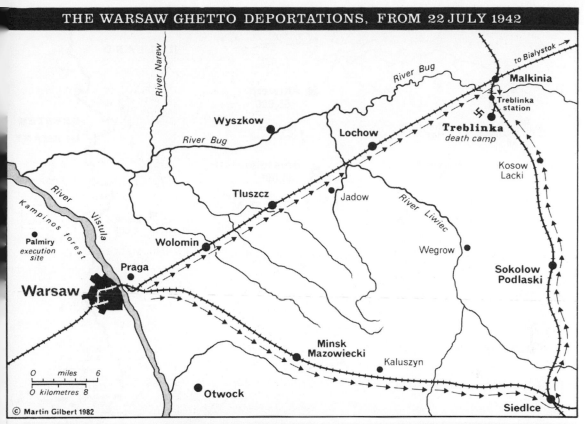

THE WARSAW GHETTO DEPORTATIONS, FROM 22 JULY 1942

River Narew

River Bug

to Bialystok

Malkinia

Wyszkow

River Bug

Lochow

Treblinka
station

Treblinka
death camp

Kosow
Lacki

Tluszcz

Jadow

River Liwiec

River Vistula

Kampinos forest

Palmiry
execution
site

Wolomin

Wegrow

**Sokolow
Podlaski**

Warsaw

Praga

Minsk
Mazowiecki

Kaluszyn

O miles 6
O kilometres 8

© Martin Gilbert 1982

Otwock

Siedlce

DISTANT DEPORTATIONS, AUGUST 1942

O miles 200
O kilometres 300

**GREAT
BRITAIN**
unconquered

1,013
3 August

987
7 August

559
10 August

Westerbork

Cottbus
12

Kosel

Auschwitz

Malines
5,990

Theresienstadt

Luxembourg
723

English Channel

Paris
14,000

Drancy

GREATER GERMANY

Pithiviers

Beaune-
la-Rolande

Belfort

Ulm
45

to Theresienstadt

SWITZERLAND
neutral

Bay
of
Biscay

Chalon-
sur-Sâone

**Bordeaux
Bacalan**

ITALY

Merignac

**Zagreb
CROATIA**
several thousands

Récébédou

Agde

Les Milles

Adriatic Sea

Noé

Rivesaltes

Mediterranean Sea

SPAIN
neutral

Pyrenees

© Martin Gilbert 1982

96

Map 134

THE JEWS OF BELGIUM AND LUXEMBOURG

North Sea

Ostend
53

HOLLAND

**Antwerp
55,000**

WEST
FLANDERS
40

Ghent
197

Malines
Dossin camp

GREATER

GERMANY

EAST
FLANDERS
39

**Brussels
35,000**

B E L G I U M

HAINAULT
434

**Liége
2,000**

Charleroi
628

Namur
50

F R A N C E

Wiltz
17

Diekirch
187

LUXEMBOURG
Redange
6

Mersch
63

E
78

C
25

Grevenmacher
79

Esch
470

Remich
99

0   miles   25
0   kilometres   40

E = Echternach
C = Capellen

**Luxembourg
2,111**

© Martin Gilbert 1982

The Belgian and Luxembourg Jews, now seized and deported, came from many cities, towns and villages *(above)*. The first deportations from Belgium took place on 4 August 1942 *(page 96)*. Henceforth, over a period of two years, a total of 26 trains set off to the 'unknown destination' from the internment camp at Dossin, near Malines. The destination was in fact, Auschwitz.

The Germans ignored protests from the Catholic Church, including one by Jean Hérinckx, a leading right-wing Catholic, and one by Cardinal van Roey, Archbishop of Malines.

The local Belgian population was active in helping Jews, of whom more than 25,000 were hidden in private homes and orphanages, and thereby saved. But of the 25,631 Belgian Jews who were deported, only 1,244 survived the war.

More than 1,000 Belgian Jews fought with the Belgian partisans; 140 of them were killed in action. Other Jews were smuggled across France, to Spain and Switzerland. But on 13 August 1942 the Swiss police began to turn back Jewish refugees who had managed to cross into Switzerland. 'Under current practice', a Police Instruction of 25 September 1942 read, 'refugees on the grounds of race alone are not political refugees'.

From France, the deportations continued without pause. On 17 August 1942, among 997 mainly Polish-born Jews deported from Paris to Auschwitz, 27 were children under the age of four, almost all of whom had been born in France, and most of whom were deported without their parents. Marguerite Jakubovitch was deported with her six brothers and sisters, the oldest of whom was only ten years old: all had been born in Paris, and were deported without their parents. All 27 young children named here *(right)* were gassed within hours of reaching Auschwitz.

SWITZERLAND TURNS BACK JEWISH REFUGEES, 13 AUGUST 1942

Chaumont

GREATER GERMANY

ALSACE

River Rhine

Schaffhausen

Boden See

Belfort

Basle

St.Gallen

Porrentruy

St.Margarethen

at least
9,751
turned away

Zurich

AUSTRIA

Les Verrières

Berne

SWITZERLAND

28,512
given refuge

ITALY

GERMAN-
OCCUPIED
FRANCE

Lausanne

Lac Leman

Geneva

Champéry

Chêne Bourg

Martigny

0   miles   50

0   kilometres   80

© Martin Gilbert 1982

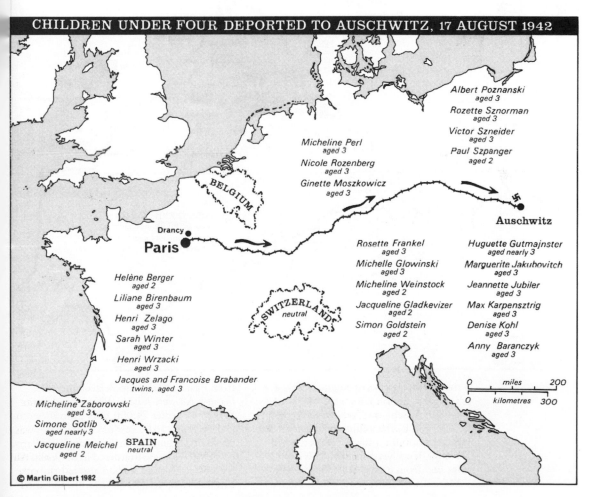

CHILDREN UNDER FOUR DEPORTED TO AUSCHWITZ, 17 AUGUST 1942

Albert Poznanski
aged 3

Rozette Sznorman
aged 3

Victor Szneider
aged 3

Paul Szpanger
aged 2

Micheline Perl
aged 3

Nicole Rozenberg
aged 3

Ginette Moszkowicz
aged 3

BELGIUM

Auschwitz

Drancy

Paris

Rosette Frankel
aged 3

Huguette Gutmajnster
aged nearly 3

Helène Berger
aged 2

Michelle Glowinski
aged 2

Marguerite Jakubovitch
aged 3

Liliane Birenbaum
aged 3

Micheline Weinstock
aged 2

Jeannette Jubiler
aged 3

SWITZERLAND
neutral

Henri Zelago
aged 3

Jacqueline Gladkevizer
aged 2

Max Karpensztrig
aged 3

Sarah Winter
aged 3

Simon Goldstein
aged 2

Denise Kohl
aged 3

Henri Wrzacki
aged 3

Anny Baranczyk
aged 3

Jacques and Francoise Brabander
twins, aged 3

Micheline Zaborowski
aged 3

Simone Gotlib
aged nearly 3

Jacqueline Meichel
aged 2

SPAIN
neutral

0   miles   200

0   kilometres   300

© Martin Gilbert 1982

98

Map 137

DEPORTATION, MASSACRE AND REVOLT, 1-13 AUGUST 1942

Radun
500
9 August

Nowogrodek
6,000
7 August

Mir
resistance
9 August
two hundred
escape to the
forests

Zdzieciol
3,000
6 August

three hundred escape
Jewish partisan unit
commanded by
Hirsch Kaplinski

G R E A T E R
G E R M A N Y

0   miles   60
0   kilometres   80

Treblinka

Chelmno

Warta
1,000

Lodz
40,000
10-22 August

Warsaw
70,000
1-13 August

Sieradz
1,400
14 August

Belchatow
5,000

Radom
30,000
5-17 August

Zolkiewka
1,000
10 August

Sobibor

Chelm
300

Zamosc
500

V O L H Y N I A
over **87,000** killed on
the spot during August
(see page 115)

Szczebrzeszyn
400

Zwierzyniec
300

Bedzin
5,000
1 August

Sosnowiec
8,000
12 August

Bilgoraj
500 *9 August*

Belzec

Krzemieniec

Glogow
500

Tarnogrod
1,000
9 August

Auschwitz

WESTERN GALICIA
over **69,000** deported and
killed during August
(see page 114)

Przemysl

Lvov

EASTERN GALICIA
over **76,000** deported and
killed during August
(see opposite)

S L O V A K I A

© Martin Gilbert 1982

In the first two weeks of August nearly a quarter of a million Jews were killed at Chelmno, Auschwitz, Treblinka and Belzec *(above)*, and by the killing squads in the east. In preparation for a single deportation to Chelmno, Jews were brought to Wielun *(opposite)* from nine nearby communities.

More than 76,000 Jews were deported from Eastern Galicia to Belzec *(opposite, below)*. All were killed within a few hours, as were a further 74,000 Jews from Western Galicia *(page 101)*. East of Greater Germany, killing on the spot continued, 87,000 Jews being murdered in the Volhynia *(page 102)*. Resistance had also led, at both Mir and Zdzieciol, to mass escapes.

JEWS ASSEMBLED FOR DEPORTATION TO CHELMNO, 1-21 AUGUST 1942

Chelmno ⌘   Dabie

Lodz

Sieradz

922 to Lodz
     22 August

Sulmierzyce
990

Lututow
1,200

10,000
to Chelmno
22 August
(see page 114)

Wieruszow
900

Wielun

Kielczyglow 200

Siemkowice 150

Boleslawiec
474

Pajeczno 1,800

Praszka
700

Dzialoszyn
1,000

© Martin Gilbert 1982

TWENTY DEPORTATIONS FROM EASTERN GALICIA, AUGUST 1942

Belzec ⌘

River

Bug

Olesko
472
29 August

Sasow
100   29 August

Lvov
40,000
1-10 August

Zloczow
2,700
28 August

Jezierna
300

Tarnopol
4,000

Skalat
500
31 August

Bobrka
1,260 to Belzec
200   shot
12 August

Mikulince
1,200
28-29 August

Sambor
4,000
4-6 August

Truskawiec
100

Chorostkow
1,500
24 August

Stary
Sambor
1,500
5-6 August

Drohobycz
2,000 3,000 17 August
6-8 August

Czortkow
2,500
28 August

Turka
5,000

Boryslaw
2,000

Dolina
3,000
3 August

Stanislawow
1,000

Tluste
300

© Martin Gilbert 1982

DEPORTATION, MASSACRE AND REVOLT, 14–31 AUGUST 1942

Gostynin
3,500
15 August

Minsk Mazowiecki
7,000
21 August

Mordy
2,000 *23 August*

Siedlce
15,000
22 August

Byten
400
29 August

0   miles   50
0   kilometres   80

Treblinka

Lenino
1,000
14 August

Warsaw
70,000
14–21 August

Chelmno

Otwock
14,000
19 August

F
R
resistance

Losice
6,900
22 August

Miedzyrzec
5,000
25 Aug

Lomazy
1,700 *shot*
17–19 August

Antopol
1,000

Sarny

Sadok
405
14 August

Radzyn
1,500
20 August

Lask
3,500
28 August

Kock
2,500

Parczew
5,000

VOLHYNIA
see opposite

Zdunska Wola
12,000
22–23 August

Wielun
10,000
22 August

Jedlinia
300

Garbatka
1,100
18 August

Goraj
800
21 August

Luck

Warta
1,000
24 August

Kielce
21,000
20 August

Wloszczowa
4,000 *26 August*

Lezajsk
Zolynia
Lancut
Radymno

10,000

Belzec

Tarnopol

WESTERN GALICIA
see below

Nowy Sacz

EASTERN GALICIA
see page 113

Czortkow

Stanislawow

F = **Falenica**
6,500
20 August

R = **Rembertow**
2,000
20 August

S L O V A K I A

© Martin Gilbert 1982

DEPORTATIONS FROM WESTERN GALICIA TO BELZEC, AUGUST 1942

0   miles   25
0   kilometres   40

Bochnia
2,600
25 August

Jaslo
and region
16,000
mid–August

Krosno
and region
5,000
mid–August

Belzec

Rzeszow
1,000

Wieliczka
8,000
27 August

Auschwitz

Cracow

Tarnow

Frysztak

Blazowa

Niebylec
Jasienica
Brzozow

Przemysl
12,500

Skawina
2,000
28 August

Biecz
700

Nowy Sacz
and region
16,000
24–28 August

Zagorz

Ropienka
Olszanica

Makow

Rabka

Szczawnica

Krynica

Dukla

Rymanow
500

Zaslaw
4,000 *to Belzec*
7,000 *shot in nearby forests*

Nowy Targ
and region
2,500
28–30 August

Stary Sacz
700
17 August

Gorlice
700
14 August

Szczawne
transit camp

© Martin Gilbert 1982

Map 142

MASSACRE. RESISTANCE AND ESCAPE IN THE VOLHYNIA. AUGUST 1942

Lubieszow
15

Pohost
2,000
16 August

Ratno
1,000
500 escape

Kamen Kashirski
2,400 10 August
600 escape

Dabrowica
2,800 1,500 escape
28 August

Wlodzimierzec
2,400 600 escape

Bereznica
1,000

Niesuchojeze
350

Rafalowka
1,600
800 escape
28 August

Tomaszgrod
150

Klesow
50

Sarny
10,500
3,500 escape

Rokitno
900
700 escape

Kowel
over 5,000

Stepan
2,000 500 escape

Berezne
1,800
200 escape

Maciejow
1,500

VOLHYNIA

Kostopol
all 700 escape

Turzysk
1,000

Rozyszcze
3,000

Zofiowka
1,500

Derazno
500

Siedliszcze
500

Torczyn
2,000

Luck
14,700
2,000 escape

Tuczyn
2,000

PODOLIA

Szumsk
over 1,000

Krzemieniec
over 3,000

Lanowce
over 400

Sarny: resistance led by
Mendel Tendler

Zofiewka: resistance led by
Chaim Wodchin
Gad Rosenblatt

Wiszniewicze
1,000
30 August

EASTERN GALICIA

Polish – Soviet border 1921–1939

River Bug

0   miles   20
0   kilometres   40

© Martin Gilbert 1982

During the last two weeks of August, more than 200,000 Jews were murdered in German-occupied Poland, most of them deported to the three death camps of Chelmno, Treblinka and Belzec. These deportations were dominated by the relentless rounding up and deportation of Jews from Warsaw to Treblinka.

For every deportation, a precise time-table was devised, and copies sent to every station en route. After the deportees had been taken off, the trains were cleaned, and returned empty along the same routes, and with the same careful planning.

Resistance also continued: at Treblinka itself, on 26 August 1942, a young deportee fom the town of Kielce, having been forbidden by one of the Ukrainian guards to say farewell to his mother, attacked the guard with a knife. Hardly had he done so, than the whole trainload of deportees was machine-gunned.

In the Volhynia (above) over 87,000 Jews were murdered in August 1942. As German units came to kill them, as many as 15,000 managed to escape. But less than 1,000 of the escapees, who included men, women and children, were able to survive nearly two years of intense hunger, severe winter cold, sickness, and repeated German and Ukrainian attacks. Some of the men later joined the small Soviet partisan units which were later parachuted into the Volhynia.

Between May and December 1942 more than 140,000 Volhynia Jews were murdered. Some, who had been given refuge in Polish homes, were murdered together with their Polish protectors in the spring of 1943, when, of 300,000 Poles living in the Volhynia, 40,000 were murdered by Ukrainian 'bandits'. In many villages, Poles and Jews fought together against the common foe.

Map 143

DEPORTATION AND MASS MURDER, 1-5 SEPTEMBER 1942

Serniki 500 killed / 500 escape

Wysock 700 killed / 300 escape

Trojanowka 50

Poworsk 20

Maniewicze 800 killed / 200 escape

Mielnica 700

Lublin 2,000 / 2 September

Majdan Tatarsky

Uscilug 2,000

Wlodzimierz Wolynski (Ludmir) 13,500 killed / 500 escape

Piatydni

Horochow 2,500 killed / 500 escape

GREATER GERMANY

Poryck 1,000

Belzec

Druszkopol 500

Bereszteczko 1,000

VOLHYNIA

Poczaje 700

resistance led by Moshe Skoczylas and Michael Majtek in nearby forest

Dzialoszyce 1,000 shot in the town / 8,000 deported to Belzec / 3 September

Bochnia 600 shot in the town / 2,000 deported to Belzec / 3 September

GENERAL GOVERNMENT

Mikolajow 500 / 4 September

Rozdol 1,000 / 4-5 September

Sambor 2,000 / 2 September

Brzozdowce 500 3-5 September

Stryj 3,000 / 1 September

Skole 2,000 / 4 September

Lvov

Chodorow 2,000 / 4 September

Zydaczow 500 / 5 September

Zurawno 500 / 5 September

Bolechow 2,000 / 3-5 September

Zbaraz 'hundreds' / 1 September

EASTERN GALICIA

© Martin Gilbert 1982

Throughout September 1942, deportation to the death camps continued. For the Wloszczowa deportation (opposite) an intricate timetable, typical of hundreds more, was devised:

Wloszczowa		depart 16.38
Kielce	arrive 19.06	depart 19.55
Skarzysko	arrive 21.41	depart 22.43
Radom	arrive 0.03	depart 0.13
Deblin	arrive 2.00	depart 3.10
Lukow	arrive 5.17	depart 6.08
Siedlce	arrive 6.58	depart 8.34
Treblinka	arrive 11.24	(depart empty) 15.59

Following the empty train's despatch from Treblinka, an equally intricate timetable was devised, to return it to the next deportation point.

East of the border of Greater Germany, the killings continued to take place, as shown above, in or near the towns themselves: at Wlodzimierz Wolynski 4,000 Jews were shot in the prison courtyard, and 14,000 driven to the gravel pits at Piatydni, and machine-gunned. Even inside the General Government, as at Warsaw (opposite) and Dzialoszyce (above), thousands were shot in the streets while the deportations were in progress.

Map 144

DEPORTATIONS TO TWO DEATH CAMPS, 1 AND 6-16 SEPTEMBER 1942

Treblinka

Dobre
500
15 September

Siedlce

Warsaw
54,069
deported
3,047
shot in the streets
6-16 September

Lukow

Biala Podlaska
1,000
6 September

Grojec
3.000

Deblin

Radom

G E N E R A L

Skarzysko Kamienna

G O V E R N M E N T

Wloszczowa
5,000
I September

Kielce

Zamosc
400

Radziechow
1,400
15 September

Checiny
4,000
13 September

Belzec

Jedzejow
6,000 *I6 September*

River Vistula

Kamionka Strumilowa
1,500
15 September

Wolbrom
8,000
6 September

River Vistula

Pustkow
slave labour camp
opened 16 September

Lvov

Brzesko
500

Tuchow
3,000

WESTERN GALICIA

Tarnow
8,000

Sanok
8,000
10 September

EASTERN GALICIA

Stanislawow
5,000
12 September

S L O V A K I A

© Martin Gilbert 1982

miles 0 40
kilometres 0 60

At Treblinka, there was a further act of resistance on 11 September 1942, by a young Jew from the Argentine, who had been trapped in Warsaw at the outbreak of war. The young man, Meir Berliner, having been deported in one of the daily September transports to Treblinka, stabbed an SS officer to death with his penknife.

Meir Berliner's action saved no lives. But it was an act of considerable courage. So too was the decision of a number of Jews from Dzialoszyce *(opposite)* to try to break out on the eve of deportation to Belzec, and make for the forests. Some of them succeeded. Led by Moshe Skoczylas and Michael Majtek, they formed two small but effective partisan units. Majtek helped to organize resistance in Pinczow *(page 118)*. Within three months, however, both had been hunted down and destroyed by German troops.

Map 145

NINE DEPORTATIONS TO BELZEC, 7 SEPTEMBER 1942

Belzec

REICHSKOMMISSARIAT UKRAINE

GENERAL GOVERNMENT

Lvov

Janowska
slave labour camp

GREATER GERMANY

EASTERN GALICIA

Zablotow
250

Kolomyja
8,700

Sniatyn
2,000

Jablonow
800

RUTHENIA

Roznow
100

Kosow
600

HUNGARY

Pistyn
500

Kuty
800

BUKOVINA

Zabie
200

© Martin Gilbert 1982

TRANSYLVANIA

0   miles   30

0   kilometres   40

The map above shows nine deportations to Belzec in a single day. The only Jews not sent to their deaths were a group of young people from Kuty. While the rest of their community was sent to Belzec, they were sent to the Janowska slave labour camp in Lvov: a camp where brutality was so savage that almost no-one survived.

In the east *(opposite, above)*, German troops had reached the Caucasus. Killing squads at once rounded up the local Jews, murdering them on the spot, or deporting them to nearby execution sites.

In the west *(opposite, below)*, the deportations to Auschwitz continued with eight trains from Holland, five from

Belgium, and 13 from Paris. The French deportees included many German Jews who had been deported to the Pyrenees two years before *(page 35)*. Deportations also continued to Theresienstadt; there, as in the Polish ghettos, tens of thousands died of starvation and disease. Of 533 Jews deported from Nuremberg in September 1942, only 27 survived the war.

Resistance also continued: at Lachwa, where all 820 Jews fought against the 'liquidation', most were killed, but a few managed to escape and join a Soviet partisan unit. At Stolin local Ukrainians handed over to the SS the two leaders of the revolt, who were then shot.

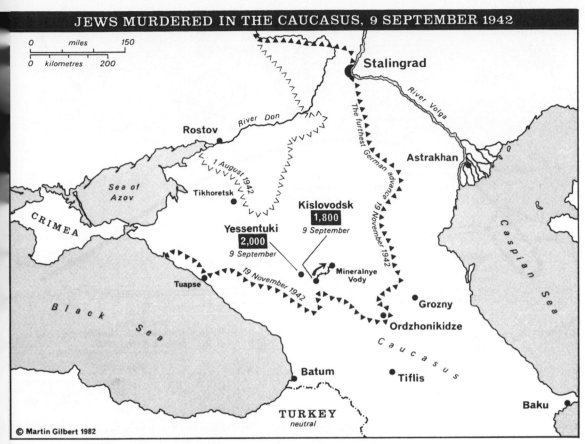

JEWS MURDERED IN THE CAUCASUS, 9 SEPTEMBER 1942

0 miles 150
0 kilometres 200

Stalingrad

River Don

Rostov

River Volga

The furthest German advance

Astrakhan

Sea of Azov

1 August 1942

Tikhoretsk

Kislovodsk
1,800
9 September

CRIMEA

Yessentuki
2,000
9 September

19 November 1942

Mineralnye Vody

19 November 1942

Tuapse

Grozny

Ordzhonikidze

Black Sea

Caucasus

Caspian Sea

Batum

Tiflis

TURKEY
neutral

Baku

© Martin Gilbert 1982

DISTANT DEPORTATIONS, MASSACRE AND REVOLT, SEPTEMBER 1942

Leningrad

led by
Dov Lopatin
700 *killed*
120 *escape*

Moscow

HOLLAND
6,675
in 8 trains

Baltic Sea

Vitebsk
8,350

Lachwa
revolt
2 September

led by *Moses Glazer*
and *Asher Shapira*

GREATER GERMANY

BELGIUM
5,750
in 5 trains

Stolin
7,000
11 September resistance

Stalingrad

Rostov
18,000

Lille
1,000
in 1 train

Paris
13,000
2·30 September

Auschwitz

Krzemieniec
armed resistance
9 September

Caspian Sea

Belfort

Theresienstadt

Bamberg
300
9 September

Noe

Nuremberg
533
10 September

Piatygorsk
300

Gurs
Rivesaltes

Les Milles

Black Sea

Yessentuki
2,000

SPAIN
neutral

Shaumyan
114

Kislovodsk
1,800

TURKEY
neutral

0 miles 400
0 kilometres 600

© Martin Gilbert 1982

106

Map 148

THE HIRSCHSPRUNG FAMILY DEPORTED, 15 SEPTEMBER 1942

North Sea

Baltic Sea

Amsterdam
their children
Nelly Hirschsprung born 8 June 1933
David Hirschsprung born 21 April 1938

Lille

Malines
The Hirschsprung family among more than a thousand Jews deported to Auschwitz 15 September 1942

Cracow

Auschwitz
Helene Hirschsprung born 22 August 1909 in the Austro-Hungarian Empire
married to
Mozes Hirschsprung born 16 October 1901 in the Austro-Hungarian Empire

0   miles   150
0   kilometres   200

© Martin Gilbert 1982

The map above tells of a single family deported from Belgium in September 1942. Hélène Hirschsprung, born in Auschwitz itself, had married a man from Cracow, and then had emigrated to Holland, where both their children were born. With the coming of war they had fled for refuge to Lille, in north-eastern France. But on 15 September 1942 they were among 1,000 Jews who were seized by the SS, transferred to Malines, and then deported to Auschwitz.

The deportees of September 15 *(opposite, above)* included many Jews born in the Polish provinces of Tsarist Russia, and others from the former Austro-Hungarian Empire.

The SS deportation lists from Paris record a total of 25 Auschwitz-born Jews, deported back to Auschwitz between 1942 and 1944. Among them was Frajdla Leiber, who had left Auschwitz with her parents shortly after

her birth in September 1932, but was deported back to Auschwitz and gassed, when she was only 11 years old.

The Lille deportation of September 15 included the 21-year-old Bernice Winer, born in neutral Switzerland *(page 131)*, and the 28-year-old Fanny Yerkowski, born in London. On the following day, from Paris, a further deportation to Auschwitz contained 40 Bulgarian-born Jews who had been seized in the French capital. The fact that no Jew had yet been deported to Auschwitz from Bulgaria itself could not save them. The names and ages of 14 of them are given opposite. Also deported was the 42-year-old Flora Landsman, born in Britain, and the 28-year-old Londoner, Lea Cohen, as well as Jews with Dutch, Estonian, Lithuanian, Latvian, Yugoslav, and even neutral Turkish citizenship.

BIRTHPLACES OF POLISH-BORN JEWS DEPORTED FROM LILLE, 15 SEPTEMBER 1942

miles 50
kilometres 80

Ciechanow

Inowroclaw

River Vistula

River Bug

Wegrow

Kutno

Warsaw   Kaluszyn   Siedlce

Ozorkow   Zyrardow

Zgierz   Mszczonow

TSARIST EMPIRE
to 1914

Kalisz   Lodz

Warta   Pabianice

Zdunska   Tomaszow   Lubartow
Wola

GERMAN EMPIRE *to 1914*

Piotrkow   Radom

Szydlowiec

Chelm

Radomsko   Konskie

Krzepice   Gidle

Czestochowa   Kielce   Izbica

Koniecpol   Zamosc

Daleszyce

Szczekociny   Jedrzejow   Tyszowce

Wolbrom

Bedzin   Stopnica   Baranow

Olkusz   Rawa
                                          Ruska
River Vistula   Kolbuszowa

Radomysl   Rzeszow

Auschwitz   Cracow   Debica

Tarnow   Tyczyn

Biala   Wielpole

Strzyzow   Przemysl

Gorlice   Rymanow

Krynica   Dukla

River San

AUSTRO-HUNGARIAN EMPIRE
to 1914

© Martin Gilbert 1982

BULGARIAN-BORN JEWS DEPORTED FROM PARIS TO AUSCHWITZ, 16 SEPTEMBER 1942

miles 75
kilometres 90

River Danube

Ruschuk (Ruse)
Anna Mayer aged 45
Djamba Mayer aged 21
Djoia Mayer aged 14

Varna
Bellina Mitrani aged 47
Rebecca Ninio aged 34
Elizer Papo aged 45

Black

Jacques Sabetai aged 41
Jeanne Tadger aged 42
Marcel Mayer aged 15   Sofia
Avram Ninio aged 40
Daniel Ninio aged 37
Esther Ninio aged 37
Moshe Ninio aged 16

BULGARIA

Sea

Kustendil
David Alkali aged 33

Plovdiv
Leon Seliktar aged 37
Joseph Illel aged 53
Israel Cohen aged 40

TURKEY
neutral

borders of 1940

GREECE

© Martin Gilbert 1982

Sea of
Marmara

Map 151

DEPORTATIONS AND REVOLT, 17-20 SEPTEMBER 1942

Treblinka

Byten
50
19 September

0 miles 50
0 kilometres 80

River Bug

Parczew
5,000
19 September
'Altana' and 'Tabor'
family camps
hideout and
resistance group led by
Yehiel Grynszpan

Sokal
2,500
17 September

mass break out from
deportation train;
almost all the would-
be escapees machine
gunned

Belzec

Brody
3,000
19 September

EASTERN
GALICIA

Zaleszczyki
2,000
20 September

© Martin Gilbert 1982

In only three days, over 10,000 Jews were deported to Belzec and Treblinka *(left)*. All were murdered. The photograph shows a group of Jews being deported from Eastern Galicia; their bundles contained everything they were allowed to take with them. At Belzec all these belongings were taken from them, sorted, and sent to Germany.

As the Parczew round-ups were in progress, several thousand Jews managed to break through the cordon, escape southwards to the hamlet of Makoszka *(opposite)*, and reach the dense woods, thickets and swamps of the Parczew forest *(photographs on page 90)*. Most of them were hunted down by German armed units, and shot. Three particular German hunts, one in November and two in December 1942, led to hundreds of Jewish families being massacred in the forest itself. Others died of starvation, cold and disease. Those few hundred who survived the repeated searches, and the ravages of winter, remained hidden in the forest, in two family camps.

One particularly unpleasant and unexpected hazard for the Jewish families hiding in the Parczew forest was the activity of a group of former Red Army soldiers, prisoners-of-war who had formed their own partisan unit. These Russians promised to give the Jews guns in return for money and jewelry, but simply took the money and disappeared. Others raped the Jewish women, one of whom, Sarah, from Parczew, was murdered by a Russian partisan when she resisted his attempt to rape her. Her murderer was killed by a Jewish partisan.

Only 200 Jews of the family camps survived the war in the Parczew forest, emerging in July 1944 as the Red Army liberated the region.

Map 152

THE 'FAMILY' CAMPS IN THE PARCZEW FOREST, 1942-1943

During the final year of the war, a Polish partisan battalion, commanded by a Jewish officer, Alexander Skotnicki, was also to make the Parczew forest its base of operations, attacking German military trains on the Lublin-Siedlce railway line. Under his command, Skotnicki had one entirely Jewish company, led by Yehiel Grynszpan. At first, Grynszpan's company had only two rifles and one pistol: but by a series of raids on German military posts, he managed to acquire seven rifles, ammunition, and even a number of grenades. About 150 of these Jewish partisans survived the war.

Map 153

DEPORTATION, MASSACRE AND REVOLT, 21-22 SEPTEMBER 1942

Baranowicze
3,000

WHITE RUSSIA

Treblinka

Jadow
1,000

Sterdyn
2,000

Wegrow
10,500

Sokolow
7,000

Warsaw
2,196

Stoczek
2,000

Serokomla
200

Pripet

River Pripet *marshes*

River Bug

UKRAINE

Aleksandrija
1,000

Kamionka Strumilowa
600

Radziechow **600**

Jozefow
1,500

Belzec

EASTERN GALICIA

Cholojow

Busk
1,000

Bursztyn
200

Narajow
1,400

Rohatyn
1,000

Brzezany
1,000

Bukaczowce
200

Podhajce
1,000

Bolszowce
1,000

0   miles   60
0   kilometres   100

© Martin Gilbert 1982

The Day of Atonement, the holiest day in the Jewish calendar, fell in 1942 on September 21. During that day and the following day, more than 30,000 Jews were murdered in eastern Europe. From Wegrow and Sokolow hundreds managed to escape to nearby woods but most were quickly hunted down and shot. In the following week *(opposite, above)* thousands more were killed or deported. At Tuczyn 2,000 Jews managed to escape. At Korzec 50 Jews who escaped built up a small partisan unit.

On September 25 the SS seized more than 700 Rumanian-born Jews in Paris, and deported them to Auschwitz. The deportees had been born throughout Rumania *(opposite, below)*, among them the 46-year-old Estera Bercovici and her six children. Many children were deported without parents or relatives, among them two 8-year-olds, Suzanne Sloim and Raymond Toutman. Sarah Sepolghi, aged 33, was deported with her ten-month-old baby, Paul. Of the 1,594 deportees on this single train, only 15 able-bodied men, who had been among those 'selected' for slave labour, survived the war.

DEPORTATION, MASSACRE AND REVOLT, 23-30 SEPTEMBER 1942

P r i p e t   m a r s h e s

0   miles   50
0   kilometres   80

Ivanova
1,000
24 September

Serniki
850 *killed*
150 *escape to the forests*
29 September
only **10** *survive the war*

Miedzyrzec
1,500

resistance led by
Misha Gildenman

1,000 *killed*
2,000 *escape to the forests*
23 September
only **15** *survive the war*

Tuczyn
revolt led by
Gecel Schwarzman
Meir Himmelfarb
Tuwia Czuwak
23 September

Korzec
2,000
30 September

Hoszcza
500

V O L H Y N I A

River Bug

G R E A T E R
G E R M A N Y

Belzec

R E I C H S K O M M I S S A R I A T
U K R A I N E

River

Zborow
1,000

from
Skala Podolska
1,500
26 September

E A S T E R N   G A L I C I A

Pomorzany
1,000

Tarnopol
1,000
30 September

© Martin Gilbert 1982

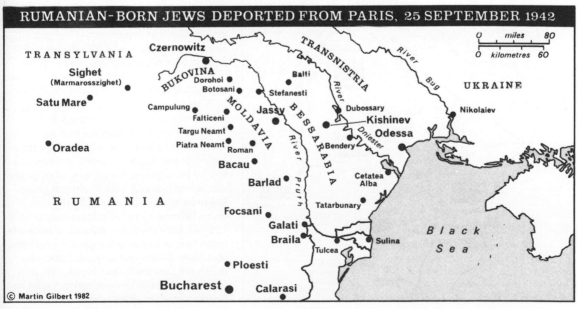

RUMANIAN-BORN JEWS DEPORTED FROM PARIS, 25 SEPTEMBER 1942

0   miles   80
0   kilometres   60

T R A N S Y L V A N I A

Czernowitz

T R A N S N I S T R I A

River Bug

U K R A I N E

Sighet
(Marmarosszighet)

B U K O V I N A

Dorohoi
Botosani

Balti

Satu Mare

Stefanesti

Campulung

Falticeni

M O L D A V I A

Jassy

B E S S A R A B I A

Dubossary

Nikolaiev

Targu Neamt
Piatra Neamt
Roman

Kishinev
Odessa

Bendery

River Dniester

Oradea

Bacau

Barlad

River Prut

Cetatea
Alba

R U M A N I A

Focsani

Tatarbunary

Galati
Braila

Tulcea

Sulina

B l a c k
S e a

Ploesti

Bucharest   **Calarasi**

© Martin Gilbert 1982

DEPORTATIONS TO CHELMNO AND TREBLINKA, 23 SEPTEMBER-5 OCTOBER 1942

River Vistula

WARTHEGAU

Chelmno

Treblinka

see map 157

Warsaw

Siedlce

Zelechow

Biala Podlaska
4,000
26 September

River Bug

Lodz
16,000
23-30 September

Kozienice
13,000
27 September

Szydlowiec
10,000
23 September

G E N E R A L

G O V E R N M E N T

Czestochowa
39,000
23 September - 5 October

River Vistula

© Martin Gilbert 1982

SEVEN FURTHER DEPORTATIONS TO TREBLINKA

Treblinka

River Bug

Kosow Lacki
5,000
23 September

Stanislawow
700 *25 September*

Kaluszyn
2,000
25 September

Warsaw

Kolbiel
1,000
27 September

River Vistula

Siedlce
2,000
26 September

Parysow
4,000 *30 September escape*

Zelechow
10,000
30 September

©Martin Gilbert 1982

In the middle of September the SS, having decided to make the Lodz ghetto an entirely 'working' ghetto, launched the 'Gehsperre' action, aimed at deporting to Chelmno all children up to the age of 10, all men and women over 60, and all who were sick or emaciated. In all, 16,000 Jews were deported and gassed within two weeks *(above)*. East of Warsaw *(left)* more than 24,000 Jews were deported to Treblinka and killed.

The deportations from the General Government also continued on a massive scale *(above)*. From one town, Zelechow, a few hundred young Jews managed to escape into the woods and form a partisan group. But most Jews were trapped by the overwhelming German military might.

From Paris the deportations to Auschwitz continued, bringing to the gas chambers Jews born throughout Asia *(opposite, above)*, the Dutch East Indies and North Africa *(opposite, below)*; men and women who had sought a new life in Paris before 1939.

JEWS BORN IN AFRICA & ASIA, DEPORTED FROM PARIS TO AUSCHWITZ

R U S S I A

Lake
Baikal

Samarkand
Henrietta Fiess aged 45

Chita
Pinchas Reznik
aged 36

C H I N A

Tashkent
Moise Rubin aged 42

Tientsin
Gerda Hecht aged 32
Eva Niwesz aged 40

AFGHANISTAN

Bukhara
Piena Slama
aged 33

Kabul
Abraham Kaufmann
aged 63

Calcutta
Murad Gubbay aged 68

Hong Kong
Henry Ullman
aged 60

INDIA

German front line October 1942

Auschwitz

Paris

Bombay
Louise Andjel
aged 43

B a y
o f
B e n g a l

S o u t h
C h i n a
S e a

German front line October 1942

Sahara desert

BELGIAN
CONGO

Stanleyville
Rosette Kadaner
aged 19

I n d i a n

O c e a n

DUTCH
EAST INDIES

Batavia
Dick Prins aged 24

Bandoeng
Rubin Zonge aged 51

Surabaja
Jacob Prins aged 28

Kimberley
Bertha Tint
aged 36

SOUTH
AFRICA

© Martin Gilbert 1982

JEWS BORN IN NORTH AFRICA, DEPORTED FROM PARIS TO AUSCHWITZ, 1942-1944

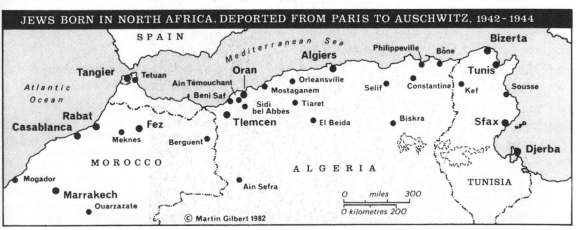

S P A I N

Mediterranean Sea

Bizerta

Tangier   Tetuan

Ain Témouchant

Oran

Algiers

Philippeville   Bône

Tunis

Atlantic
Ocean

Beni Saf

Orléansville

Selif

Constantine   Kef

Sousse

Rabat

Mostaganem

Sidi
bel Abbès

Tiaret

Fez

Tlemcen

El Beida

Biskra

Sfax

Casablanca

Meknes

Berguent

Djerba

M O R O C C O

A L G E R I A

TUNISIA

Mogador

Ain Sefra

Marrakech

Ouarzazate

0   miles   300

0 kilometres 200

© Martin Gilbert 1982

DEPORTATIONS AND REVOLT, 1–14 OCTOBER 1942

Treblinka

Radzymin
3,900
2 October

Miedzyrzec
6,000
6 October

Kobryn
4,000
14 October

Wolomin
2,400
4 October

Siedlce

Biala
Podlaska
1,200
6 October

Lukow
7,000

Sobienie
Jeziory
4,000
2 October

Ludwisin
1,000
4 October

Radzyn
1,000
1 October

Piotrkow
22,000
14-21 October

Firlej
317

Sobibor

Resistance group 'Lions' led by
Julian Ajzenman
sabotage railway line

Konskowola
1,000

Lubartow
4,500
11 October

Luboml

Opoczno

Gorzkowice
1,500

Przedborz
4,500
9 October

Konskie

Skarzysko
2,200

Opole
3,000

Belzyce
3,000

Majdanek

U

Radomsko
14,000
10-12 October

A D

Zakrzowek
1,176
to Belzec

Koniecpol
1,600
7 October

Ostrowiec
11,000
11 October

Modliborzyce
2,002
to Belzec

Zarki
800
6 October

Chmielnik
8,000
6 October

Lagow
2,000
7 October

Belzec

Wislica
3,000
3 October

Busko
Zdroj
2,000
1 October

from Holland
1,014 *2 October*
2,012 *5 October*
1,703 *9 October*
1,711 *12 October*

Auschwitz

© Martin Gilbert 2008

0   kilometres   60

0   miles   40

A	Annopol	
	1,943	*to Belzec*
U	Urzedow	
	500	*to Belzec*
D	Dzierkowice	
	146	*to Belzec*

MORE KILLINGS, SEPTEMBER – OCTOBER 1942

0   miles   100

0   kilometres 150

Baltic
Sea

Koziany
400 *30 September*

Korzeniec
2,000
9 Sept

Kobylnik
150 *29 September*

Grodek
1,600 *11 September*

Wolozyn
1,000 *29 September*

Danzig

Rakow
112 *21 September*

GREATER
GERMANY

Warsaw

Janow
2,000
24 August

Kiev

CZORTKOW
REGION
Jezierzany
900
Kopyczynce
1,500
Korolowka
700
Mielnica
1,000
Probuzna
1,500

Belzec

to Belzec

Buczacz
1,500

Horodenka
1,500 *8-10 September*

© Martin Gilbert 1982

Among the Jews murdered in September 1942 *(left)* were 1,000 from the town of Wolozyn, formerly a centre of Jewish spiritual learning. In Eastern Galicia Jews had been deported to Belzec from seven communities, some of them small villages in the Czortkow region.

Throughout October 1942 the deportations continued. From Holland *(above)* and Belgium *(opposite, above)*, Jews were brought to Auschwitz *(see also page 117)*. From central Poland and Theresienstadt they were deported to Treblinka, with as many as 30 deportations during the last two weeks of October *(opposite, below)*; and from eastern Galicia to Belzec *(opposite, above)*. East of Greater Germany, the Jews were killed in the streets, or in nearby woods and quarries, including 10,000 in the Volhynian town of Luboml.

DEPORTATION, MASSACRE AND REVOLT, 1-31 OCTOBER 1942

Baltic Sea

German front line

Bystrzycza
hundreds

Kiemieliszki
hundreds

Oszmiana
406
23 October

Nowogrodek
*50 Jews escape to join
resistance led by*
Tobias Bielski

from Belgium

Bielsk Podlaski
11,000
2 October

Kosow
300 *14 October*

Antopol **1,000**

Treblinka

Drohiczyn **2,500**
15 October

Siedlce

Ryki

Szack **150**

Kamen Kashirsky
300 *14 October*

Parczew
108

999
10 October

675
16 October

GREATER

GERMANY

995
20 October

476
24 October

822
31 October

875
31 October

Theresienstadt

1,000
5 October

1,998
15 October

2,018
22 October

1,000
8 October

1,984
19 October

Luboml
Warkowicze

Belzec

Zdolbunow
1,000

Mizocz

Ostrog

EASTERN GALICIA

Auschwitz

Czortkow
500

Kolomyja
4,500
3 October

Tluste
1,000
5 October

Bar
12,000

Luboml
10,000 *1 October*
*hundreds escape but
later hunted down*

Warkowicze
400 *killed*
1,600 *escape*

Mizocz
850
850

Ostrog
2,200
800
escape

0 *miles* 150
0 *kilometres* 200

© Martin Gilbert 1982

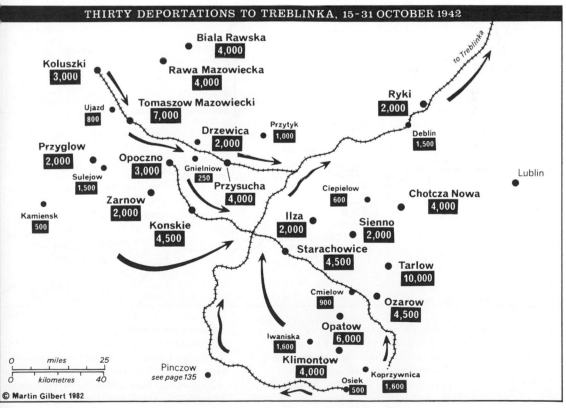

THIRTY DEPORTATIONS TO TREBLINKA, 15-31 OCTOBER 1942

to Treblinka

Biala Rawska
4,000

Koluszki
3,000

Rawa Mazowiecka
4,000

Ryki
2,000

Ujazd
800

Tomaszow Mazowiecki
7,000

Drzewica
2,000

Przytyk
1,000

Deblin
1,500

Przyglow
2,000

Opoczno
3,000

Gnielniow
250

Przysucha
4,000

Lublin

Sulejow
1,500

Zarnow
2,000

Ciepielow
600

Chotcza Nowa
4,000

Kamiensk
500

Konskie
4,500

Ilza
2,000

Sienno
2,000

Starachowice
4,500

Tarlow
10,000

Cmielow
900

Ozarow
4,500

Opatow
6,000

Iwaniska
1,600

Klimontow
4,000

Pinczow
see page 135

Osiek
500

Koprzywnica
1,600

0 *miles* 25
0 *kilometres* 40

© Martin Gilbert 1982

Map 164

DEPORTATIONS TO AUSCHWITZ, 15 – 31 OCTOBER 1942

The map above shows ten of the deportations from western Europe and Norway to Auschwitz in the second half of October 1942. In addition to these deportations, and four from Belgium *(page 116)*, the Auschwitz calendar records a further train reaching the camp from Slovakia on October 23.

Within six months of the German occupation of Norway in April 1940 *(page 32)*, Jews had been forbidden to participate in professional life. Forcible registration of

Map 165

FURTHER DEPORTATIONS, MASSACRE AND REVOLT, 15–31 OCTOBER 1942

0 miles 40
0 kilometres 60

Ciechanowiec **3,000** *15 October*

Bereza Kartuska **3,500** *16 October*

Treblinka ⛨

Pinsk **10,000** *28 October*

Latowicz **800** *15 October*

✳ Brest-Litovsk **25,000** resistance led by Hana Ginsberg *15 October*

Siennica **700** *18 October*

for the other Treblinka deportations 15–31 October 1942 see page 129

Wlodawa **2,000**

Sobibor

REICHSKOMMISSARIAT UKRAINE

Leczna **1,000**

Siedliszcze **1,000**

Przytyk

Lublin **1,800**

Opole **2,000**

Chelm **3,300**

Demidowka **500**

Targowica **700** *killed* **200** *escape*

Mlynow **500**

Krasnystaw **10,000**

Izbica

Krasnik **1,000**

Zawichost **5,000**

Szczebrzeszyn **1,000**

Zamosc **4,000**

Hrubieszow **2,000**

Dubno **3,000**

Sokal **2,500**

✳ Murawica **150**

Sandomierz **3,200**

Ulanow **500**

Bilgoraj **500** Belzec ⛨

Lopatin **400**

Radzwillow **1,800** **600** *escape*

✳ Pinczow **3,000**

resistance led by Michael Majtek Zalman Fajnsztat

GENERAL

Kamionka Strumilowa **500**

Zbaraz **1,000**

⛨ Auschwitz

Cracow **6,000** *deported* **300** *children killed on the spot 28 October*

GOVERNMENT

Sambor **3,000** *deported naked to prevent revolt*

Drohobycz **2,300**

Stryj **2,000**

Skalat **3,000**

Podhajce **1,500**

Monasterzyska **2,500**

Buczacz **1,500**

SLOVAKIA

© Martin Gilbert 1982

---

all Jews took place in June 1942, and the confiscation of all Jewish property in October 1942. Then, on October 25, all Jewish men and boys over the age of sixteen, some 209 in all, were seized throughout the country, sent by sea from Norway to Stettin, and then on by rail to Auschwitz. A further 531 women and children were seized on November 25 *(page 120)*, and likewise sent to their deaths. Only 12 of the 740 deportees survived the war.

Helped by the Norwegian people, often at the risk of their own lives, as many as 930 Norwegian Jews succeeded in escaping into neutral Sweden. About 60 were imprisoned or interned inside Norway itself.

The map above shows some of the deportations to the eastern death camps during the same two-week period. Before the deportation from Drohobycz, nearly 200 old

and sick Jews were shot in the streets of the town. Among the executions on the spot was the killing of 25,000 Jews in Brest-Litovsk. Almost all the other Jews of Brest, some 5,000, had been murdered in June 1941 *(page 54)*. Most of the few hundred Jews still alive managed to join partisan units.

Among the deportations during these two weeks was one from Przytyk to Treblinka *(page 116)*. It was the murder of three Jews in Przytyk before the Second World War *(page 8)* that had created such alarm among Polish Jewry, reviving memories of the Tsarist pogroms. But in the autumn of 1942 the deportation and immediate murder of 1,000 Jews from the same village, deaths horrific in themselves, were dwarfed by the total number of deaths in only two weeks, in eastern Poland alone, of more than 100,000 men, women and children.

Map 166

DEPORTATION AND RESISTANCE, 1-6 NOVEMBER 1942

Ciechanow
1,000

Bielsk

BIALYSTOK REGION
over **110,000**
see map opposite

Plonsk
12,000
1 November–5 December

Treblinka

Miedzyrzec
1,500
7 November

Sobibor

Tomaszow Mazowiecki
7,000
3 November

Gowarczow
1,000

Skarzysko-Kamienna
slave labour camp

Chelm
10,000
6 November

Krasnik
resistance led by
Abraham Braun
Eduard Forst

Radoszyce
4,000
3 November

Konskie
6,000
6 November

Frampol
600

Jozefow
600 *2 November*

Belzec

Zloczow
2,500
2 November
including the poet
S. J. Imber

Stopnica
5,000
5 November

Krzeszow
500 *shot*
2 November

Tarnogrod
3,000
2 November

Szczucin

Bilgoraj
4,000
2 November

Lvov
8,000

Auschwitz

GENERAL

GOVERNMENT

Komarno
2,000

Brzezany
1,000
4 November

Boryslaw
600
5 November
deported naked to prevent revolt

© Martin Gilbert 1982

S L O V A K I A

miles 0 — 50
kilometres 0 — 80

In November 1942 the Dutch, French and Norwegian deportations continued *(opposite, above)*. Further east, Jews were slaughtered at Slutsk; and at Proskurov, where 1,700 Jews had been killed in 1919 *(page 2)*, the last 7,000 Jews were murdered.

On November 2 one of the most carefully organized and intensive round-ups of the war took place throughout the Bialystok region *(opposite, below)*, where more than 20,000 Jews had already been murdered during the first two months of the German invasion *(page 54 and 55)*. The remaining 110,000 Jews, who had been strictly confined to their towns and villages, were now seized and sent to camps at Zambrow, Wolkowysk, Bogusze and Kielbasin, before being taken by train to Treblinka and Auschwitz. When the Jews of Marcinkance resisted deportation, all were shot in the village.

At Siemiatycze a few dozen Jews managed to escape to nearby forests and to form a small resistance group. Most were then killed by Polish partisan bands.

Further south, at Stopnica *(above)*, 1,500 men were sent to the slave labour camps at Skarzysko Kamienna, while 400 children and old people were shot in the town cemetery. The remaining 3,000 Jews were marched to Szczucin, many being shot on the way, and the survivors sent on by train to Treblinka, at which, with Belzec and Auschwitz, more than 170,000 Jews were killed within one week *(above)*.

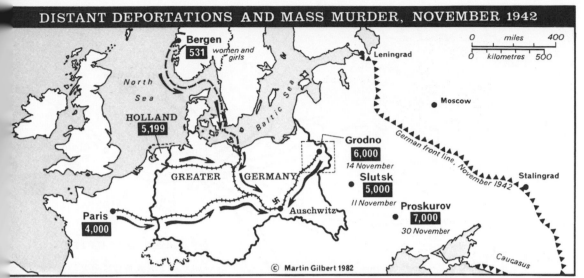

DISTANT DEPORTATIONS AND MASS MURDER, NOVEMBER 1942

Bergen 531 *women and girls*

North Sea

Baltic Sea

Leningrad

Moscow

HOLLAND 5,199

GREATER **GERMANY**

Grodno 6,000 *14 November*

German front line, November 1942

Stalingrad

Slutsk 5,000 *11 November*

Auschwitz

Proskurov 7,000 *30 November*

Paris 4,000

Caucasus

miles 0 — 400
kilometres 0 — 500

© Martin Gilbert 1982

SIXTY-FIVE DEPORTATIONS FROM THE BIALYSTOK REGION, 2 NOVEMBER 1942

to the Leningrad front

360 *killed on the spot*

to Konigsberg and the Baltic

Marcinkance

Porzecze 1,000

GREATER EAST PRUSSIA

Augustow 2,000

Sopockinie 2,000

Druskieniki 500

Ostryna 2,000

Rajgrod 400

Dabrowa Bialostocka 1,000

Grodno 4,500

Jeziory 2,000

Bogusze *slave labour camp*

Grajewo 2,500

Suchowola 5,100

Kuznica 1,000

River

Skidel 3,000

Szczuczyn 1,500

Goniadz 1,280

Janow 950

Sidra 350

Kielbasin *slave labour camp*

Lunna 1,500

Niemen

Wasosz 50

Stawiski 60

Radzilow 22

Korycin 1,000

Sokolka 8,000

BIALYSTOK

Indura 2,500

Mosty 350

GREATER

Jedwabne 30

Trzcianne 1,200

Knyszyn 1,300

Wasilkow 1,180

Suprasl 170

Krynki 5,000

REGION

Ros 1,000

Wolpa 1,500

Nowogrod 36

Lomza 7,000

Zawady 180

Bialystok

Choroszcz 440

Grodek 1,300

Michalowo 750

Wolkowysk 7,000

to the Moscow front

GERMANY

Rutki 20

Sniadowo 650

Zambrow 2,000

Wysokie 3,700

Lapy 600

Zabludow 2,000

Swisłocz 3,000

Rozana 3,000

Sokoly 850

Narew 400

Jalowka 850

Porozow 1,000

Lyskow 600

Lubotyn 174

Czyzew 200

Bielsk 5,000

Klukowo 68

Bransk 2,600

Orla 2,000

Malkinia Junction

Ciechanowiec 700

Bocki 756

Pruzana 3,000

to Germany

Treblinka

River Bug

Milejczyce 1,000

Kleszczele 1,000

resistance led by Herschl Shabbes

GENERAL GOVERNMENT

Siemiatycze 6,000

Drohiczyn 500

miles 0 — 20
kilometres 0 — 30

© Martin Gilbert 1982

Map 169

JEWS DEPORTED FROM PROVINCIAL FRANCE, 3 NOVEMBER 1942

English Channel

St.Quentin
37

Rouen

to Auschwitz

Caen
5

Drancy

Châlons
sur Marne
52

Paris

Nancy
234

Melun
69

Troyes
3

Rennes
36

GERMAN-OCCUPIED

FRANCE

Angers
296

Poitiers
617

Bay

VICHY

of

FRANCE

Lyons

Biscay

Angoulême
9

Merignac

Bordeaux
135

0   miles   100

0   kilometres   140

© Martin Gilbert 1982

Among the deportations to Auschwitz in November 1942 was one, from Paris on November 3, which included several hundred Jews who had been seized in provincial France *(above)*.

Of the 1,000 Jews deported on that day, 200 were children, deported with their parents or grandparents; including the 4-year-old twins, Annie and Lydia Kirzner, the 2-year-old Jacques Wlademirski, the 4-year-old Daniel Szulc, and the Zajdenwerger children, David aged 4 and his sister, Solange, aged 3. All were gassed.

The map opposite *(top)* shows some of the other birthplaces of those deported from Paris to Auschwitz on November 3. Some were old people, such as Gabriel Erlich, from Warsaw, aged 70, deported with his wife, and his two daughters, aged 36 and 38.

Many of the deportees, like the Erlich daughters, were in the prime of life: Magalta

Poulios, from the Greek island of Chios, was 35; Jean Blumenthal, from Berlin, was 27; so also was Joseph Rozio from the Turkish port of Smyrna; Robert Geyer from Metz was just 20; Gabrielle Bruski from Budapest was only 18. Deported all alone was a boy, the 4-year-old Jankiel Ciesielski, who had been born in Lodz.

The two smaller maps *(opposite, below)* give the birthplaces and names of some of the hundreds of Jews deported from Paris to Auschwitz between 1942 and 1944 who had been born in the Americas. At least 10 were still United States citizens at the time of their deportation. Between the wars all had chosen to come to Europe; to teach, to work, to marry and to bring up children.

The photograph was taken during one of the Paris deportations; more than 80,000 Jews were deported from Paris to Auschwitz in little over two years.

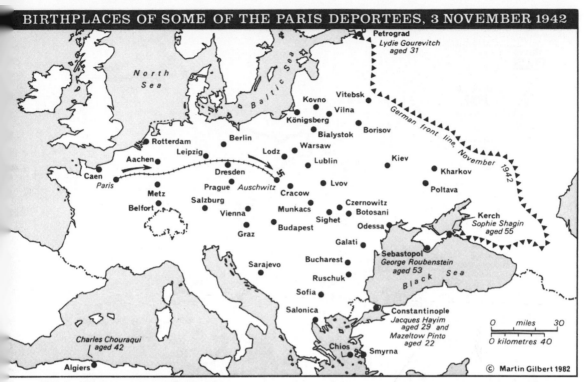

BIRTHPLACES OF SOME OF THE PARIS DEPORTEES, 3 NOVEMBER 1942

North Sea

Baltic Sea

Petrograd
*Lydie Gourevitch
aged 31*

Kovno
Vitebsk
Vilna
Königsberg
Bialystok
Borisov

German front line, November 1942

Berlin
Rotterdam
Leipzig
Aachen
Warsaw
Lodz
Lublin
Kiev
Kharkov

Caen
Paris
Dresden
Prague
Auschwitz
Lvov
Poltava

Metz
Salzburg
Cracow
Czernowitz
Belfort
Munkacs
Botosani
Kerch
*Sophie Shagin
aged 55*
Vienna
Sighet
Odessa
Graz
Budapest

Galati
Sebastopol
*George Roubenstein
aged 53*
Sarajevo
Bucharest
Black Sea
Ruschuk
Sofia
Salonica
Constantinople
*Jacques Hayim
aged 29 and
Mazeltow Pinto
aged 22*
Chios
Smyrna

*Charles Chouraqui
aged 42*

Algiers

0 miles 30
0 kilometres 40

© Martin Gilbert 1982

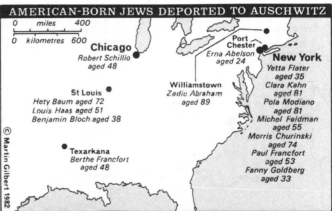

AMERICAN-BORN JEWS DEPORTED TO AUSCHWITZ

0 miles 400
0 kilometres 600

Chicago
*Robert Schillio
aged 48*

Port Chester
*Erna Abelson
aged 24*

New York
*Yetta Flater
aged 35
Clara Kahn
aged 81
Pola Modiano
aged 81
Michel Feldman
aged 55
Morris Churinski
aged 74
Paul Francfort
aged 53
Fanny Goldberg
aged 33*

Williamstown
*Zadie Abraham
aged 89*

St Louis
*Hety Baum aged 72
Louis Haas aged 51
Benjamin Bloch aged 38*

Texarkana
*Berthe Francfort
aged 48*

© Martin Gilbert 1982

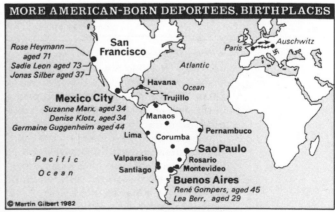

MORE AMERICAN-BORN DEPORTEES, BIRTHPLACES

*Rose Heymann
aged 71*
San Francisco
*Sadie Leon aged 73
Jonas Silber aged 37*

Paris → Auschwitz

Atlantic
Havana
Ocean
Trujillo

Mexico City
*Suzanne Marx, aged 34
Denise Klotz, aged 34
Germaine Guggenheim aged 44*

Manaos
Lima
Corumba
Pernambuco

Sao Paulo
Rosario
Valparaiso
Montevideo
Santiago
Buenos Aires
*René Gompers, aged 45
Lea Berr, aged 29*

Pacific Ocean

© Martin Gilbert 1982

Map 173

DEPORTATION, MASSACRE AND REVOLT, 7-30 NOVEMBER 1942

Mlawa
6,300
10 November

Makow
500
14 November

Treblinka

Wyszogrod
2,700
19 November

Warsaw

Miedzyrzec Podlaski
1,500   7 November

Danilowicze
900
21 November

Serokomla
200 shot
22 November

Lukow
3,000
7 November

Wisznice
120 shot
20 November

Szydlowiec
10,000
23 November

Gniewoszow
1,000
15 November

Leczna
1,000
11 November

Komarow Osada
1,000
10 November

Konskie
4,500
7 November

Zwolen
10,000
29 November

Majdanek

Piaski
4,000
9 November

Wlodzimierz Wolynski
2,500
13 November
resistance

Szczekociny
1,500
21 November

Suchedniow
4,000
21 November

Goraj
30 shot
30 November

Zamosc
4,000
15 November

Belzec

Brody
250 to Belzec
20 shot
26 November

Sedziszow
1,000
21 November

Staszow
6,000
7 November

Kolbuszowa
2,500

Lubaczow

Zolkiew
2,500
22 November

Busk
1,000 shot

Zbaraz
1,000
8 November

Ksiaz Wielki
500 shot

Cracow

Rzeszow
2,000

Sasow
400
25 November

Skalat
1,100
9 November

Bochnia
570
10 November

Tarnow
3,000
15 November

Przemysl
4,000
18 November

Rudki
800

Lvov
5,000
18 November

Zakliczyn
500

'Amsterdam' Jewish resistance group active, November 1942 – November 1944

Stryj
1,500
to Belzec

Buczacz
2,750
27 November

Jaworow
1,500
7 November

Tlumacz
2,000
27 November

SLOVAKIA

Mosciska
2,500
28 November

Szczerzec
600

© Martin Gilbert 1982

miles 50
kilometres 80

123

During the last three weeks of November more than 50,000 Jews were deported to the death camps of Treblinka and Belzec, sent to the concentration camp at Majdanek, now a death camp; or, as in Wlodzimierz Wolynski, massacred in the streets *(above)*.

In the course of a few hours ancient communities were totally destroyed: the Jews of Wyszogrod could trace their first settlement in the town to the early fifteenth century, those of Buczacz to the late sixteenth century.

It was in Buczacz that the author S. Y. Agnon, a Nobel prizewinner, had been born in 1907; at the age of 20, he had emigrated to Palestine. After a visit to Buczacz in 1930, he published a nightmarish picture of his home town, its synagogues empty, its society collapsed, its people shattered: a 'city of the dead'.

In Buczacz, following the first killings in August 1941 *(page 56)*, and the deportations of October 1942 *(page 118)*, young men and women had searched for arms, and tried to

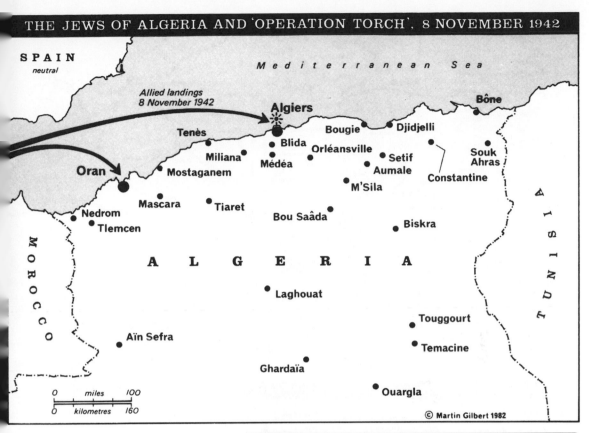

THE JEWS OF ALGERIA AND 'OPERATION TORCH', 8 NOVEMBER 1942

SPAIN
neutral

Mediterranean Sea

*Allied landings
8 November 1942*

Algiers

Bône

Tenès

Bougie **Djidjelli**

Oran

Blida

Orléansville

**Souk
Ahras**

Miliana

Médéa

Setif

Mostaganem

Aumale

Constantine

M'Sila

Mascara   **Tiaret**

Nedrom

Bou Saâda

Tlemcen

Biskra

A   L   G   E   R   I   A

MOROCCO

Laghouat

TUNISIA

Touggourt

Aïn Sefra

Temacine

Ghardaïa

Ouargla

0 — miles — 100
0 — kilometres — 160

© Martin Gilbert 1982

train themselves for a breakout. In mid-1943 *(page 148)*, when the SS liquidated the ghetto, some Jews managed to escape to the forest. But most were murdered near the Jewish cemetery on the outskirst of the town.

It was not only in Europe, but also in North Africa *(above)* that Jews were at risk. Jews were active throughout the Algerian resistance, and it was a Jew, Jose Abulker, who led the uprising in Algiers, tying down the Vichy French and 'neutralizing' the capital, as the Allies carried out 'Operation Torch', the landings of 8 November 1942. For the 117,000 Jews of Algeria, the Allied landings brought security from deportation.

With the almost simultaneous German defeats at Stalingrad and El Alamein *(right)* the Allied landings in North Africa marked a major turning point of the war. But a full year and a half were to pass before the Red Army reached the first of the death camps on Polish soil, Majdanek *(page 187)*, or the western Allies landed on the Normandy beaches *(page 188)*. During those eighteen months the deportation of Jews continued without respite throughout Nazi-dominated Europe.

STALINGRAD, EL ALAMEIN, 'TORCH'

0 — miles — 400
0 — kilometres — 800

Leningrad
besieged

*North
Sea*

Baltic Sea

SOVIET RUSSIA

*Atlantic
Ocean*

Warsaw

Stalingrad
relieved

**GREATER
GERMANY** **Cracow**

Black Sea

Oran   Algiers
Allied landings

Mediterranean Sea

EGYPT

**El
Alamein**
Germans defeated

© Martin Gilbert 1982

BIRTHPLACES OF DEPORTEES FROM PARIS, 9 NOVEMBER 1942

Joseph Misrachi aged 44

Esther Cohen aged 60

© Martin Gilbert 1982

GREEK-BORN DEPORTEES FROM PARIS

© Martin Gilbert 1982

On 9 November 1942 it was the turn of Jews who had been born in Greece to be seized in Paris and deported to Auschwitz. More than 800 of these deportees had been born in Salonica *(above)*: nearly 100 or them were children under 12. Among those from the ancient town of Drama were Jacques and Nicoula Benveniste, and their daughter Liza, aged 19. From Canea, in Crete, had come the 67-year-old Moise Cohen.

As with each of the previous Paris deportations, there were Jews who had been born throughout Europe *(above)*, North Africa and Asia Minor. Esther Cohen had been born in Cairo 60 years before, Joseph Misrahi in Jerusalem 44 years before, Solomon Moscowitz in the port of Kerch in 1877.

In the General Government several thousand Jews, from four communities, had been in hiding in the forests since the spring *(opposite, above)*. On November 10 a German promise of the security of a new ghetto led more than 6,000 of them to agree to come out in return for safe conduct. Starving and freezing, they were taken to Sandomierz: but two months later, on 10 January 1943, almost all of them were deported to Treblinka and gassed, only a few hundred being sent to labour camps at Skarzysko Kamienna and Sandomierz itself.

In the province of Zamosc *(opposite, below)* it was Poles who faced Nazi brutality. To enable SS men, ethnic Germans and Ukrainians to settle in the province's rich pastureland, tens of thousands of Poles were driven from their homes, and hundreds killed. At the same time, thousands of Polish children were deported to concentration camps. In all more than 100 villages were emptied of their inhabitants, and more than 40,000 Poles expelled.

ESCAPE, DECEPTION AND DEPORTATION, 10 NOVEMBER 1942

0 miles 40
0 kilometres 60

Treblinka

GREATER GERMANY

GENERAL GOVERNMENT

Ujazd

Szydlowiec

6,000

Skarzysko Kamienna
slave labour camp

200

Radomsko

Zamosc

Sandomierz
slave labour camp

400

© Martin Gilbert 1982

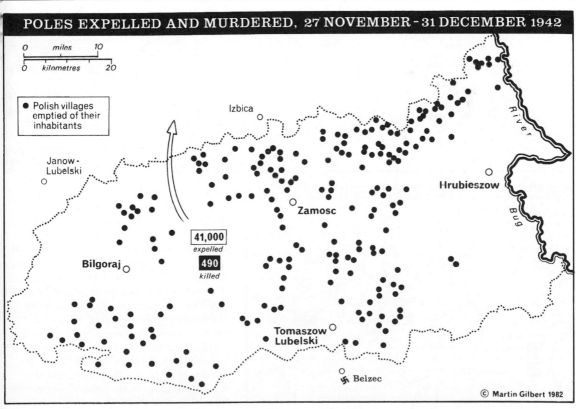

POLES EXPELLED AND MURDERED, 27 NOVEMBER – 31 DECEMBER 1942

0 miles 10
0 kilometres 20

● Polish villages
emptied of their
inhabitants

Izbica

River

Janow-
Lubelski

Hrubieszow

Zamosc

Bug

41,000
expelled

490
killed

Bilgoraj

Tomaszow
Lubelski

Belzec

© Martin Gilbert 1982

126

DEPORTATION, MASSACRE AND REVOLT, DECEMBER 1942

0 miles 40
0 kilometres 60

Dworzec

Slonim
300
and 500 escaped to
join the partisans

Baranowicze
3,000
17 December

3,000 killed
slave labour camp
19 December

to Treblinka
4,000
8 December
to Auschwitz
1,500
6 December

Makow

Treblinka

Minsk Mazowiecki
slave labour camp
218
24 December

Nowy Dwor
and

Czerwinsk
2,000
12 December

Karczew
slave labour camp
400
1 December

Miedzyrzec
500

Biala Podlaska
231 shot
17 December

Pinsk
150
23 December
the last artisans
murdered

Radzyn
1,500
20 December

Sobibor
4 escape, betrayed in
a nearby village and shot
25 December

Kruszyna
slave labour camp
557 killed
17 December

Kielce
ghetto resistance
organized

Trawniki
slave labour
camp

Luck
500
slave labour camp
remnant murdered
12 December

Czestochowa
ghetto resistance
organized

Parczew
forest
resistance groups
active

Belzec

Rawa Ruska
several thousands
7-11 December

Brody acts of
resistance led by

Jakub Linder

Samuel Weiler and

Solomon Halberszstadt

Stalowa Wola
slave labour camp
2 Jews shot for mutiny
28 December

Auschwitz

Cracow
attacks on Gestapo officers
20 Jews killed including
the resistance leader
Adolf Liebeskind
24 December

Krosno
600
4 December

Rohatyn
1,250
8 December

Bursztyn

Bolszowce

Bukaczowce

Buczacz

Czortkow
acts of resistance led by

Meir Waserman

Ryuwen Rosenburg

Heniek Nusbaum

Mundek Nusbaum

© Martin Gilbert 1982

THREE DEPORTATIONS, THREE MASSACRES

North
Sea

Baltic Sea

Westerbork

Postawy
2,500
25 December 1942

Iwje
150
31 December 1942

Berlin

Korelicze
1,000

Auschwitz

HOLLAND
817 4 December
927 8 December
757 12 December 1942

GREATER
GERMANY

0 miles 300
0 kms 400

Black
Sea

© Martin Gilbert 1982

From western Europe the deportations from Holland to Auschwitz continued (left). But by the end of 1942 the deportation of Polish Jews to Belzec and Treblinka had almost ended, and in many regions (above) only the remnants of communities now remained. In slave labour camps Jews were also murdered.

Throughout German-occupied Poland, as in the Parczew forest, Jewish resistance had become more organized. In Buczacz the Jews were preparing to break out of the ghetto. In Cracow the Jewish Fighters' Organization, set up in July 1942, carried out acts of sabotage. Elsewhere, acts of resistance, escape to the forests, preparation for uprisings, and even escape from the

Map 182

GYPSY DEPORTATIONS, MASSACRES, AND REVOLT, 1939-1945

NORWAY 60

ESTONIA 1,000

LATVIA 2,500

LITHUANIA 1,000

REICHSKOMMISSARIAT OSTLAND 30,000

HOLLAND 500

BELGIUM 500

Bergen Belsen

Ravensbrück
Sachsenhausen
Chelmno

Treblinka

POLAND 35,000

Bialystok 2,600

Nieswiez *revolt*

Sobibor

Babi Yar *hundreds*

VOLHYNIA 4,000

GREATER

Gross Rosen

Majdanek

Buchenwald

Belzec

revolt Auschwitz

Lierenfeld *sterilization*

GERMANY 15,000

LUXEMBOURG 200

Valogne *sterilization*

Dachau

Natzweiler

Mauthausen

SLOVAKIA 1,000

HUNGARY 28,000

Nikolaiev

Tiraspol

AUSTRIA 6,500

BOHEMIA 6,500

FRANCE 15,000

SWITZ.

RUMANIA 36,000

Simferopol 800

ITALY 1,000

CROATIA 28,000

Zemun
Jasenovac

ALBANIA *thousands*

SERBIA 12,000

Black Sea

Baltic Sea

© Martin Gilbert 1982

death camps, continued, against formidable odds.

Like the Jews, Europe's Gypsies were marked for destruction by the Nazis *(above)*. Following a decree of 16 December 1942, all German Gypsies were deported to Auschwitz. On 29 March 1943 the order was given to deport all Dutch Gypsies to Auschwitz. All over Europe, as shown above, Gypsy communities were destroyed. Several Gypsy revolts are recorded. But like the Jews, the Gypsies had to face a combination of artificially intensified 'race' hatred, meticulous planning, continual deception, and overwhelming military power.

Many Gypsies were deported to Jewish ghettos. In Lithuania the Gestapo locked 1,000 Gypsies in a synagogue until they died of starvation. Hundreds were killed alongside Jews, as at Babi Yar. At Valogne, Lierenfeld and Ravensbrück, hundreds of Gypsy women were sterilized. By 1945 more than 220,000 of Europe's 700,000 Gypsies had been murdered by the Nazis. The photograph is of a Gypsy family in Volhynia.

Map 183

DEPORTATION, MASSACRE AND REVOLT, JANUARY 1943

Grodno **10,000** to Auschwitz

Jasionowka **2,120** 25 January

Sokolka **200**

Wolkowysk

Zambrow **20,000** 12 January to Auschwitz

Lomza **8,000** 14 January to Auschwitz

Bialystok

several hundred 28-30 January to Auschwitz

Narewka

acts of resistance

Hajnowka

Bialowieza

Pruzana **12,000** 28 January to Auschwitz

Treblinka

Warsaw first acts of resistance 18 January **6,000** deported to Treblinka **1,000** murdered in the streets

Minsk Mazowiecki Kopernik labour camp uprising 10 January

Ujazd 2,000 6 January

Radom 1,500 13 January

Przytyk 1,000 13 January

Opoczno 120 3 January

escape led by Hayyim Sabatkowski and his two brothers

Szydlowiec 5,000 13 January

Radomsko 4,500 5 January

Ostrowiec 1,000

Bilgoraj 27 the last Jews in hiding, discovered and murdered

Czestochowa armed resistance 3 January led by Mendel Fiszlewicz **250** old people and children killed as reprisal

Konskie 300 6 January

Sandomierz slave labour camp **6,000** 10 January

Lubaczow several hundred 6 January

G E N E R A L

Grodek Jagiellonski 1,300 shot 27 January

Lvov 15,000 5-7 January

Auschwitz

G O V E R N M E N T

Jaryczow Nowy 2,500 shot 15 January

Stanislawow 1,000 26 January

S L O V A K I A

© Martin Gilbert 1982

During January 1943, as the deportation of the remaining Jews of Poland continued, many were murdered on the spot, such as the last 200 in Sokolka (*above*) who had been working in a boot factory, the last 27 Jews in Bilgoraj, and the last 17 craftsmen of Dzisna (*opposite*). Deported to Auschwitz (*opposite, above*) were more than 10,000 Jews from Holland, Theresienstadt and Belgium, as well as 2,000 from Berlin. The last Dutch transport contained 869 invalids and children; all were gassed on arrival.

Jewish resistance was also growing in scale and confidence. In Czestochowa a Jewish resistance group killed 25 German soldiers. But as a reprisal, the SS shot 250

DISTANT DEPORTATIONS TO AUSCHWITZ, JANUARY 1943

HOLLAND
Westerbork

750	11 January
748	18 January
921	21 January
516	23 January
869	29 January

Baltic Sea

Dvinsk

Soviet forces advancing

Vitebsk

Berlin

1,000	12 January
1,000	29 January

Augustow
4,000
7 January

WHITE
RUSSIA

Soviet
German
battle zone

40,000

forced labourers
killed in battle
zone (see page 184)

Malines
BELGIUM

948
15 January

612
15 January

Theresienstadt

GREATER
GERMANY

Auschwitz

1,582	21 January
1,802	24 January
709	27 January
783	30 January

Black
Sea

0	miles	300	
0	kilometres	400	

© Martin Gilbert 1982

THE LAST SEVENTEEN CRAFTSMEN OF DZISNA, MURDERED

Dvinsk

River Dvina

Polotsk

Dzisna

17

22 January 1943

River Disna

Swieciany

Vitebsk

Vilna

Lake Narocz

0	miles	30	
0	kilometres	60	

© Martin Gilbert 1982

old people and children. Reprisals on this scale made acts of resistance all the more perilous. At Pruzana a small group of Jews made contact with nearby Polish partisans, but even this course of action was not free from danger. When the three Sabatkowski brothers, Hayyim, Mordekhai and Herzke, finally reached the forests near Konskie, they were murdered by Polish partisans. While fleeing many Jews were killed by anti-semitic Poles, many other Jews were saved when Poles risked their lives to shelter them.

As the sealed trains reached Treblinka, the Ukrainian guards drove the starving, frightened passengers with whips and rifle butts along the short road to the gas chamber. The road itself was flanked by bogus shops, and the station disguised as a transit point. But by January 1943 it was no longer fear of the unknown but fear of death which filled the deportees, and when one of the trains from Grodno reached Treblinka late in the evening, 1,000 Jews turned on the guards and attacked them with wooden clubs torn from a nearby fence, with knives and with razors. The fight lasted several hours. In the morning all the Jews and the guards were found dead in the snow, killed by SS machine-gun fire and grenades aimed indiscriminately at both.

BIRTHPLACES OF SOME WHO DIED AT DRANCY DURING 1943

Paris
Max Bybeleser aged 28
Ernest Fernbach aged 73
Daniel Halphein aged 62
Yvette Menasse aged 10

Warsaw
Jacob Altglass aged 62
Alexander Imbryezeck aged 67
Ida Prussak aged 88
Mrs Maltz aged 23

Petrograd
Simon Gordon
aged 71

North Sea

Baltic Sea

Gulf of Finland

0 miles 200
0 kilometres 300

Vilna
Hirsch Linkever
aged 81

Poltava
Olga Apostol
aged 71

Warsaw

Pinsk
Nicolas Piekmann
aged 78

Amsterdam
Louis Voorzanger
aged 47

Kalisz
Abraham Szymkiewiecz
aged 61

Radom
Lazare Berman
aged 62

Kiev
Samuel Bistritzky
aged 71

Brody
Mathilde Barbasch
aged 76

Odessa
Sarah Dimonte aged 66
Abraham Lichtenstein aged 71

Drancy
Paris

Reims
Maxime Hirtz aged 57

Nancy
Lucien Weill aged 67

Vienna
Richard Treibb
aged 57

Bacau
Rosa Moscovltch
aged 70

Orleans
Octave Lion
aged 67

Mulhouse
Jean Dreyfus
aged 64
Marcel Bloch
aged 53

Lyon
the widow Weil
aged 71

Adriatic Sea

Black Sea

Dardanelles
Isaac Capsuto
aged 51

Isaac Beressi aged 66
Isaac Emram aged 60
Hugo Mosseri aged 65

Salonica

Constantinople
Bernard Brittman aged 72
Abraham Mires aged 44

New York
Henry Weille aged 60

© Martin Gilbert 1982

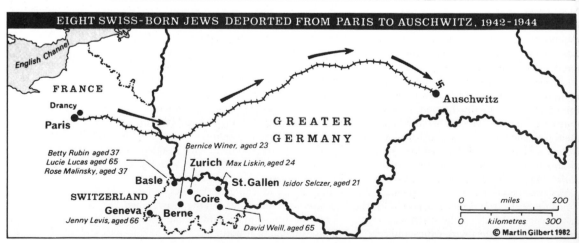

EIGHT SWISS-BORN JEWS DEPORTED FROM PARIS TO AUSCHWITZ, 1942-1944

English Channel

FRANCE

Drancy
Paris

**GREATER
GERMANY**

Auschwitz

Betty Rubin aged 37
Lucie Lucas aged 65
Rose Malinsky, aged 37

Bernice Winer, aged 23

Zurich Max Liskin, aged 24

Basle

St. Gallen Isidor Selczer, aged 21

SWITZERLAND

Coire

Geneva
Jenny Levis, aged 66

Berne

David Weill, aged 65

0 miles 200
0 kilometres 300

© Martin Gilbert 1982

THE JEWS OF TUNIS AT RISK

Bizerta
Utica
Mateur
Béja • Tunis
Souk el Arba
Menzel
Bou Zelfa
Chemtou
Testour
Soliman
Nabeul
Lekef
Ebba-Ksour
Sousse
Thala
Monastir
Kairouan
Moknine
Hadjeb-el-
Mahdia
Sbeitla
Aioun

under Axis military control

Sfax

Gafsa
El Guettar
Nefta • Tozeur
El Hamma
Hara Kebira
Djerba Island
Gabès
Hara Sghira
Kebili
Zarzis
Médenine
Foum Tatahouine
Ben
Gardane

TUNISIA

ALGERIA

LIBYA

0 miles 100
0 kilometres 160

© Martin Gilbert 1982

In preparing to deport Jews from Paris, the Gestapo confined them at Drancy, where conditions were primitive. More than 100 Jews died there during 1943, including many old people *(opposite, above)* who could not stand the continuous privation. Henry Weille had been born in New York in 1883, and Ida Prussak had been born in Warsaw at the time of the Crimean War. Some young people also died in the camp, including the 10-year-old Yvette Menasse.

The photograph was taken by the Germans at Drancy detention camp in 1942.

Even Jews who had been born in neutral Switzerland were not immune from deportation. The Gestapo's own lists of those deported fom Paris record 39 Swiss-born Jews deported to Auschwitz between March 1942 and May 1944: their birthplaces are shown on the map opposite *(below)*: both Max Liskin from Zurich and Bernice Winer from Berne were in their early twenties at the time of their deportation.

The Jews of Tunis *(right)* suffered five months of confiscation of property, plunder, forced labour, ill-treatment and execution under German rule. More than 4,000 of them had been sent to labour camps near the front lines, and many had died from ill-treatment, disease, and even during Allied aerial bombardments. Shown here are the principal towns in which more than 50,000 Tunisian Jews lived. Their suffering came to an end in May 1943, as the Allied armies drove the Germans from North Africa.

THE ADVANCE OF THE ALLIES

Mediterranean Sea

ITALY
GREECE
CORFU
SICILY
Tunis
captured 7 May 1943
MALTA

Algiers
Allied landing 8 November 1942

battle area January–April 1943

ALGERIA

Tripoli
captured 23 January 1943

Benghazi
captured 20 November 1942

0 miles 200
0 kilometres 300

LIBYA

© Martin Gilbert 1982

Map 190

SOME CHILDREN DEPORTED TO AUSCHWITZ, 11 FEBRUARY 1943

GREAT BRITAIN

North Sea

Amsterdam

| Miriam Sluizer | aged 5 |
| Abel Sluizer | aged 2 |

Antwerp

| Joseph Skoulsky | aged 10 |
| Augusta Skoulsky | aged 5 |

Straits of Dover

English Channel

Luxembourg

| Gaston Kahn aged 9 |

Rouen

| Leon Eskenazi aged 6 |

Metz

Anna Checinski	aged 7
Elise Checinski	aged 12
Simon Checinski	aged 14

Le Havre

| Claire Leibel | aged 6 |
| Nelly Leibel | aged 4 |

Paris

| Pauline Leibel aged 9 |

Nancy

| Joseph Haber | aged 8 |
| Samy Gryn | aged 9 |

St. Nazaire

| Maxime Borenheim aged 3 |

Angers

Mina Sternchuss	aged 10
and her sisters	
Lola	aged 6
Simone	aged 4

Mulhouse

| Pierre Roth | aged 3 |
| Germaine Roth | aged 7 |

SWITZERLAND *neutral*

Bay of Biscay

Angoulême

| Joseph Wapniarz | aged 11 months |
| Frieda Reiss | aged 11 months |

Bordeaux

Henri Ayzenberg	aged 3
Helene Zavidowitcz	aged 8
Simone Zavidowitcz	aged 6

| 0 | miles | 100 |
| 0 | kilometres | 160 |

Gulf of Lions

SPAIN *neutral*

Pyrenees

Mediterranean Sea

© Martin Gilbert 1982

Map 191

OLD PEOPLE DEPORTED TO AUSCHWITZ, 11 FEBRUARY 1943

Suwalki
Théodore Baera
aged 82

Sosnowiec
Berta Schmulevitz
aged 84

Piotrkow
Leja Granek
aged 85

Novomoskovsk
Kiva Makline
aged 80

Drancy

Paris

Cracow
Gitla Wajslfisz
aged 83

Kuppenheim
Marie Dreifuss
aged 85

Teschen
Caroline Neumann
aged 82

Kishinev
Githel Mandelevitch
aged 91

© Martin Gilbert 1982

Odessa
Esther Krimer   aged 84
and
Fania Krinitchevsky   aged 86

North Sea

Baltic Sea

Black Sea

miles 300
kilometres 400

As the deportations from France to Auschwitz continued, neither children nor old people were spared. Among 1,000 Jews deported on 11 February 1943, of whom only 10 survived the war, were several hundred children and old people who were gassed immediately the deportation train reached the camp.

The children whose names and birthplaces are shown opposite were deported together with their parents, except for Joseph and Augusta Skoulsky who were deported alone, and the two Leibel sisters who were deported with their sister Pauline, aged 9, who had been born in Paris.

The young Maxime Borenheim was deported with his 19-year-old mother, who had been born in Warsaw. The three Sternchuss sisters were deported with their 74-year-old grandmother, also born in Warsaw. The Zavidowitcz sisters were deported with their father, who had been born in Brest-Litovsk.

In addition to the old people in their eighties and nineties whose birthpalces are given in the above map, a further 15 old people in their seventies were deported in this particular train: all were likewise gassed on arrival at Auschwitz.

On February 12 the Gestapo reported that three Jews had tried to escape from the train at the French frontier. But each had been caught and forced to continue the journey.

The photograph shows a group of Jewish children from Beregszasz and Bilke arriving at Auschwitz in 1944 *(page 184)*.

Map 192

DISTANT DEPORTATIONS AND THE 'FACTORY ACTION', FEBRUARY 1943

890	2 February
1,184	9 February
1,108	16 February
1,101	23 February

Baltic Sea

also | 952 | 3 February
1,000 | 19 February
913 | 26 February

HOLLAND

Hamburg
1,000

Berlin
7,000

Treblinka

GREATER

FRANCE

Essen
Cologne
1,000

Theresienstadt
1,000
1 February

Frankfurt

GERMANY

Majdanek

Bedzin
Auschwitz

Sobibor

1,000
9 February

998
11 February

1,000
13
February

Munich
1,000

SWITZERLAND
neutral

0   miles   150

0   kilometres   200

© Martin Gilbert 1982

In February 1943 transports reached the eastern death camps from Holland, Berlin, Theresienstadt and Paris *(above)*. Among those deported fom Paris to Auschwitz on February 13 was Gisele Lustiger, who had been born in Bedzin. Her son, Aaron, who had converted to Catholicism before the war, survived the war; in February 1981 he was appointed Archbishop of Paris.

At the beginning of 1943 more than 10,000 Jews were working in factories throughout Germany. On February 27 the SS put into operation the 'Factory Action', deporting these workers to the east *(above)*, where few survived. The photograph, taken in 1980, shows some of the fences and watchtowers at Majdanek.

The destruction of slave labour camps also continued, 1,000 labourers being sent from Chrzanow to Auschwitz *(opposite)*.

In Eastern Galicia the deportations to Belzec had ceased: those Jews still alive were killed in local cemeteries or nearby woods.

At Bialystok eight SS men were killed

Map 193

DEPORTATION, MASS MURDER, AND REVOLT, FEBRUARY 1943

Rakow 1,000
2 February Maly Trostenets **Minsk**
1,500
1 February

Nowogrodek
450
4 February

*bringing the total
number of Jews
murdered in Minsk
since July 1941 to*
86,632
*according to Nazi
calculations*

resistance led by
Eliyahu Boraks
Eight S.S. men killed ☀**Bialystok**
10,000 1,000
deported *killed on
5 February* *the spot
to Treblinka* *5 February
and
Auschwitz*

☀**Treblinka**
guards attacked

River Vistula

River Bug

VOLHYNIA

*hundreds of Jews hiding in the
woods since August 1942
hunted down and shot. Of*
40,000 *in hiding in February
1943 more than* 37,000
*were killed, or died of hunger
during 1943.*

Belzec ⋙

Chrzanow *slave labour camp*
1,000 *18 February*

⋙**Auschwitz**

Boryslaw—
600 men
15 February
600 women
& children
16 February

EASTERN
River **GALICIA**
Chodorow 200
5 February

Stryj
2,000

☀

*Szeparowce
forest*

Buczacz
2,000
1 February
Fedor Hill

Tluste
40
12 February

Dniester

Kolomyja
1,500

0 *miles* 50
0 *kilometres* 80

Stanislawow
10,000
22 February
resistance led by Oskar Friedlender
Anda Luft

© Martin Gilbert 1982

when members of a Zionist youth movement
resisted deportation. Captured and deported,
the remnants of the group then attacked the
guards at Treblinka, using one, possibly two,
remaining pistols. But they were quickly
killed: at Treblinka the 150-strong SS and
Ukrainian garrison had a large armoury of
machine-guns and grenades. They also
wielded their whips and clubs without mercy
against men, women and children staggering
from the trains. Even then, individuals
resisted, as when a young women, stripped
naked, snatched a rifle from a Ukrainian,
shot dead two Nazis and wounded a third,
before being overpowered and viciously
tortured until she was dead.

Map 194

THE JEWS OF MACEDONIA AND THRACE DEPORTED, 3-22 MARCH 1943

SERBIA
under German
military
occupation

YUGOSLAVIA

4 barges

River Danube   RUMANIA

Lom
Palanka
left 20-22
March

Nis

Pirot
185

Pristina
249

Sofia

BULGARIA

Radomir
labour camp

Kriva
Palanka
5

Kumanova
13

Dupnitsa
internment camp
18-19 March
Gorna Dzhumaia
internment camp
18-19 March

Didimoticon
867

Skopje
3,351

Tobacco factory camp
11-31 March

Veles
18

Stip
551

Drama
589

Paranestion
19

Nea
Orestia
194

Xanthi
526

MACEDONIA

EASTERN THRACE

Bitola
3,315

occupied by Bulgaria

Ziliahovo
18

Komotini
878

Souflion
32

Gevgelija
11

Seres
471

THRACE

Kavalla
1,484

Sarzhshaban
12

Dedeagatch
137

Salonica

Thasos
16

Samothrace
3

Aegean

Dardanelles

GREECE

Sea

TURKEY
neutral

© Martin Gilbert 1982

Mount
Athos

O   miles   40
O   kilometres   60

137

After the Bulgarian occupation of the Greek province of Thrace in April 1941, the Germans imposed direct German rule on Eastern Thrace, which lay along the Turkish border *(left)*. In this zone were some 1,250 Jews, most of them in the town of Didimoticon, where the Jewish community could trace its origins back to 1542, to the arrival of refugees from Spain. After 300 years these 'Sephardi' (or Spanish) Jews still spoke a Spanish dialect, Ladino.

On 3 March 1943 the Germans seized the Jews of Eastern Thrace, including the three Jews living on the island of Samothrace. Five days later they were deported by train to Treblinka. Other than 40 who managed to escape the round-up at Nea Orestia, and 33 who evaded deportation from Didimoticon, none of the Jews of Eastern Thrace survived the war.

A day after the round-up in Eastern Thrace, the Jews of Bulgarian-occupied Thrace and Bulgarian-occupied Macedonia were likewise seized, taken to internment camps at Skopje, and inside Bulgaria, and then deported in a total of 20 trains *(right)*, some direct to Treblinka, others to the Danube town of Lom, where they were transferred first by barge through the Iron Gates to Vienna, and then by train.

Within three weeks 23 communities had been destroyed. The Bitola community had been established shortly after the expulsion of the Jews from Spain in 1492.

The photographs were taken on board one of the barges *(left)* and at a deportation centre.

TWENTY BALKAN TRAINS, MARCH 1943

GREATER GERMANY

Baltic Sea

Vilna · Danzig · Bialystok · Treblinka · Poznan · Siedlce · Radom · Breslau · Kielce · Zhitomir · Myslowice · Teschen · Czernowitz · Vienna · River Danube · Jassy · Zagreb

one deportation barge sank
several hundred drowned

Bucharest · Belgrade · Iron Gates · River Danube · Sarajevo · Lom · Nis · Radomir 4 trains · Pirot 2 trains · Sofia · Dupnitsa 3 trains · Skopje 5 trains · Gorna 3 trains · Souflion · Bitola 3 trains · Bari · Athens

Adriatic Sea · Ionian Sea · Aegean Sea

© Martin Gilbert 1982

0 miles 150
0 kilometres 200

Map 195

Map 196

THE SALONICA DEPORTATIONS, FROM 15 MARCH 1943

GREATER GERMANY

Auschwitz

SLOVAKIA

Vienna

Graz
Maribor

Zidani Most

Trieste

Zagreb

miles   0   150

kilometres   0   200

CROATIA

Belgrade

SERBIA

Nis

Sofia

Skopje

BULGARIA

Adriatic Sea

ITALY

ALBANIA

Salonica
43,850

Kastoria
655

Veroia
424
1 May

GREECE

Aegean Sea

© Martin Gilbert 1982

Within two weeks of the deportation of the Jews of Thrace and Macedonia to Treblinka, the Jews of Salonica were being seized, interned, and deported to Auschwitz *(left)*. The photograph shows the preliminary indignities to which they were subjected: compulsory drills until they collapsed.

Jews had lived in Salonica since the time of St Paul. In the twelfth century they had their own mayor. In 1430 their rabbis were placed on the same footing as the spiritual heads of the Greek Church. In the fifteenth and sixteenth centuries, both German and Spanish Jews found in the city a safe haven from persecution. In the nineteenth century the Jews of Salonica were active as artisans, traders, shopkeepers and dock workers. Between the wars many emigrated to Palestine, France and the United States. Others stayed as part of a flourishing community: doctors, lawyers, teachers, and above all stevedores and dock workers.

The first deportation of Salonica Jewry began on 15 March 1943, when 2,800 Jews were forced into 40 cattle trucks and told that they were to be 'resettled' in Poland. Five months later, on 7 August 1943, the last train left Salonica for Auschwitz, where more than 43,000 of Salonica's 56,000 Jews had been killed *(pages 141, 144 and 147 to 149)*.

The insanity of the German policy towards the Jews was clearly shown in Salonica, where the Jewish dock workers and port labourers were essential to the efficient operation of the port. But even this practical consideration was of no interest to the Nazis: nothing was to be allowed to stand in the way of the destruction of every one of Europe's Jewish communities.

Map 197

THE SAVING OF THE JEWS OF BULGARIA, 17 MARCH 1943

North-east of Salonica, the Jews of Bulgaria (above) were likewise marked out by the Nazis for deportation. In 1934 there were 48,398 Jews in Bulgaria, out of a total Bulgarian population of six million. On 22 January 1941 a 'Law for the Defence of the Nation' gave Jews one month to leave all public posts, and forced almost all Jewish doctors, dentists and lawyers to give up their practices. In addition, a special tax was imposed on all Jewish homes, shops and other property, amounting to a quarter of its value. By the end of 1941, there were some 400 Bulgarian Jews serving in local Bulgarian partisan units.

On 10 March 1943 the SS demanded the deportation of all Bulgarian Jews to Poland, on the same pattern as the deportation from Thrace, Macedonia and Salonica. The Bulgarian Government had already bowed to the demand that 12,000 Jews under Bulgarian occupation in Thrace and Macedonia should be deported. But the demand for the deportation of the 49,000 Jews of Bulgaria proper was resisted by the

Bulgarian people: by the King, the Parliament, the intellectuals, and the farmers. The farmers, indeed, were said to be ready to lie down on the railway tracks to prevent any such deportations, and on 17 March 1943 the Bulgarian Parliament voted unanimously against the deportation order.

Not only the King, but the Archimandrite Cyril, and the Papal Nuncio in Turkey, Angelo Roncalli (later Pope John XXIII) protested strongly against the proposed deportations.

As a result of these protests, no Bulgarian Jews were deported to the gas chambers from Bulgaria itself. A few, who were living in Paris at the time of the outbreak of war, has already been deported to Auschwitz (page 108). Others were sent to labour camps at Samovit and Radomir. But these were not punitive camps, as in Germany.

Bulgaria was the only country under German influence or control whose Jewish population actually increased during the war years, from 48,565 in 1934, to 49,172 in 1945.

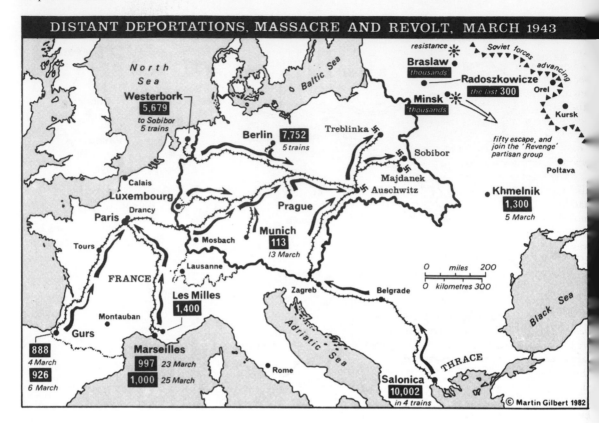

DISTANT DEPORTATIONS, MASSACRE AND REVOLT, MARCH 1943

North Sea

Baltic Sea

Westerbork
5,679
to Sobibor
5 trains

Berlin **7,752**
5 trains

Treblinka

Sobibor

resistance

Braslaw
thousands

Soviet forces advancing

Radoszkowicze
the last 300

Orel

Minsk
thousands

Kursk

fifty escape, and join the 'Revenge' partisan group

Poltava

Calais

Luxembourg

Drancy

Paris

Tours

FRANCE

Mosbach

Prague

Majdanek
Auschwitz

Khmelnik
1,300
5 March

Munich
113
13 March

Lausanne

Les Milles
1,400

Montauban

Gurs

888
4 March
926
6 March

Marseilles
997 *23 March*
1,000 *25 March*

Zagreb

Belgrade

Adriatic Sea

Rome

Salonica
10,002
in 4 trains

THRACE

Black Sea

0   miles   200
0   kilometres   300

© Martin Gilbert 1982

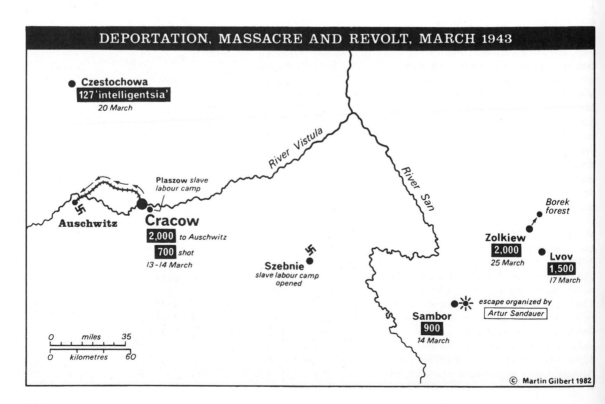

DEPORTATION, MASSACRE AND REVOLT, MARCH 1943

● **Czestochowa**
127 '**intelligentsia**'
20 March

River Vistula

River San

Plaszow *slave labour camp*

Auschwitz

Cracow
2,000 *to Auschwitz*
700 *shot*
13–14 March

Szebnie
slave labour camp opened

Borek forest

Zolkiew
2,000
25 March

Lvov
1,500
17 March

escape organized by
Artur Sandauer

Sambor
900
14 March

0   miles   35
0   kilometres   60

© Martin Gilbert 1982

Map 200

During March 1943 five trains left Holland for Sobibor, one train left Paris for Auschwitz and two trains left Paris for Majdanek *(opposite, above)*. Among the deportees to Majdanek was the German Jewish painter, Hermann Lismann, who had studied in Lausanne, Rome and Paris. A post-impressionist, he had emigrated to France in 1933. At first he had lived near Tours. Then he escaped to Montauban, from where he was deported.

From Gurs were deported to their deaths all but two of the 51 Jews of Mosbach, who had been deported from Germany to Gurs more than two years before *(page 35)*.

Also deported to Majdanek from Paris in March 1943 were Nathan Lewinsztejn, aged 29, and Lajwa Krysztal, aged 40, who had both been born in Lublin, in a suburb of which the Majdanek concentration camp and gas chamber was situated.

From the General Government *(opposite, below)*, 10,000 Jews were seized, deported from Cracow to Auschwitz, sent to the slave labour camp in the suburb of Plaszow, or shot in the streets. At Sambor 900 Jews were shot in the town's main square, many mothers being forced to watch their children being shot first. Resistance plans, carefully nurtured, were cut short by the 'liquidation'. At Braslaw *(opposite, above)* the resistance fighters fell at their posts. During the slaughter at Minsk, while thousands were shot, only 50 were able to break out of the armed cordons and reach the partisans.

Among those deported from France in March 1943 were 4,000 Jews from the Marseilles region *(right)*, most of whom had been seized two months earlier during 'action Tiger'. Sent to Drancy, they were deported on 23 March 1943 to Sobibor. All the deportees, were gassed on arrival. A second train left Drancy for Sobibor two days later, with 1,000 Jews. All but 15 were gassed. Only five survived the war.

Among the Jews in these two trains were Vidal Farhi and Lea Klauser, both of whom had been born in Jerusalem, Dick and Jacob Prins from the Dutch East Indies *(page 114)* and the 18-year-old twins, Jean and Victor Nerver, who had been born in Calais.

At Les Accates, in the Marseilles region, 16 Jewish children were sheltered, and saved. But the 30 orphans from La Rose, photographed by the author in 1976, were deported to Auschwitz, together with their guardian, Alice Salomon, who insisted on sharing their fate.

THE JEWS OF MARSEILLES AND AIX

Aix-en-Provence
55 Jewish properties confiscated

les Milles
detention camp
1,400 deported

Meyreuil
labour camp
20

Calas
Jewish families emigrate

Bouc-Bel-Air
Jews deported

Gardanne
Jewish families emigrate

Cabriès
Jewish property confiscated

Biver coal mines labour camp

Plan-de-Cuques
Jewish property confiscated

Allauch
Jewish property confiscated

Port

La Rose
30 *orphans* deported

Vieux Port

les Accates
16 Jewish and 27 Spanish children sheltered

les Camoins
a Jew deported

Mediterranean Sea

Marseilles
4,000 deported

miles 0 — 4
kilometres 0 — 6

© Martin Gilbert 1982

Map 201

DEPORTATION, MASSACRE AND REVOLT, APRIL 1943

Wlodawa
2,000
30 April

On arrival at the unloading ramp, Jews in the transport from Wlodawa attacked the S.S. All the Jews were killed by S.S. machine-gun fire and grenades

Sobibor

0   miles   5
0   kilometres   8

Leczna
slave labour camp
the last
300
slave labourers
killed
29 April

Izbica
300
28 April

REICHSKOMMISSARIAT
UKRAINE

GREATER

VOLHYNIA

River Bug

Belzec

GERMANY

Leszniow
100

Jaworow
3,489
18 April

Zloczow
5,000
5 April

Przemysl
revolt

Rudki
1,700
9 April

EASTERN
GALICIA

Komarno
500
9 April

resistance led by
Michael Glanz

Sambor
1,000
14 April

Brzezany
2,000
12 April

Kozowa
1,000
9,17 April

Skalat
750   7 April

© Martin Gilbert 1982

The killings in Eastern Galicia continued during April 1943 *(above)*, as did the distant deportations to Auschwitz and Treblinka *(opposite, above)*: nine from Salonica, four from Holland, one from Belgium and one from France.

The 300 Jews of Soly and Smorgonie *(opposite, above)* were brought by train to Vilna, having been told that they were to be resettled in the Kovno ghetto. But instead of going to Kovno, the train stopped at nearby Ponary. A 15-year-old Vilna schoolboy, Yitskhok Rudashevski, noted in his diary the story that reached Vilna within a few hours: 'Like wild animals before dying, the people began in mortal despair to break the railroad cars, they broke the little windows reinforced by strong wire. Hundreds were shot to death while running away. The railroad line over a great distance is covered with corpses.'

All who survived the rail-side massacre of April 5 were shot in the pits at Ponary by the German and Lithuanian SS men. A few hours later 4,000 Jews reached Ponary station from Swieciany, where the ghetto had been virtually unmolested since the Polygon slaughter of September 1941 *(page 64)*. They too resisted, with revolvers, knives and fists. A few dozen managed to escape to Vilna. The rest were shot down on the spot.

From Jaworow *(opposite, below)*, the Jews already expelled from six nearby village communities, and held in the town, were murdered on 18 April 1943, the Jews of Jaworow itself having already been killed at Belzec the previous November *(page 123)*.

From Jaworow, most of those who reached the forests fell in battle against the Germans. There was also resistance in Skalat and Przemysl *(above)*, in Belgium *(opposite, above)* and, on a massive scale, in Warsaw *(page 145)*.

DISTANT DEPORTATION, MASSACRE AND REVOLT, APRIL 1943

HOLLAND

2,020	6 April
1,204	13 April
1,166	20 April
1,204	27 April

Berlin
938
19 April

Brussels
1,400
19 April

Westerbork

derailment

Paris

Drancy

Warsaw
ghetto revolt
19 April

Treblinka

Sobibor

Auschwitz

Kovno
5,000

Widze
1,800

Moscow

Soly

Vilna
Ponary

Smorgonie

Oszmiana
2,500

Swieciany
4,000

Soviet forces advancing April 1943

EASTERN GALICIA

Siedlce
slave labour camp liquidated
14 April

Trembowla
800
7 April

Borszczow
800 19 April

Kopyczynce
600
15 April

Buczacz
2,000
13 April

Avignon
20
17 April

Black Sea

24,921
in 9 trains
Salonica

| 0 | miles | 300 |
| 0 | kilometres | 400 |

Baltic Sea

© Martin Gilbert 1982

SIX COMMUNITIES DESTROYED, 18 APRIL 1943

Lubaczewski forest

EASTERN GALICIA

Wielkie Oczy
547.

Skolin
7

Krakowiec
529

Jaworow
3,489 *shot*

acts of resistance led by Artur Henner *and* Henry Gleich

Szklo
53

River San

Lvov

Przemysl

Mosciska
2,328

Sadowa Wisznia
25

| 0 | miles | 10 |
| 0 | kilometres | 75 |

© Martin Gilbert 1982

Map 204

THE WARSAW GHETTO REVOLT, 19 APRIL 1943

Marymont

Zoliborz

Powazki

Targowek

Praga

ghetto

city centre

Grochow

Kolo
Wola

Ujazdowski

W a r s a w

Mokotow

municipal boundary

© Martin Gilbert 1982

On 18 January 1943 the Jewish underground in Warsaw had resisted a new wave of deportations. In four days 6,000 Jews had been deported and 1,000 murdered in the streets *(page 129)*. But so fierce was the Jewish resistance and street fighting that the deportations had been suspended.

The Jewish underground, led by Mordecai Anielewicz, prepared to resist any further attempt to renew the deportations.

On 19 April 1943 a German military force, equipped with tanks and artillery, entered he ghetto in order to resume the death camp deportations. The Jewish units fought back, and the Germans were driven out of the ghetto altogether.

Within a few hours the Germans returned no longer seeking open conflict with Jewish armed units, but systematically burning down houses in the ghetto street by street, while at the same time killing or driving out with smoke and hand grenades those who were hiding in bunkers or sewers.

On 8 May 1943 the German forces reached the Jewish underground headquarters. In the ensuing battle Anielewicz, and more than 100 of his fighters were killed. A week later the German commander, General Stroop, reported to his superiors: 'The Warsaw ghetto is no more.'

During the fighting more than 56,000 Jews had been burned alive, shot as they emerged from the burning buildings, or rounded up and deported to Treblinka.

The map shows the municipal boundary of Warsaw, the original extent of the ghetto, and, in solid black, the three much smaller areas to which the ghetto had been reduced following the massive deportations between July and September 1942. The photograph on the left, taken in 1980, shows two of the very few buildings in the ghetto area which survived the otherwise total destruction.

The photographs on the right are both taken from the special album prepared by General Stroop to celebrate his 'victory'. The upper photograph shows a Jewish fighter being brought out of a bunker. The lower photograph shows German officers and soldiers, and (left), two captured Jewish fighters, a man (sitting) and a woman (standing).

As many as 15,000 Jews escaped to the 'Aryan' part of Warsaw. Some were later caught or betrayed. But most, sheltered by the Poles, survived the war, and many were to fight in the Warsaw uprising in August 1944 *(pages 193–4)*.

145

Map 205

SEVEN DEPORTATIONS, MASSACRE AND RESISTANCE, 4-25 MAY 1943

HOLLAND
1,187	4 May
1,446	11 May
2,511	18 May
2,862	25 May

Baltic Sea

Nowogrodek
the last 370
7 May

Bryuchovo ● 40

The Red Army advances, May 194.

Germans capture headquarters bunker of Ghetto revolt
The commander of the revolt
Mordechai Anielewicz
killed 8 May

Warsaw 56,000

Berlin
at least 395 *17 May*

Sobibor

Brody 2,500 *1 May*
Jewish resistance against German army and Ukrainian police, 17 May

Auschwitz

GALICIA

Skalat 660
9 May

Sokal 2,500
27 May

Busk 1,000
21 May

Tluste 3,000
27 May

Stryj 1,000
22 May

CROATIA

miles 0 — 250
kilometres 0 — 400

Zagreb
at least 1,000 *7 May*
at least 1,000 *13 May*

from Salonica
10,930
in four trains

Black Sea

© Martin Gilbert 1982

At the very moment when the Warsaw ghetto uprising was being crushed, and 56,000 Warsaw Jews were being burned to death, shot, or deported, the deportations continued from outside Greater Germany: four from Holland and two from Croatia.

In the Eastern Galician town of Brody, as well as in Warsaw, Jewish resistance had led to German deaths: but with Soviet forces still more than 300 miles to the east, the Germans were able to devote considerable strength and efforts during May and June 1943 to wiping out the remaining Jewish communities of Eastern Galicia, as seen above and in the map opposite (below).

The photograph is of a mother and her three children at the moment of deportation. Most of those marked out to die in Galicia were now taken, not to one of the death camps, but to local forests or gravel pits, or, as at Tluste, to the Jewish cemetery. Here, the executions were carried out with savagery and sadism, a crying child often being seized from its mother's arms and shot in front of her, or having its head crushed by a single blow from a rifle butt. Hundreds of children were thrown alive into pits, and died in fear and agony under the weight of bodies thrown on top of them.

Throughout June the Dutch and French deportations continued (opposite, above).

NINE EASTWARD DEPORTATIONS, JUNE 1943

HOLLAND
- 3,006 *1 June*
- 1,266 *children* 5 June
- 3,017 *8 June*
- 2,397 *8 June*

Baltic Sea

Bialystok

Berlin

Brest-Litovsk

Sobibor

Bamberg 16 *18 June*

Breslau

Belzec

Auschwitz

GALICIA

434,329
Jews deported to Belzec between June 1942 and June 1943, or killed in their towns, according to an S S report

Orancy

Würzburg 57 *17 June*

Nuremberg 70 *18 June*

Paris 1,002 *23 June*

SWITZ. *neutral*

sterilization rate reported to Berlin on 7 June as 1,000 women a day

from Salonica 880 *8 June*

0 miles 200
0 kilometres 300

© Martin Gilbert 1982

Soviet forces June 1943

Black Sea

DEPORTATION, MASSACRE AND REVOLT, JUNE 1943

0 miles 40
0 kilometres 60

Warsaw
the last resistance crushed

Minsk Mazowiecki
Rudzi factory all 150 *shot 5 June*

Wlodawa
1,000

Sobibor

B = **Brzezany** 100 *12 June*

K = **Kozowa** 400 *4 June*

T = **Trembowla** 900 *3 June*

Borszczow 700 *5 June*

Skala Podolska 800 *9 June*

SILESIA

Czestochowa
armed resistance 25 June
1,000 *deported*

Dabrowa Gornicza
2,000 *26 June*

Sosnowiec
resistance led by Zevi Dunski

Auschwitz

Belzec
the corpse-burning squad deported to Sobibor, revolted on arrival, and shot 8 June

GALICIA

Rawa Ruska 100 *shot 8 June*

Lvov 13,000 *21 - 27 June*
armed resistance 25 June

Tarnopol 4,000 *20 June*

T

Podhajce 300 *6 June*

Moravska Ostrava
all residents of the Jewish old peoples home deported 23 June

Drohobycz
all Jewish workers in the municipal factories murdered 21 June

Rohatyn 1,000 *6 June*

B K

Buczacz
ghetto liquidated escape and resistance

Tluste 1,000 *6 June*

© Martin Gilbert 1982

On June 5 a total of 1,266 children under the age of 16 were deported from Holland to Sobibor. All were gassed on arrival. Among 1,000 Jews deported from Paris to Auschwitz on June 23, more than 100 were likewise under 16 years. There were also 13 babies and many mothers with young children, all of whom were murdered on arrival, including the eight-months-old

Henry Kaminka deported with his mother Salomée, born in Bialystok, and his father Vital, born in Brest-Litovsk.

In Galicia and Silesia as the killings continued, so too did the resistance *(above)*. But with arms almost impossible to obtain, and the local population often unwilling to give shelter, both defence and escape were equally hopeless. But both continued.

Map 208

DEPORTATION, MASSACRE AND REVOLT, JULY 1943

As the Red Army began its advance westward in the summer of 1943, the Nazis murdered several thousand Jews who had not been deported to the death camps earlier, but who had been kept alive in order to serve as slave labourers in factories and labour camps. At the same time, the deportations to Auschwitz continued from the furthest extremities of German rule *(above)*, including two from Paris, one from Belgium, three from Holland, and the remaining Jews in Salonica *(page 139)*.

Six eastern ghettos had escaped 'liquidation' by the Nazis during 1942:

Vilna, Kovno, Shauliai (known to the Jews as Shavli), Riga, Minsk and Lida.

In Vilna *(above and opposite)*, where 20,000 Jews lived in the ghetto, a group of 21 young men and women who had been active in the Jewish underground movement decided to try to make contact with the Soviet partisans who were now increasingly active behind the German front line.

The escape of the 21 was successful, but they were ambushed by German soldiers at the Mickun bridge, and nine were killed in the ensuing fighting.

Three days after the ambush at the bridge,

Map 209

ESCAPE, AMBUSH AND RESISTANCE, 24 JULY 1943

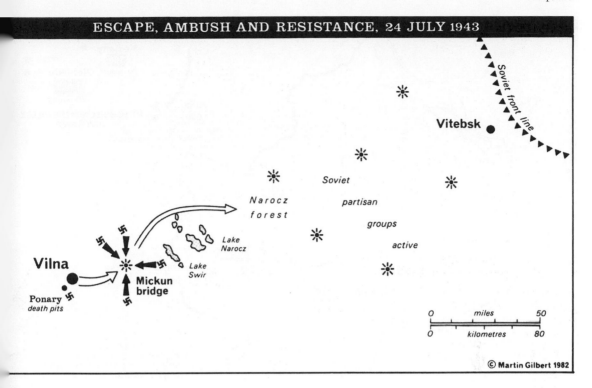

32 relatives of the nine Jews who had been killed were seized by the Gestapo in Vilna, taken to Ponary, and executed.

Those who survived the ambush continued eastwards to the Narocz forest where they joined the Soviet partisans, and were active in disrupting German military supplies and communications with the front line.

In Vilna itself, the execution of the 32 relatives proved a tragedy for all those who remained in the ghetto. To prevent any further such escapes, the head of the Gestapo in the city, Bruno Kittel, at once made it known that in future the whole family of anyone who escaped to the forest would be killed as a reprisal, while if the man who got away had no family then those who shared his room, or even lived in the same tenement building, would likewise be executed. The Gestapo also decreed that if, from any of the labour gangs of 10 Jews sent out of the ghetto, even a single man failed to return, the remaining nine would be shot. Escapes to the forest ceased. But inside the ghetto the Jewish resistance groups continued to make plans, and to collect arms.

In 1940 the SS had set up a concentration camp at Natzweiler, in Alsace, with 20 satellite labour camps. Between the first executions on 18 September 1942 and the liberation of Natzweiler on 31 August 1944, at least 25,000 prisoners, Jews and non-Jews, died there of starvation and ill-treatment, or were murdered.

Many Jewish and non-Jewish women, active in the French resistance, were executed in Natzweiler, as well as many Russian and Polish prisoners. The meticulous camp records show, for example, eight civilians from Luxembourg shot in the camp on 19 May 1944.

On 6 November 1942 Heinrich Himmler had given his support to a plan to establish a collection of Jewish skulls and skeletons at the Reich Anatomical Institute in Strasbourg, near Natzweiler. On 21 June 1943, 73 Jews and 30 Jewesses were selected in Auschwitz, and sent to Natzweiler, where they were measured, weighed and gassed, and their corpses sent on to the Anatomical Institute in Strasbourg. On 15 October 1944, as Allied forces approached Strasbourg, Himmler ordered the skeleton collection to be destroyed. But all the documents relating to it survived the war.

At Auschwitz itself, medical experiments *(page 94)* continued, and led to the deaths of hundreds of people, especially women. Many hundreds were maimed for life by sterilization and other experiments. Others were deliberately murdered so that the SS doctors could study their bone structure.

Map 210

DEPORTATION, MASSACRE AND REVOLT, AUGUST 1943

Baltic Sea

Koziany
100
20 August

revolt ✷ ●

Glebokie
3,000
20 August

Vilna
1,000
*deported to Estonia
dozens who resisted deportation
killed, 6 August*

✷

**REICHSKOMMISSARIAT
OSTLAND**

Stutthof

revolt led by
Mordecai Tenenbaum
and Daniel Moszkowicz

*slave labour camp revolt
led by*
Rabbi Joshua Aaronson

Bialystok
40.000
✷
*revolt
16·23 August*

Konin

River Vistula

Treblinka
✷
*revolt
2 August*

among the leaders,
Dr. Julian Chorarzycki
*a physician who worked in the camp
hospital, and was killed before the revolt*
Engineer Alfred Galewski *and*
Zelo Bloch

from Holland
1.001 26 August
1.004 21 August

River Bug

Sobibor

Krychow
✷ *slave labour camp
revolt
16 August*

*members of the corpse-burning
squad dig a tunnel to escape.
Their tunnel came out in the
camp minefield.* All **150**
*members of the squad were
executed.*

Sosnowiec
15,000

Bedzin
many thousands

Dabrowa Gornicza
thousands
3 August

River Vistula

Auschwitz

revolt ✷ ●

Sasow
slave labour camp
liquidated

Borszczow
360 *shot*
14 August

Lackie Wielkie
armed resistance ✷ *slave labour camp*
liquidated

armed resistance ✷ **Jaktorow**
slave labour camp
liquidated

SLOVAKIA

0   miles   60
0   kilometres   80

© Martin Gilbert 1982

In August 1943 more than 2,000 Jews were deported from Holland to Auschwitz *(above)*, while several slave labour camps in the General Government were 'liquidated', and their inmates murdered.

The deportation of 40,000 Jews from the Bialystok ghetto to Treblinka led to two major revolts: inside Bialystok itself, when the Germans used artillery and tanks to crush the rebellion, and at Treblinka *(above)*,

JEWISH PARTISAN ACTIVITY IN THE BIALYSTOK REGION, 1943

to the Leningrad front

to Konigsberg and the Baltic

GREATER
EAST
PRUSSIA

Augustow

Marcinkance

Porzecze

Druskieniki

Sopockinie

Ostryna

Bogusze
slave labour
camp

Rajgrod

Grajewo

Dabrowa

Grodno

Jeziory

Skidel

Szczuczyn

Suchowola

River

Wasosz

Goniadz

Sidra

Kielbasin
slave labour
camp

Lunna

Niemen

Stawiski

Radzilow

Janow

Kuznica

GREATER

Trzcianne

Korycin

Sokola

Indura

Jedwabne

Knyszyn

Suprasl

Krynki

Nowogrod

Wasilkow

BIALYSTOK

to the
Moscow
front

Lomza

Bialystok

Grodzisk

GERMANY

Zawady

Choroszcz

Michalowo

REGION

Wolkowysk

Rutki

Sniadowo

Sokoly

Lapy

Zabludow

Zambrow

Wysokie

Narew

Lubotyn

Czyzew

Bielsk

Malkinia
Junction

Klukowo

Bransk

Orla

Bocki

Treblinka

Ciechanowiec

Kleszczele

Pruzana

to Germany

GENERAL
GOVERNMENT

Milejczyce

Siemiatycze

River Bug

Drohiczyn

0   miles   20
0   kilometres   30

© Martin Gilbert 1982

where several hundred prisoners battled with guards, and tried to break out across the minefields. But at Treblinka, as elsewhere, all acts of resistance were brutally suppressed. After the Bialystok revolt more than 1,000 Jewish children were seized in the city and deported, first to Theresienstadt, and then to Auschwitz *(right)*, while at Glebokie 3,000 Jews who tried to resist being taken out to the nearby woods were massacred in a single day. But those Jews who did manage to escape built up small but active networks of partisan activity. Throughout the Bialystok region *(above)* Jews who had managed to escape from the deportations of 2 November 1942 *(page 120)* did whatever they could to disrupt German rail communication with the Leningrad and Moscow fronts: the arrows show the main partisan attacks.

THE KILLING OF 1,260 CHILDREN OF BIALYSTOK

0   miles   100
0   kilometres   150

Bialystok

1,260
children deported
23 August 1943

Warsaw

Theresienstadt

Czestochowa

Auschwitz

1,260
arrived and gassed
7 October 1943

arrived 24 August 1943
deported 6 October 1943

© Martin Gilbert 1982

152

Map 213

S k a g e r r a k

SWEDEN
neutral

K a t t e g a t

Aalborg

Nibe

Viborg

Randers

Aarhus

Hälsingborg

DENMARK

Helsingor

Horsens

Hillerod

Copenhagen

Fredericia

Roskilde

Middlefart

Ringsted

Malmö

T h e   B a e l t s

Odense

Slagelse

Haderslav

Nyborg

Nestved

Assens

Svenborg

escape of

5,919	Jews
1,301	half-Jews
686	Christians married to Jews

Nakskov

Baltic   Sea

Kiel

Stralsund

GERMANY

| 0 | *miles* | 40 |
| 0 | *kilometres* | 60 |

Lübeck

Hamburg

© Martin Gilbert 1982

Map 214

Following the German occupation of Denmark in the spring of 1940, the Germans had embarked on a policy of cooperation and negotiation with the Danish authorities, as embodied in the Danish-German Agreement of 9 April 1940. As a result, the Jews had been left unmolested. But on 28 August 1943, as Danish resistance to the German occupation undermined any chance of continued cooperation, the Germans abolished the Agreement, and declared martial law.

The SS hoped to use this opportunity to deport all Denmark's 7,200 Jews, most of whom lived in Copenhagen, a few hundred in each of the towns and villages shown opposite. Forewarned, however, of the planned deportation, Danes and Jews plotted to ensure that, on the eve of the deportation, Danish sea captains and fishermen ferried 5,919 Jews, 1,301 part Jews (designated Jews by the Nazis), and 686 Christians married to Jews, to safety in Sweden, a country where, between 1933 and 1943, more than three thousand European Jews, including many from Germany itself, had already found refuge (right).

On 1 October 1943 the Germans found only 500 Jews still in Denmark. All were sent to Theresienstadt; 423 survived the war.

The photograph is of Danish Jews waiting in a cellar for the moment of rescue.

SWEDEN AND THE JEWS, 1939-1945

A SLAVE LABOUR CAMP ESTABLISHED, 30 SEPTEMBER 1943

© Martin Gilbert 1982

SLAVE LABOUR CAMPS, 1943-1944

Alderney
deaths include:
Chayim Goldin
7.12.1943
Robert Perlestein
22.12.1943
Seib Becker
30.12.1943
Lucien Worms
7.1.1944
Isaac Stekovsky
8.2.1944
Wilfred Gordeson
26.2.1944
Henry Lippman
2.3.1944
Szmul Kirschenblatt
26.4.1944

© Martin Gilbert 1982

As Soviet forces advanced westwards more and more Jews were taken to slave labour camps in White Russia and Greater Germany. With the disbanding of a Krupp armaments works at Mariupol (above), it was relocated at Funfteichen in Silesia. Jews who had just been deported from Sosnowiec to Auschwitz were sent by train to work at Funfteichen, where many died.

In all labour camps, deaths from brutality were a daily occurrence. The map on the left names eight of the 100 Jews who died on Alderney, a British island captured by the Germans in 1940.

One use of slave labour was to obliterate all trace of earlier mass murders. At Himmler's instigation, a series of special units, known collectively as 'Unit 1005', were being forced to dig up the corpses of those slain, to burn them, and to scatter the ashes. This work took nearly two years and involved exhuming more than two million corpses (opposite, above).

One such unit was at work at Babi Yar (opposite). Others, working at different times at the murder sites shown above, were

Map 217

© Martin Gilbert 1982

themselves murdered once their work was done. The SS wanted no trace to survive either of their crimes, or of the slave labourers who were being forced to hide them. Nevertheless, a few did manage to escape. The Janowska unit, which had begun its grim work in July 1943, revolted four months later *(page 161)*. Even from Borki, where there was an equal number of armed guards as of prisoners, three prisoners survived an attempted break-out.

At Plaszow, in January 1945, a 'unit 1005' was forced to exhume 9,000 bodies from 11 mass graves. At Ponary more than 58,000 bodies were exhumed and cremated between September 1943 and April 1944. The Ponary unit, made up of 70 Jews and 10 Soviet prisoners-of-war who were suspected of being Jewish, was chained while working, and kept at night in a deep pit, access to which was by a wooden ladder which was withdrawn each evening. After digging an escape tunnel for three months with hands and spoons, 40 escaped on the night of 15 April 1944 *(page 168)*. Twenty-five were caught and killed; 15 eluded their pursuers.

The photograph is of a group of prisoners at the slave labour camp at Plaszow.

Map 218

THE JEWS OF THE SOUTHERN DALMATIAN COAST

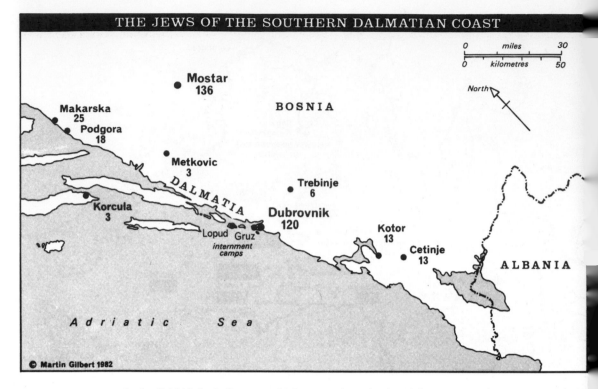

© Martin Gilbert 1982

In April 1941 the Italian army had occupied Dalmatia, whose small Jewish communities *(above)* dated back to the fourteenth century. The numbers shown are according to the Yugoslav census of 31 March 1931. In November 1942, following German pressure, the Jews of Dalmatia were interned at Gruz and Lopud. In June 1943 they were transferred to the island of Rab *(opposite, above)*. With Italy's withdrawal from the war in September 1943, many escaped, and joined the Yugoslav partisans. But the old, the sick, and women with children, were deported to Zemun, and killed.

From France, Belgium, Holland and the north of Italy, newly occupied by Germany, *(opposite, above)* more than 5,000 Jews were deported to Auschwitz, as were Jews from Theresienstadt, Moravia and Galicia. Before the deportation from Tarnow to Auschwitz *(opposite, below)*, hundreds of Jews were murdered in the streets, then 5,000 forced into a single train, with an average of 160 in each sealed truck. The train stopped at Bochnia, where more trucks were added, containing a further 3,000 Jews. When it reached Auschwitz, only 400 of the deportees were still alive. The 'survivors' were sent to the gas chambers.

In the east *(opposite, above)*, with the deportation of more than 7,000 Vilna Jews to

the slave labour camps of Estonia at the end of August and in early September, several hundred Jews managed to escape from Vilna to the forests, and to join the partisans.

Meanwhile, as the Soviet army advanced steadily westward, and the Allied armies were on European soil south of Rome, 2,000 Jews were deported from Minsk to Sobibor.

At Miedzyrzec, and at Sobibor itself, virtually unarmed Jews challenged German troops and SS. At Treblinka, on 2 September 1943, a group of 13 Jewish slave labourers killed their Ukrainian SS guard with a crowbar while working just outside the camp wire. The leader, an 18-year-old Polish Jew, Seweryn Klajnman, put on the dead guard's uniform, took his rifle, and 'marched off' his fellow prisoners as if to a new work detail further off, cursing and bellowing at them as they went, as befitted an SS guard. Guided by one of their number, a carter, who knew the area well, they escaped their pursuers and evaded capture.

Near Kiev, on 30 September 1943, a work unit of 325 Jewish and Soviet prisoners who were being forced, in chains, to dig up and burn victims of the Babi Yar massacre *(page 63)* resisted when they too were about to be killed. The SS overseers opened fire with machine-guns and grenades. Only 14 of the prisoners survived the revolt.

DISTANT DEPORTATIONS, ESCAPE AND REVOLT, SEPTEMBER 1943

NORWAY

SWEDEN
neutral

Leningrad

Klooga

ESTONIA

7,906
escape

Riga

Moscow

Dvinsk

North Sea

HOLLAND

987 7 September

1,005 14 September

979 21 September

DENMARK

7,130
deported

hundreds escape

Vilna

Minsk

2,000
18 September

Soviet front line

Baltic Sea

GREATER   GERMANY

Treblinka

13 escape

Sobibor

Jews attack the
S.S. with stones
and bottles.
All attackers
killed.

Kiev

revolt of
Jewish & Soviet
prisoners of war
29 September

311 killed

14 escape

BELGIUM

631 both
on
794 20
September

Auschwitz

MORAVIA

GALICIA

Paris

1,000
2 September

Miedzyrzec
Jewish youths attack
Germans. 2 Germans
killed. 5 Jews shot
10 September

Vilna
escape organized by

Izik Wittenberg

Joseph Glazman

Abba Kovner

Merano

24
16-18 September

0   miles   200

0   kilometres 300

ITALY

RAB

Adriatic Sea

Zemun

Black Sea

Split 500

Dubrovnik

Rome

under
Allied
control

© Martin Gilbert 1982

FIVE DEPORTATIONS TO AUSCHWITZ, 2-8 SEPTEMBER 1943

Theresienstadt
5,007
8 September

Tarnow
5,000
2 September

Auschwitz

0   miles   80

0 kilometres 100

resistance

MORAVIA

Moravska
Ostrava
3,442
8 September

WESTERN

Przemysl
3,500
2 September

Bochnia
3,000 3 September

GALICIA

© Martin Gilbert 1982

Map 221

THE JEWS OF ITALY DEPORTED, 9 OCTOBER – 21 NOVEMBER 1943

G R E A T E R

G E R M A N Y

Auschwitz

Moravska Ostrava

SLOVAKIA

Vienna

SWITZERLAND
neutral

HUNGARY

Merano

Bolzano

Villach

Milan
9 November

Trieste
9 October

Vercelli

Verona Padua

La Risiera di San Sabba

Turin

Asti
Alessandria

Mantua

Venice
9 November

3,000 *Italian prisoners-of-war
murdered by the S.S.
and Ukrainian guards,*

620 *of Trieste's* **1,920** *Jews
also murdered*

DALMATIA

Parma

Fossoli

Ferrara
14 September

Modena

Bologna

Genoa
3 November

La Spezia

85

San Remo

Pisa
Livorno

Florence
9 November

*A
d
r
i
a
t
i
c

S
e
a*

Borgo San Dalmazzo

325
21 November

Sienna

**NORTHERN
ITALY**
*occupied by
Germany
16 September
1943*

Termoli

Rome
1,015
18 October

Foggia

under
Allied

*The front line on 15 November
The front line on 12 October*

Naples

control

Salerno

T y r r h e n i a n

S e a

Ferramonte
di Tarsia

0 *miles* 80

0 *kilometres* 120

© Martin Gilbert 1982

Map 222

DEPORTATIONS, MASSACRE AND REVOLT, OCTOBER 1943

© Martin Gilbert 1982

On 16 September 1943 more than 37,000 Italian Jews had come under Nazi rule. Some escaped to Switzerland. Several thousand found refuge in Catholic homes. On 16 October 1943, 1,000 Jews were seized in Rome and deported to Auschwitz. Within a month 8,360 Italian Jews, mostly from the towns shown opposite, had been deported to Auschwitz, where 7,749 were murdered.

The deportations from Holland and France to Auschwitz continued. From Kovno 3,000 Jews were sent to the Klooga slave labour camp in Estonia *(above)*.

In September *(page 158)* 2,000 Jews and Soviet prisoners-of-war had been deported from Minsk to Sobibor: 80 had been selected

to work as carpenters and joiners. The rest had been gassed. One of the 80, Alexander Pechersky, a Soviet officer and also a Jew, together with other prisoners, planned a break-out. On October 14 the revolt took place: 11 or 12 SS men, and more than a dozen Ukrainian SS guards, were killed. Of the 600 Jews then in the labour camp, 200 were shot while escaping, or were blown up in the camp minefields; 400 escaped, of whom 100 were subsequently captured and killed; others joined Soviet partisan units, and were mostly killed fighting; others died of typhus, or were killed by hostile Polish gangs. Only 64 survived the war, including Pechersky.

Map 223

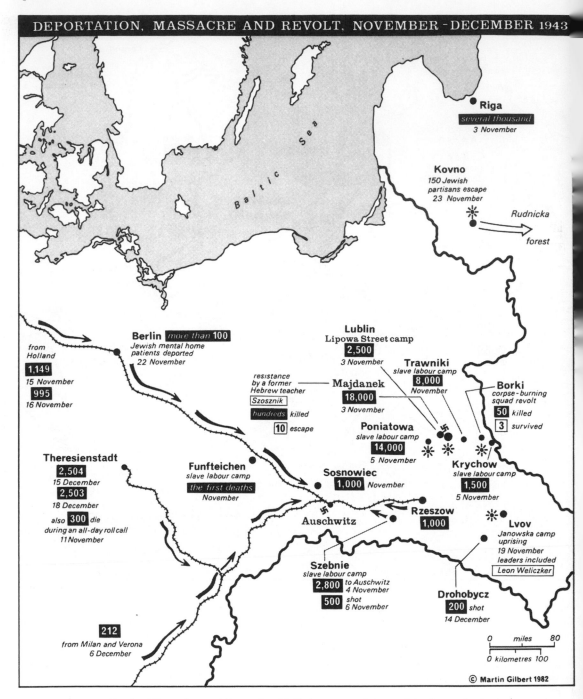

DEPORTATION, MASSACRE AND REVOLT, NOVEMBER – DECEMBER 1943

Riga
several thousand
3 November

Kovno
150 Jewish
partisans escape
23 November

Rudnicka

forest

Berlin *more than* 100
Jewish mental home
patients deported
22 November

Lublin
Lipowa Street camp
2,500
3 November

Trawniki
slave labour camp
8,000
November

Borki
corpse-burning
squad revolt
50 killed
3 survived

*from
Holland*
1,149
15 November
995
16 November

resistance
by a former
Hebrew teacher
Szosznik
hundreds killed
10 escape

Majdanek
18,000
3 November

Poniatowa
slave labour camp
14,000
5 November

Krychow
slave labour camp
1,500
5 November

Theresienstadt
2,504
15 December
2,503
18 December
also 300 die
during an all-day roll call
11 November

Funfteichen
slave labour camp
the first deaths
November

Sosnowiec
1,000 November

Auschwitz

Rzeszow
1,000

Lvov
Janowska camp
uprising
19 November
leaders included
Leon Weliczker

212
from Milan and Verona
6 December

Szebnie
slave labour camp
2,800 to Auschwitz
4 November
500 shot
6 November

Drohobycz
200 shot
14 December

0 miles 80

0 kilometres 100

© Martin Gilbert 1982

Baltic Sea

During November and December 1943 the deportations to Auschwitz continued from Italy, Holland and Theresienstadt *(above)*. At Majdanek 18,000 prisoners were murdered in a single day of slaughter, called by the SS the 'harvest festival'. Elsewhere, the SS continued to destroy slave labour camps. Jews tried to resist execution, as at Majdanek, Janowska and Poniatowa *(above)*.

Many of the Jews who had managed to escape the ghettos and camps joined Soviet partisan groups, or formed small units of their own. The map opposite shows 35 towns and villages from which Jews had managed to escape to the forests. From Kovno almost all who tried to escape were killed.

Map 224

ESCAPE AND RESISTANCE, JULY - DECEMBER 1943

0   miles   40
0   kilometres   60

REICHSKOMMISSARIAT
OSTLAND

Russo Polish border, 1921 – 1939

Kovno

Lake Narocz   Miadziol

Vilna

*24 December 1943
Sixty-four escape
from the Ninth Fort.*
45 *caught and
killed.*
19 *survive*

*Narocz
forest*

Wilejka

Krasnoe

Horodok

Olkieniki

*Rudnicka
forest*

Werenow

Iwje

Minsk

Lida

Wasiliszki

Grodno

Bielce

Nowogrodek

Korelicze   Stolpce

Szczucin   Zoludek

Mir

*River
Niemen*

Nowojelnia

Dworzec

Nieswiez

**GREATER
GERMANY**

Dereczyn

Baranowicze

Kleck

Slutsk

Zelwa

Slonim

Lachowicze

**BIALYSTOK
REGION**

Hancewicze

**BARANOWICZE
REGION**

95,000 *executed*
6,000 *escape*
in August 1942

Lenino

Pruzana

**Brest-
Litovsk**

Kobryn

Drohiczyn   Janow

Pinsk

*River
Bug*

Russo Polish border, 1921 – 1939

REICHSKOMMISSARIAT
UKRAINE

*Pripet
marshes*

© Martin Gilbert 1982

Map 225

JEWS DEPORTED TO AUSCHWITZ AND GASSED, JANUARY-FEBRUARY 1944

BIRTHPLACES OF TWENTY-FOUR OF THOSE DEPORTED TO AUSCHWITZ, 22 JANUARY 1944

North Sea

Baltic Sea

Vilna
Jankel Lewin,
aged 51

Bialystok
Riwka Golombek, aged 19
Anna Golombek, aged 15

Manchester
Maurice Braunstein,
aged 39

Drancy

Auschwitz

London
Joseph Terasfeld,
aged 28
Rebecca Gabay,
aged 29

Paris
Jean Navon, aged 19
Odette Navon, aged 6

Bordeaux

Jacqueline Dray, aged 4
Michel Dray, aged 1

Nice
Rachael Haim, aged 14
Fanny Haim, aged 13
Renée Haim, aged 5

Black Sea

Bursa

Albert Navon, aged 45
Sol Navon, aged 37
Mordechai Haim, aged 40
Esthera Haim, aged 37

Baghdad
David Somekh
aged 37

Casablanca
David Dray, aged 11
Leon Dray, aged 8

Tunis
Albert Dana
aged 62
Nina Dana
aged 62

Mediterranean Sea

Damascus
Isaac Saal,
aged 59

Cairo
Jacques Menache
aged 23

© Martin Gilbert 1982

0 miles 400
0 kilometres 600

The map opposite shows the deportations to Auschwitz during January and February 1944. The dates are those of the arrival of each train at Auschwitz; the figures show the actual numbers gassed, according to the records kept by the SS in Auschwitz itself. In all, the SS recorded 13 deportations for these two months, from the Baltic to the Adriatic.

The map above shows the birthplaces, and ages, of 24 of the deportees in one of these 13 deportations, that which reached Auschwitz from Drancy on 22 January 1944. It had left Paris two days earlier, with 632 men, 515 women and 221 children under the age of 18. Of these 1,368 Jews, 749 were gassed on arrival at Auschwitz. As well as those named on the map, the deportees included Jews who had been born in every country in Europe.

Among the Jews deported from Paris to Auschwitz were more than 1,000 who had been born in Turkey, but whose nationality was no protection, despite Turkish neutrality. Some of their birthplaces are shown on the right-hand map.

The photograph is of children in the Dutch deportation centre of Westerbork, on the eve of deportation.

TURKISH-BORN JEWS DEPORTED FROM PARIS

BULGARIA

Black Sea

Edirne

TURKEY -IN- EUROPE

Istanbul

EASTERN THRACE

Silviri

Izmit

Gallipoli

Sea of Marmara

Adapazari

Chanak
(Canakkale)

Bursa

Pazarcik

TURKEY
neutral

Bergama

Aegean

Manisa

Izmir
(Smyrna)

Sea

Aydin

0 miles 60
0 kilometres 80

© Martin Gilbert 1982

164

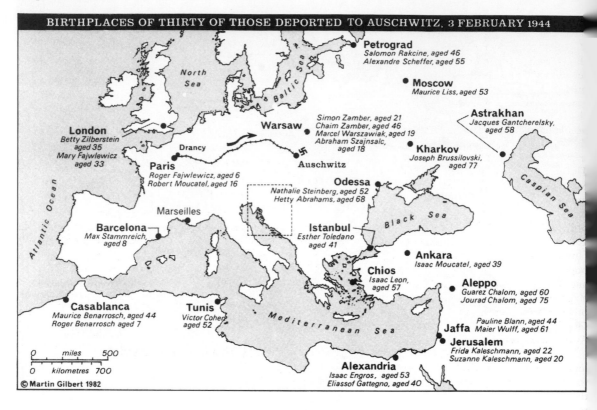

BIRTHPLACES OF THIRTY OF THOSE DEPORTED TO AUSCHWITZ, 3 FEBRUARY 1944

Petrograd
Salomon Rakcine, aged 46
Alexandre Scheffer, aged 55

Moscow
Maurice Liss, aged 53

Simon Zamber, aged 21
Chaim Zamber, aged 46
Marcel Warszawiak, aged 19
Abraham Szajnsalc, aged 18

Astrakhan
Jacques Gantcherelsky,
aged 58

Warsaw

London
Betty Zilberstein
aged 35
Mary Fajwlewicz
aged 33

Drancy

Kharkov
Joseph Brussilovski,
aged 77

Paris
Roger Fajwlewicz, aged 6
Robert Moucatel, aged 16

Auschwitz

Odessa
Nathalie Steinberg, aged 52
Hetty Abrahams, aged 68

Marseilles

Istanbul
Esther Toledano
aged 41

Ankara
Isaac Moucatel, aged 39

Barcelona
Max Stammreich,
aged 8

Chios
Isaac Leon,
aged 57

Aleppo
Guarez Chalom, aged 60
Jourad Chalom, aged 75

Casablanca
Maurice Benarrosch, aged 44
Roger Benarrosch aged 7

Tunis
Victor Cohen,
aged 52

Pauline Blann, aged 44
Maier Wulff, aged 61

Jaffa

Jerusalem
Frida Kaleschmann, aged 22
Suzanne Kaleschmann, aged 20

Alexandria
Isaac Engros, aged 53
Eliassof Gattegno, aged 40

© Martin Gilbert 1982

THE JEWS OF NORTHERN DALMATIA

GREATER GERMANY

Lake Balaton

AUSTRIA

HUNGARY

SLOVENIA

Trieste

ISTRIA

Kraljevica 2
Crikvenica 30

Jasenovac

Senj 6
Rab 4

CROATIA

DALMATIA
Gospic

Obrovac 1
Bencovac 1

Knin 1

Drnis 1

BOSNIA

Sibenic 28
Split 210

Dalmatian Coast

Adriatic Sea

ITALY

© Martin Gilbert 1982

On 3 February 1944 yet another train left Paris for Auschwitz. It was the 67th such deportation in nearly two years. The map above shows the names, birthplaces and ages of 30 of the deportees. Also deported, and gassed on arrival at Auschwitz, was the 39-year-old Chief Rabbi of Strasbourg, René Hirschler, who had been born in Marseilles, and his 32-year-old wife Simone. In 1939 Hirschler had been chaplain to those Jewish refugees who had joined the French Foreign Legion in order to fight against Germany. In March 1943 he had become chaplain of all foreign-born Jews in the detention camps in France. He and his wife had been arrested in Marseilles in December 1943.

In all, 1,214 Jews were deported in this one train. Fourteen of the deportees were over 80. More than 100 were under 16 years old. Only 26 survived the war.

The deportees of February 3 included four American-born deportees, the 89-year-old Zadie Abraham, the 81-year-old Clara Kahn, the 81-year-old Pola Modiano, the 57-year-old Michel Feldman *(page 122)*, Murad Gubbay, born in Calcutta *(page 114)*, and the 17-year-old Raymond Strauss, born in the Brazilian city of Sao Paulo.

The Jewish communities, and individual Jews, of northern Dalmatia, according to the Yugoslavia census of 31 March 1931, are shown in the map opposite *(below)*. The Jews of Split could trace their Jewish predecessors to the third century AD.

On 11 March 1944, 300 women and children from northern Dalmatia, having been interned at Gospic, were deported to the Croat concentration camp at Jasenovac *(right, below)*. Not a single one survived. The men had already been deported to the Sajmiste death camp near Belgrade five months earlier *(page 160)*.

In 1941, following the Italian occupation of Dalmatia, the island of Rab which in 1931 had been the home of a single Jewish family, became the centre of a large refugee population, of Jews from Austria, Croatia and Bosnia. Many had been able to join the Yugoslav partisans in September 1943; others mostly women and children, were seized in March 1944, and deported to Auschwitz *(right, below)*.

The Jews of Albania had survived unmolested under Italian rule. The first Jews to settle in Albania had been refugees from the Spanish expulsions of 1492. Other refugees had joined them in the sixteenth century from Sicily and southern Italy. By 1927 most of Albania's Jews were living in Koritza *(right, top)*. After 1938 several hundred Jewish refugees from Germany and Austria took refuge in Tirana and Durazzo. Following the collapse of Italy in September 1943, they were, at first, unmolested. Then in April 1944, at German insistence, they were interned at Pristina, and consequently deported to Bergen-Belsen. Of 400 Albanian deportees, only 100 survived the war.

These deportations of March and April 1944 took place as the Allied armies in southern Italy were approaching Rome, and after Soviet forces had already crossed the eastern border of Greater Germany and were approaching Lvov.

Meanwhile in Warsaw, on 7 March 1944, the historian Emanuel Ringelblum, who had struggled to collect and preserve as much material as possible about the Warsaw ghetto, and who had managed to hide in 'Aryan' Warsaw after the ghetto revolt, was discovered by the Gestapo, and, together with his family, tortured and killed. Elsewhere in 'Ayran' Warsaw, Polish families, at the risk of their own lives, gave shelter to several thousand Jews, most of whom survived the war.

THE JEWS OF ALBANIA INTERNED

© Martin Gilbert 1982

THREE DEPORTATIONS, MARCH - APRIL 1944

© Martin Gilbert 1982

Map 232

GREEK JEWS DEPORTED TO AUSCHWITZ, 23 MARCH - 2 APRIL 1944

YUGOSLAVIA

ALBANIA

YUGOSLAV MACEDONIA
occupied by BULGARIA

THRACE
Occupied by BULGARIA

Gorgopotamo

GREEK MACEDONIA

Florina 336

Salonica

Kastoria 865

Veroia 329

*Jews active in
Greek resistance*

EPIRUS

Trikala 160

Larisa 394

Katerina 3 shot

33 saved by local Greeks

CORFU

Yanina 1,687

23 March 1944

Volos 237

Aegean

THESSALY

Arta 320

Jews active in Greek resistance

EUBOEA

Preveza 235

Ionian Sea

GREECE

Chaicis 155

Sea

Patras 213

Athens **1,500**

2 April 1944

0 miles 50

0 kilometres 80

PELOPONNESE

Salamis 6

ZANTE

Piraeus 167

© Martin Gilbert 1982

On 15 March 1944 the German authorities assembled trucks and guards throughout mainland Greece, and began a systematic search for more than 10,000 Greek Jews. Half were able to flee into the mountains to find shelter with local peasants, to join Greek partisan units, or to escape across the Aegean to neutral Turkey. Many survived as a result of an instruction issued by Archbishop Damaskinos to all monasteries and convents in Athens and the provincial towns to shelter any Jew who knocked on their doors. But over 5,000 Greek Jews were caught, and deported to Auschwitz. It was an eight-day journey in sealed cattle trucks. Hundreds died during the journey itself.

From the west the French and Dutch deportations continued *(opposite)*: there were Jews on these two Paris trains from Hong Kong, Senegal, Liverpool and Samarkand.

In the east there were two rebellions. On 22 March 1944, at Koldyczewo, 10 SS guards were killed, and hundreds of prisoners escaped to join the partisans. Twenty-five escapees were caught, including the leader, who committed suicide. On 15

April 1944 *(see also page 156)* a group of prisoners whose task was to destroy the evidence of mass murder, tried to escape from Ponary. Twenty-five were killed; 15 got away. Five days later, the remaining 40 members of the unit were killed.

Thousands of individual Jews served and fought in the French resistance, and in Yugoslav and Greek partisan units *(above)*. More than 300 Jewish soldiers from the Greek Army, and 1,000 other Jews, joined Greek partisan units. A group of 40 Jewish partisans took part in the blowing up of the Gorgopotamo Bridge, breaking German rail communications between Greece and the north. The main Greek national resistance organization in the Trikala, Larisa and Volos region was commanded by Moses Pesah, a Greek rabbi.

Jews also served in Soviet partisan forces which were parachuted behind the German lines in order to disrupt German troops and munition movements. In the Lublin region, by March 1944, were many Jews who had been parachuted into Poland as members of Soviet partisan units. Among these Jews

Map 233

DEPORTATION, MASSACRE AND REVOLT, MARCH - APRIL 1944

North Sea

Baltic Sea

Riga

Siauliai (Shavli) *ghetto*

Kovno *ghetto*
1,200 *children killed March 1944*

Ponary ☀
25 **15** revolt 15 April
70 20 April

Danzig
Stutthof

Mogilev

Koldyczewo ☀
slave labour camp revolt 22 March led by Shlomo Kushnir

Berlin

HOLLAND
732 *3 March*
599 *23 March*

Bialystok ☀
region
Jews in Soviet partisan units

Lodz

Lublin ☀ **Chelm**
region

Kiev

Zhitomir

Soviet forces advancing

from Paris
1,501 *7 March*
1,025 *27 March*

Auschwitz

Plaszow

Boryslaw
600
28 March

Czernowitz

Vienna

SWITZLD.
neutral

Jassy

Odessa

Black Sea

Verona

☀ *Jews in French underground units*

Fossoli **Mantua**
559 *5 April*

Jasenovac

RAB
300

Gospic ☀
300 *Jews in Yugoslav partisan units*
11 March

Split

Jews in Italian underground units

miles 0 — 200
kilometres 0 — 300

Pristina
300

Rome
57 *Jews among 335 Italians, murdered as a German reprisal, Ardeatine Caves, 24 March*

Allied forces

Jews in Greek partisan units

6,469
deported from Greece to Auschwitz

CORFU

SICILY

Lamia
1

Patras

Amalias
12

Kalamata
4

Aegion
1

Athens

TURKEY
neutral
1,500
escape to Turkey by boat

CRETE

RHODES

TUNIS

© Martin Gilbert 1982

were the commander of the Special Soviet Parachute Battalion, Lieutenant Colonel Henryk Torunczyk, from Lodz; his deputy commander, Joseph Kratko, from Chelm; and the only woman officer in the battalion, Lieutenant Lucyna Herz, who was killed in action while leading a company against a German position on the Vistula. For her bravery she was posthumously awarded the rank of Captain in the Red Army.

Map 234

SLAVE LABOUR CAMP EVACUATIONS, MARCH 1944

© Martin Gilbert 1982

As Soviet forces advanced further and further westward, the Germans began the systematic evacuation of the slave labour camps in their path *(above)*. From the camp at Plaszow, many hundreds were sent to Auschwitz, others westward to Mauthausen and Flossenbürg, some northward to the concentration camp at Stutthof.

Majdanek itself was evacuated on 20 March 1944, when all sick prisoners were sent direct to Auschwitz to be gassed, while the rest were sent to Gross Rosen, and the women to Ravensbrück and Natzweiler.

The photograph, taken in 1980, shows some of the hundreds of thousands of shoes which the Germans had collected from their victims at Majdanek between 1942 and 1944, hoping to find a technical process which would enable used shoe leather to be turned to some practical or even military purpose. But no such process had been discovered before the camp was evacuated. The shoes remained in their original storehouse.

Even while the first westward evacuations were in progress, the eastward deportations were continuing. Those from Holland, Italy and Paris are shown on the two small maps *(opposite)*. More than half of the Dutch Jews sent to Bergen-Belsen and Theresienstadt survived. But most of those sent to Auschwitz perished.

FIVE DUTCH DEPORTATIONS

Bergen-Belsen | 101 | 5 April
| 232 | 19 May

HOLLAND

Theresienstadt
289
5 April

Auschwitz
240
5 April
453
19 May

miles 300
kilometres 500

© Martin Gilbert 1982

FOUR FURTHER DEPORTATIONS

North Sea

miles 200
km 300

Treblinka
Warsaw

Paris
1,500 including Simone Jacob (Simone Veil)
13 April
1,004 including Itzak Katznelson
29 April

Auschwitz

Fossoli
518
16 May

Backa Topola
3,000
29 April

Adriatic Sea

© Martin Gilbert 1992

Among those deported from Paris on 13 April 1944 were several hundred Jews who had been born in Alsace, the French province annexed by Germany, first in 1870 and again in 1940. The map on the far right shows some of the towns, villages and hamlets in which these deportees were born, many of them during the period of German rule before the First World War.

In all, 1,500 Jews were deported from Paris to Auschwitz on 13 April 1944, among them 148 children under 12, and a 16-year-old girl, Simone Jacob, who had been born in Nice. Miss Jacob was one of 100 deportees from this particular train who survived Auschwitz. Later, as Simone Veil, she became Minister of Health in the French Government, and, in July 1979, President of the European Parliament at Strasbourg.

From the second Paris deportation that month, on 29 April 1944, those killed included the Yiddish poet from Warsaw, Yitzak Katznelson. His wife and most of his family had already been killed at Treblinka.

ALSACE-BORN DEPORTEES, 13 APRIL 1944

Niederbronn, Oberbronn, Struth, Ingwiller, Mertzwiller, Neuwiller, Ringendorf, Haguenau, Phalsbourg, Mommenheim, Schwindratzheim, Saverne, Wingersheim, Brumath, Romanswiller, Küttolsheim, Strasbourg, Quatzenheim, Molsheim, Lingolsheim, Urmatt, Düttlenheim, Duppingheim, Rosheim, Wishes, Fegersheim, Eschau, Ottrott, Obernai, Westhausen, Benfeld, Gerstheim, ALSACE, Muttersholz, Rhine, Bergheim, River, Grussenheim, BADEN, Colmar

miles 10
kilometres 15

© Martin Gilbert 1982

170

Map 238

THE JEWS OF HUNGARY AND THE GERMAN OCCUPATION, 19 MARCH 1944

FELVIDEK
78,000
annexed from Czechoslovakia
2 November 1938

GREATER GERMANY

EASTERN GALICIA

RUTHENIA
72,000
annexed from Czechoslovakia
2 November 1938 and
15 March 1939

SLOVAKIA

MORAVIA

Kassa
(Kosice)

Munkacs
(Mukacevo)

AUSTRIA

River Danube

Budapest

Lake
Balaton

HUNGARY
444,567

Kolozsvar
(Cluj)

RUMANIA

CROATIA

**NORTHERN
TRANSYLVANIA**
149,000
annexed from Rumania
30 August 1940

BACSKA
20,000
annexed from Yugoslavia
7 April 1941

Novi Sad
(Ujvidek)

BANAT

SREM

© Martin Gilbert 1982

0 miles 100
0 kilometres 160

On 19 March 1944 German control was imposed on Hungary. Suddenly more than three quarters of a million Jews who had hitherto seemed safe from Nazi terror, and in particular from deportation, came under Nazi dominance.

More than a quarter of a million of these Jews lived in areas which Hungary itself had annexed between 1938 and 1941, as shown on the map above. One such area was the Bacska, whose Jewish communities are shown on the map opposite, according to the Yugoslav census of 1931.

In the autumn of 1941 more than 10,000 Jews whose Hungarian citizenship was in doubt had been deported to Kamenets Podolsk, and murdered (page 55). A few months later, in January 1942, 1,000 Jews had been massacred in the Bacska (page 74).

In January 1943, after more than 50,000 Hungarian Jews had been forced to serve in labour battalions on the eastern front as part of Hungary's war effort against Russia, at least 40,000 had been killed during the fighting or had died after the

Soviet army's victory on the River Don (page 130).

Despite the deaths of so many Jews, the Hungarian Government had adamantly rejected two German requests for the deportation of Hungarian Jews to Greater Germany in 1943, and had even begun to institute court proceedings against those responsible for the Bacska killings of 1942.

Hitler himself had protested twice to the Hungarian Government about what he called its 'irresolute and ineffective' handling of the Jewish question, and on 12 March 1944, a week before the German occupation of Hungary, the SS began to plan the complete destruction of Hungarian Jewry.

Within a few weeks of the imposition of German control over Hungary, tens of thousands of Jews were driven from their towns and villages, and forced into ghettos and special camps (page 173).

The photograph shows a deportation from a town in the Felvidek region, which Hungary had annexed from Czechoslovakia in November 1938.

Map 239

THE JEWISH COMMUNITIES OF THE BACSKA, INTERNED

River Danube

HUNGARY

RUMANIA

Baja
5

Bacsalmas

Horgos
42

Martonos
17

Stare Kanjiza
40

Subotica
3,758

Senta
1,457

Bajmok
131

Cantavir
78

Stanisic
80

Ada
342

River Tisza

Topola
411

BANAT

Bezdan
74

Conoplja
49

BACSKA

Petrovo Selo
282

Monostor
22

Sombor
1,175

Feketic
48

Stari Bečej
500

Kupusina
7

Prigrevica
13

Kula
88

Nadalj
2

Gradiste
4

Apatin
94

Sonta
47

Srbobran
50

Curug
72

Bogojevo
10

Odzaci
16

Dubrava
20

Temerin
92

Zabalj
41

Karavukovo
16

Mosorin
10

YUGOSLAVIA

Bac
14

Novi Sad
2,445

Kac
25

Titel
67

River Danube

SREM

0 miles 15
0 kilometres 20

© Martin Gilbert 1982

Map 240

JEWS ASSEMBLED FOR DEPORTATION, 16 APRIL – 23 MAY 1944

GREATER GERMANY

EASTERN
GALICIA

S L O V A K I A

Kassa (Kosice)
12,000
11 May

Ungvar
14,000
6 May

Havasko
3 May

Nevicke
3 May

Munkacs
26,000
15·22 May

Csap

RUTHENIA

Iza 3,000

B U K O V I N A

Satoraljaujhely
15,000
11 May

Beregszasz
10,000

Huszt
10,000 *11 May*

Miskolc
21,000
11 May

Kisvarda
2,000 *15 May*

Nyiregyhaza

Maramarossziget

Vad

Petrova

NORTHERN
TRANSYLVANIA

Eger
9,000

Nagykallo
23 May

Szatmarnemeti
24,000

Szekelyhid
3 May

H U N G A R Y

Nagybanya
3,500

Felsoviso
8,000
5 May

Monostor-
Kapolnok
3 May

Bethlen
3 May

Nagyszollos
8,000 *15 May*

Szilagysomlyo
7,000
3 May

Des
10,000
3 May

Beszterce
8,000 (Bistriza)
3 May

Nagyvarad (Oradea
Mare)
36,000
3 May

Kolozsvar (Cluj)
22,000
3 May

Szaszregen
8,000
3 May

Szamosujvar
1,600

Marosvasarhely
6,000
3 May

R U M A N I A

Sepsiszentgyorgy
3 May

0   miles   50
0   kilometres   80

© Martin Gilbert 1982

Beginning on 15 April 1944, tens of thousands of Hungarian Jews were forced to leave their homes, and to move into specially designated ghetto areas. The map above shows some of these ghettos, with the approximate numbers held in them.

On entering each Hungarian town or village, one Gestapo method was to seize several leading citizens, and then threaten to kill them unless the community agreed to a punitive ransom. In this way, the Jews of the town were impoverished overnight, without even the money to buy railway tickets. The ransom exercise also made the SS seem plausible: they had said they would release the hostages as soon as the money was paid, and they had kept their word. When the SS then said: 'we have orders to put you in brick factories and timber yards *and no harm will come to you*', it could be believed. 'Quite soon', the SS told those who had been thus confined, 'you will go east to help with the harvest.'

On 15 May 1944 *(opposite, above)* the deportations to Auschwitz began. By mid June a total of 289,357 Jews had been deported to Auschwitz from Ruthenia and northern Transylvania *(see also pages 183–88)*.

The map opposite, gives the approximate number of Jews known to have been deported to Auschwitz and then gassed there, from 63 towns and villages in eastern Hungary. The places shown here amount to no more than half of the towns and villages in this region alone from which Jews were deported. At Miskolc and Satoraljaujhely hundreds of Jews were shot as they tried to resist boarding the trains.

An indication of the size of the destruction elsewhere in Hungary during the summer months of 1944 can be seen from the maps on pages 183 to 188.

DEPORTATIONS FROM EASTERN HUNGARY, 15 MAY - 7 JUNE 1944

GREATER

Auschwitz

Tarnow

Cracow

Rzeszow

Nowy Sacz

GERMANY

Sanok

Lvov

Przemysl

GENERAL

Stryj

Lubotin

Radvan

GOVERNMENT

Presov

Lawoczne

SLOVAKIA

Kysak

Voloc

Szolyva

Munkacs

see map 255

RUTHENIA

Kassa

Bilke

Korosmezo

Beregszasz

Kisvarda

Tecso

Miskolc

Mateszalka

CENTRAL
HUNGARY
see map 254

Nyiregyhaza

Terebesfejerpatak

Eger

Nagykallo

see
map 242

NORTHERN
TRANSYLVANIA

HUNGARY

0   miles   60
0   kilometres   100

© Martin Gilbert 1982

SOME HUNGARIAN JEWISH COMMUNITIES DESTROYED, 15 MAY - 7 JUNE 1944

0   miles   15
0   kilometres   30

Gonc
150

Goncruszka
25

Zahony
50

Tiszaszentmarton
50

Szendro
280

Tiszabezded
50

Satoraljaujhely
3,600

Encs
260

Sarospatak
800

Ricse
160

Barabas
86

Edeleny
250

Erdobenye
150

Cigand
180

Tornyospalca
90

Tiszaszalka
65

Ibrany
200

Patroha
130

Kisvarda
2,500

Szikszo
900

Mad
250

Tokaj
380

Rakamaz
160

Nagyhalasz
220

Vasarosnameny
440

Tarpa
250

Szerencs
800

Nyirkarasz
130

Szatmarcseke
85

Miskolc
13,500

Tarcal
260

Tiszaeszlar
50

Demecser
300

Baktaloranthaza
200

Fehergyarmat
550

Taktaharkany
65

Tiszalok
350

Kemecse
300

Or
50

Mateszalka
1,400

Onod
150

Niregyhaza
3,500

Hodasz
150

Porcsalma
200

Tiszavasvari
620

Nagykallo
750

Nyirbator
1,400

Nagyecsed
600

Csenger
400

Polgar
450

Hajdunanas
750

Nyirbogat
300

Hajdudorog
250

Ujfeherto
400

Balkany
300

Nyiradony
200

Fabianhaza
75

Mezocsat
407

Hajduboszormeny
600

Hajduhadhaz
250

Nyiradony
200

Nyirbeltek
100

River Tisza

© Martin Gilbert 1982

THE PARIS DEPORTATIONS OF 15 MAY 1944

FINLAND

Leningrad

Reval
*arrived
19 May*

*North
Sea*

Baltic Sea

Kovno
*arrived
18 May*

Stutthof

Proyanovska
*slave labour
camp*

Soviet forces

Drancy

Auschwitz

Soviet forces

Paris
878
15 May — *including Israel Kopelov, aged 38
born in Kovno*

0   miles   200
0 kilometres 300

© **Martin Gilbert 1982**

BIRTHPLACES OF SOME OF THE PARIS DEPORTEES OF 15 MAY 1944

*also
Moses Algaze–Razon,
born in Havana, Cuba,
aged 23*

Reval   Petrograd (Leningrad)

Riga

*North
Sea*   Dvinsk

Baltic Sea

Moscow
*Jacob Boguslavski
aged 26*

*Atlantic
Ocean*

London   Vilna   Molczacz

Amsterdam   Kovno

Brussels   Berlin   Warsaw   Kobryn   Kiev

Drancy   Lodz   Lublin

Paris   Frankfurt   Cracow   Lvov

Strasbourg   Brno   Sokal

Dijon   Vienna   Budapest   Kishinev   Odessa

Zurich   Szombathely   Mako   Jassy

Lyons   Geneva   Pecs   Ismail

Avignon   Belgrade   Bucharest   Sulina   Sevastopol

Varna   *Black Sea*

Bordeaux

*Caspian
Sea*

Baku
*Abraham
Jakoubovitch
aged 22*

Marseilles   *Adriatic Sea*   Edirne

Rome   Salonica   Constantinople

Bursa

Aegean Sea

Smyrna
Aidin

Oran   Algiers   Tunis   Baghdad
*Arnold David
aged 32*

Rabat   Tlemcen   Constantine   Emmanuel
Cohen
aged 54   Damascus

*Simon Kadosh
aged 20*

*Georges Quaziz
aged 19*

Mediterranean   Sea   Safed

Jaffa

Jerusalem
*Haim Epstein
aged 39*

0   miles   500
0 kilometres 800

Georges Sirkis, aged 37   © **Martin Gilbert 1982**

Map 245

BIRTHPLACES OF SOME OF THE PARIS DEPORTEES TO AUSCHWITZ, 20 MAY 1944

Chita
Pinchas Reznik
aged 36

Liverpool
Jaffa Hermann
aged 55

Baghdad
Lily Haim
aged 48

Mogador
David Dahan
aged 60

Cairo
Allegra Cori
aged 31

Havana
Dorothée Salomontchik
aged 29

Jerusalem
Tobias Salomon
aged 49

Lima
Rosita Lindow
aged 59

Sao Paulo
Denise Levy
aged 34

Buenos Aires
Sigismund Syskind
aged 30

© Martin Gilbert 1982

On the very day that the first deportations took place from Hungary to Auschwitz, a train left Paris with 878 Jews locked into its 15 cattle trucks. All were men. Their destination was not Auschwitz, but Kovno.

After three days and three nights, on 18 May 1944 they reached their destination, and were sent to the Proyanovska slave labour camp. There, 160 of them were shot and the rest evacuated with other Jews from Kovno six weeks later *(page 187)*.

Nearly 260 of the deportees had been sent on to Reval. Six days after their arrival, 60 were taken for work but never seen again. The rest worked on airfield repairs, 60 being taken to a nearby forest and shot on July 14. On August 14 a hundred of the sick were sent to an 'unknown destination'. Four days later the 34 survivors were evacuated to Stutthof *(page 193)*: 15 survived the war.

The lower map *(opposite)* shows some of the birthplaces of the May 15 deportees; the map above shows the birthplaces of 10 of the deportees in the train sent from Paris to Auschwitz five days later. Like several thousand of those murdered at Auschwitz, they had emigrated to western Europe between the wars. The photograph is of a Jew at the moment of departure from Paris.

Map 246

JEWS EXECUTED IN FRANCE FOR RESISTANCE, 1 JANUARY - 5 JUNE 1944

London

BRITAIN

Dover

North Sea

Portsmouth

English Channel

NORMANDY

BELGIUM

Cologne

GREATER
GERMANY

LUX.

LORRAINE

ALSACE

Suresnes
18

Paris
3

Argentan
1

Sougé
5

GERMAN - OCCUPIED
FRANCE

Les Ponts de Cé
1

Mezières
1

Dole
1

SWITZERLAND
neutral

Poitiers
1

Garnat
1

Morez
1

Gex
1

Nanteuil
4

Limoges
28

Eymoutiers
1

Cours
1

Lyon
9

Champier
1

Bay
of
Biscay

Cognac
1

Tourtoirac
3

Uzerche
3

Puy de Dôme
2

Voiron
1

St. Etienne
2

Grenoble
1

Brantôme
9

Salignac
5

Thenon
1

Brive
4

Hauteforte
4

GERMAN-OCCUPIED
ITALY

Martignas
1

DORDOGNE
78

Mane
1

Nice
5

Villematier
4

Toulouse
6

Marseilles
1

0   miles   60

0 kilometres 80

Miremont
9

Mediterranean   Sea

Pyrenees

SPAIN
neutral

© Martin Gilbert 1982

177

Map 247

SOME BIRTHPLACES

In the six months before the Allied landings in Normandy, more than 250 Jews had been executed in France for resistance and acts of sabotage. The place of execution of 229 of them is shown here *(opposite)*. More than half of them had come to France as immigrants, or as refugees, in the decade before the Second World War, when France offered both work and haven.

Among the 28 Jews executed at Limoges was the 67-year-old Victor Rubinstein, who had been born in New York. Nineteen of those executed had been born in Warsaw, eight in Budapest, five in Berlin, five in Vienna and three in Algiers.

One of the six Jews executed in Toulouse, Mandel Langer, had been born in Auschwitz in 1903. Haim Matem had been born in Jerusalem in 1898 when it formed part of the Ottoman Empire.

The map on the left shows some of their other birthplaces.

The photograph shows a Gestapo firing squad in France executing a Jewish member of the Resistance.

Map 248

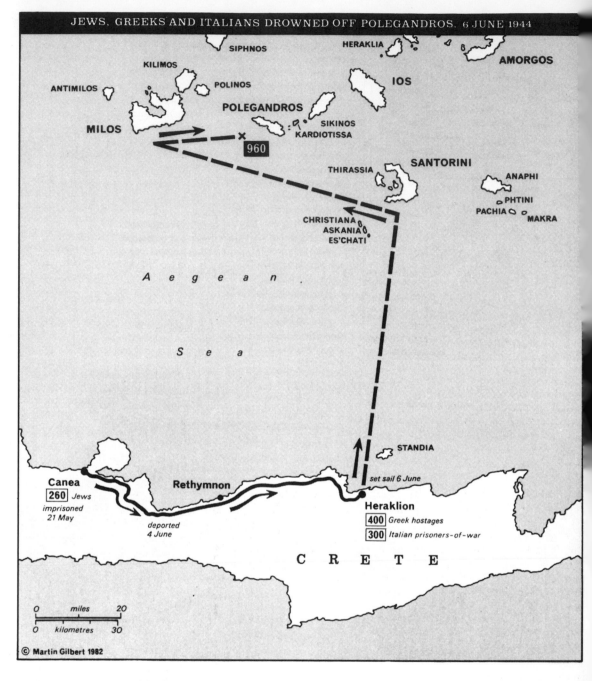

JEWS, GREEKS AND ITALIANS DROWNED OFF POLEGANDROS. 6 JUNE 1944

SIPHNOS

HERAKLIA

AMORGOS

KILIMOS

POLINOS

IOS

ANTIMILOS

POLEGANDROS

MILOS

SIKINOS
KARDIOTISSA

960

SANTORINI

THIRASSIA

ANAPHI

PHTINI
PACHIA
MAKRA

CHRISTIANA
ASKANIA
ES'CHATI

A e g e a n

S e a

STANDIA

set sail 6 June

Canea
260 *Jews*
imprisoned
21 May

Rethymnon

deported
4 June

Heraklion

400 *Greek hostages*
300 *Italian prisoners-of-war*

C R E T E

0   miles   20
0   kilometres   30

© Martin Gilbert 1982

Jews had lived on Crete since Roman times. Often oppressed, in AD 440 they put their faith in a pseudo-Messiah, who offered to lead them 'dry shod' through the sea to the Promised Land. Hundreds were drowned.

On 21 May 1944 the Gestapo imprisoned all 260 Jews of Canea, and the five families of Rethymnon. On June 4 they were all deported to Heraklion, and two days later, put on board ship and sent across the Aegean Sea towards the island of Santorini.

Deported with the Jews were 400 Greek civilians, who had been seized as hostages, and 300 Italian prisoners-of-war, who for more than four years had been Germany's allies. All were taken 120 miles across the sea, where the ship was deliberately sunk, and all on board were drowned.

Only 7 Cretan Jews managed to survive the war, in hiding.

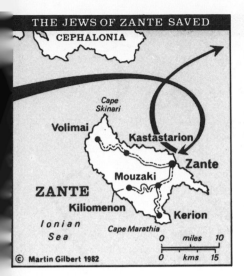

THE JEWS OF ZANTE SAVED

CORFU JEWS DEPORTED, 14 JUNE 1944

Despite the presence of Allied forces in southern Italy, and the Soviet advance into Eastern Galicia, the SS still sought out Jews to deport to Auschwitz. One of the areas of their search was the islands of the Ionian Sea, among them Zante, and Corfu, then only 50 miles from the Allied forces in south Italy.

Jews had lived on Corfu (right) since the thirteenth century. During the seige of the island by the Turks in 1716, the Jews had distinguished themselves in defence of the island. During the Italian occupation, from April 1941 to September 1943, there had been no serious hardship, nor did the German occupation on 27 September 1943 lead to any immediate persecution. But on 6 June 1944 all 1,800 Jews were seized by the Gestapo, and eight days later they were deported to what they were told would be 'resettlement' in Poland. The women went overland to Larissa, the men by sea. While at sea they were given nothing to eat or drink and several died. On June 20 all were sent northwards by train, reaching Auschwitz nine days later: 1,600 were sent at once to the gas chamber, and 200 to forced labour.

On Zante (above) both Archbishop Chrysostomos and Lukos Karrer, the mayor, refused to obey the Gestapo order that all 257 Jews on the island should be assembled at the quayside to board the boat from Corfu. 'If the deportation order is carried out', the Archbishop declared, 'I will join the Jews and share their fate.' All 195 able-bodied Jews were sent to safety in remote villages. Sixty old people and children were seized by the Gestapo and taken to the quayside to await the Corfu boat: but the boat was already so overcrowded that it did not stop.

Map 251

DISTANT DEPORTATIONS, JUNE 1944

North Sea

Baltic Sea

Stutthof

20,000 *women* 29 June

Soviet forces

D – Day landings 6 June

HOLLAND 496 3 June

Auschwitz

Paris 1153 30 June

13 June

Boryslaw 700 22 June

Mauthausen

Oradour

0   *miles*   200
0   *kilometres*   300

Verona Fossoli 485 26 June

ITALY

HUNGARY 381,000 15 May · 30 June

Florence 16 4 June

Adriatic Sea

Allied forces

Aegean Sea

Corfu 1,800 14 June

Mediterranean Sea

Zante

© Martin Gilbert 1982

As Soviet forces drew nearer and nearer to Auschwitz, and Allied forces landed on the Normandy beaches on 6 June 1944, the deportations to Auschwitz continued. Trains reached Auschwitz throughout June *(above)* from Paris, Italy, Holland, the Eastern Galician town of Boryslaw and from Corfu, as well as from the massive continuing deportations from Hungary *(pages 183–8).*

At the same time as these deportations into Auschwitz, the first evacuation of Jews away from Auschwitz had begun, when prisoners in the slave labour camps drawing their labour force from Birkenau were sent out by train, the men westwards to Mauthausen, the women northwards to Stutthof.

The concentration camp at Stutthof had

STUTTHOF AND ITS SATELLITE SLAVE LABOUR CAMPS

Baltic Sea

Gulf of Danzig

Seerappen

Königsberg

EAST PRUSSIA

Lauenburg

Stolp

POMERANIA

Gdynia

Troyl *shipyard*

Danzig
Wrzeszcz
Pruszcz

River Vistula

Stutthof

49,000 *deaths in 1944*

Heiligenbeil

Reimansfelde

Schichau *shipyard*

Elbing

Gerdauen

Schippenbeil

Brusy

| 0 | miles | 30 |
| 0 | kilometres | 40 |

© Martin Gilbert 1982

been set up in September 1939 *(page 21)*. But it was not until August 1943 that any large number of Jews, several hundred survivors of the Bialystok ghetto revolt, were deported there *(page 151)*.

It was in the area around Stutthof that the Germans had begun, in the spring of 1944, to set up more than 60 new labour camps, to replace those which had already been overrun by the Soviet forces. The map above shows the principal towns and camps to which prisoners were sent from Stutthof throughout the summer and autumn of 1944 *(pages 198)*.

In the labour camps around Stutthof, conditions were barbaric: of 100 Jewish girls in the slave labour camp at Gerdauen, only three survived the war.

In Stutthof itself, tens of thousands of prisoners died of dysentery, typhus and starvation. Others were brutally clubbed to death while working in the nearby forests, or sadistically drowned in mud. Many were killed by means of phenol injections, and their bodies then burned in the crematorium, in specially designed 'high capacity' ovens.

Altogether more than 52,000 Jews passed through Stutthof, of whom at least 30,000 were women. Only about 3,000 survived the brutal treatment.

In France, four days after the Allied landings, the Germans killed more than 600 French villagers at Oradour-sur-Glane *(right)*. The women and children were burned alive in the church, and the men were machine-gunned, as a reprisal against the

SEVEN JEWS KILLED AT ORADOUR, 10 JUNE 1944

North Sea

Baltic Sea

Ickern
Joseph Bergman aged 27

Warsaw
Marie Goldman aged 45

Nancy
Raymond Enciel aged 10

Strasbourg
*Dora Kanzler aged 14
Simon Kanzler aged 9
Serge Bergman aged 8*

Oradour-sur-Glane
massacre
642

Budapest
Joseph Kanzler aged 50

| 0 | miles | 200 |
| 0 | kilometres | 300 |

© Martin Gilbert 1982

killing in another village of an SS army commander by a resistance sniper. Seven of the 642 men, women and children killed at Oradour were Jews: refugees who had earlier been able to escape deportation to Auschwitz by hiding among the friendly villagers. Now they became the victims of another repeated feature of Nazi tyranny, reprisals against civilians. Among the seven were Joseph Kanzler, born in Budapest, and his two children, born in Strasbourg.

Map 254

DEPORTATIONS FROM CENTRAL HUNGARY, 15 MAY - 8 JULY 1944

from Theresienstadt

| 2,503 |
| 15 May |
| 2,500 |
| 16 May |
| 2,500 |
| 18 May |

GALICIA

Auschwitz
Dziedzice
Bielsko Biala
Zywiec
Zwardon

GREATER   GERMANY

Zilina

MORAVIA

Danube

AUSTRIA

S L O V A K I A

Zvolen

Szecseny 250

Balassagyarmat 2,100
Nagyoroszi
Losonc

Mosonmagyarovar 350

Oroszvar 120
Ersekujvar 7,000
Dunaszerdahely 8,000
Vamosmikola 113
Bercel 170

Putnok 509
Sajoszentpeter 500
Ozd 500
Petervasara 50
Eger 1,400
Saly 40
Harsany 50
Kisterenye 75
Emod 60

Miskolc
see map 242

4,000
Gyor
Acs 100
Komarom 100
Tata 450
Budapest and region
Paszto 380
Gyongyos 1,600
Mezokovesd 750

Kapuvar 300
Tet 120
Gyomore 170
Beled 300

Kal 100
Fuzesabony 200
Heves 350
Tiszafured 650

Cerseg 225

Papa and region
see map 258

H   U   N   G   A   R   Y

Jaszbereny 560
Jaszkiser 55
Tiszaroff 45

Szombathely 4,228

Balaton region
see maps 256 and 262

Danube

see maps 257 and 259

Korosladany 100
Gyoma 48
Mezobereny 100
Sarkad 159

Szarvas
Izsak 25
Kiskoros 580
Kiskunfelegyhaza 700
Szentes 400
2,000
Bekescsaba
Gyula 450

Kecel 30
Dunapataj 100
Kalocsa 250
Kiskunhalas 750
Kiskunmajsa 126
Kistelek 200
Janoshalma 200
Melykut 70
Hodmezovasarhely 650
Totkomlos 100
Mezokovacshaza 250

Baja 700
Nagybaracska 50
Bacsalmas 160
Mako 1,400

CROATIA

RUMANIA

B A C S K A
see page 185

BANAT
see page 59

| 0 | miles | 40 |
| 0 | kilometres | 60 |

© Martin Gilbert 1982

Map 255

DEPORTATIONS FROM RUTHENIA AND NORTHERN TRANSYLVANIA, 15 MAY - 8 JULY 1944

The deportation of Hungarian Jews to Auschwitz had begun on 15 May 1944 from eastern Hungary *(page 174)* and central Hungary *(opposite)*. Also starting on May 15, Jews were deported from two of the areas annexed in 1938 and 1940, Ruthenia and northern Transylvania *(above)*, where the number of victims exceeded 250,000 in just under eight weeks. The maps show some of these deaths and give an indication of the speed, scale and effectiveness of the Nazi plan; a plan put into operation more than four and a half years after the German invasion of Poland.

Each deportation train bore the deceptive inscription 'German worker-resettlers'. Up to 100 people were forced into each wagon. Like the earlier French, Dutch, Belgian and Greek deportees, they were allowed only a single bucket of water and a single waste bucket to each wagon. Hundreds died during the journey. Many committed suicide or were driven insane by confinement and fear. Others were killed or robbed whenever the train had to stop for traffic control.

The deportations were still in mid course on 'D-Day' when the forces of the Western allies landed on the Normandy beaches *(page 181)*. For more than two years the Nazi authorities, and even Hitler himself, had failed to persuade the Hungarian Government, or the Hungarian Regent, Admiral Horthy, to agree to these deportations. Now, in control of Hungary, the Germans hastened to destroy this last unmolested mass of Jewry before Soviet forces, steadily advancing towards Eastern Galicia, entered eastern Hungary.

THE HUNGARIAN DEPORTATIONS CONTINUE: THE LAKE BALATON REGION

Sarvar
600

Papa (and region)
see map 258

Lovasbereny
50

Kapolnasnyek
80

Janoshaza
300

Varpalota
180

Szekesfehervar
1,750

Devecser
150

Csabrendek
50

Veszprem
800

Polgardi
50

Seregelyes
80

Nagyvazsony
30

Racalmas
25

Zalaszentgrot
100

Aba
50

Dunapentele
60

Balatonfured
130

Balatonkiliti
50

Tapolca
600

Kovagoors
40

Enying
170

Siofok
190

Keszthely
see map 262

Lake Balaton

Balatonszemes
50

Simontornya
70

Dunafoldvar
300

Balatonboglar
190

Ozora
70

Cece
50

Kethely
45

Iregszemcse
56

Pincehely
100

Tamasi
200

Nagydorog
70

Nagykanizsa
1,800

Somogyszil
30

Gyonk
55

Nagybajom
90

River Danube

Danube River

0 — miles — 15
0 — kilometres — 20

© Martin Gilbert 1982

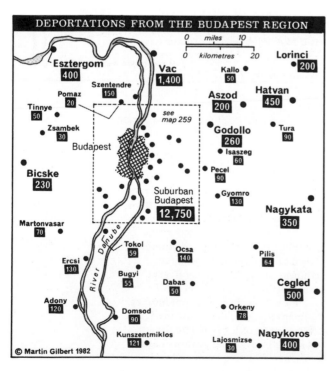

DEPORTATIONS FROM THE BUDAPEST REGION

0 — miles — 10
0 — kilometres — 20

Esztergom
400

Vac
1,400

Lorinci
200

Szentendre
150

Kallo
50

Pomaz
20

Aszod
200

Hatvan
450

Tinnye
50

see map 259

Zsambek
30

Godollo
260

Tura
90

Budapest

Isaszeg
60

Bicske
230

Pecel
90

Gyomro
130

Suburban
Budapest
12,750

Nagykata
350

Martonvasar
70

Tokol
59

Ocsa
140

Pilis
64

Ercsi
130

Bugyi
55

Dabas
50

Cegled
500

Adony
120

Domsod
90

Orkeny
78

Kunszentmiklos
121

Lajosmizse
30

Nagykoros
400

© Martin Gilbert 1982

The Hungarian deportations to Auschwitz continued throughout May and June: and were carried out systematically from region to region. Towards the end of June, and in the first week of July, the deportations were focused on the regions of Lake Balaton *(above)*, Budapest *(left)*, and the outer suburbs of Budapest *(opposite, below)*. Jews from even the smallest of communities were seized *(opposite, above)*, the Nazi aim being to deport every Hungarian Jew to Auschwitz. To this end, Adolf Eichmann personally supervised the deportations from an office in Budapest.

On reaching Auschwitz, only a few from each train, sometimes only a dozen men out of as many as 4,000 deportees, were kept alive for use as slave labourers; the vast majority was taken straight to the gas chambers, and murdered. The corpses were cremated.

The map opposite *(above)* shows the Jewish communities and families from the Papa region, who were deported to Auschwitz on 4 July 1944 and murdered there. In 1942 many of the young Jews of Papa had been sent

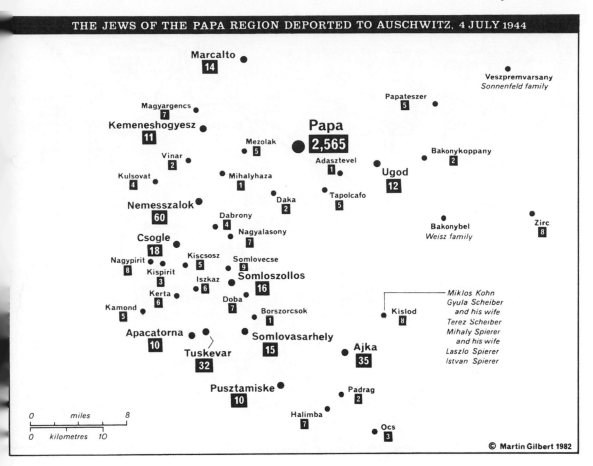

THE JEWS OF THE PAPA REGION DEPORTED TO AUSCHWITZ, 4 JULY 1944

Marcalto
14

Veszpremvarsany
Sonnenfeld family

Magyargencs
7

Papateszer
5

Kemeneshogyesz
11

Mezolak
5

Papa
2,565

Bakonykoppany
2

Vinar
2

Adasztevel
1

Ugod
12

Kulsovat
4

Mihalyhaza
1

Tapolcafo
5

Nemesszalok
60

Daka
2

Dabrony
4

Bakonybel
Weisz family

Zirc
8

Nagyalasony
7

Csogle
18

Kiscsosz
5

Somlovecse
9

Nagypirit
8

Kispirit
3

Iszkaz
6

Somloszollos
16

Kerta
6

Doba
7

Borszorcsok
1

Kislod
8

Miklos Kohn
Gyula Scheiber
and his wife
Terez Scheiber
Mihaly Spierer
and his wife
Laszlo Spierer
Istvan Spierer

Kamond
5

Apacatorna
10

Somlovasarhely
15

Ajka
35

Tuskevar
32

Pusztamiske
10

Padrag
2

Halimba
7

Ocs
3

0   miles   8

0   kilometres   10

© **Martin Gilbert 1982**

to forced labour on the Russian front *(page 171)*. On 24 May 1944 the remaining 2,565 Jews of the town, and more than 200 Jews from nearby villages, had been confined to a ghetto. A few weeks later they were moved to a concentration camp set up in a factory in the town, in readiness for deportation.

As news of the deportations reached the West, together with the first accounts, by escapees, of the working of the gas chambers at Auschwitz, and of the gassing of Jews from the first trains from Hungary, protests poured in to Budapest: from the Allied leaders, from the King of neutral Sweden, from the President of the International Red Cross, and from the Vatican. These protests reached a climax in the first days of July, as the Papa Jews were about to be deported. Tragically, for them, the protests came too late. Even as the Hungarian Government was deciding to order a halt to the deportations, the 2,800 Jews of Papa were being made ready to be sent to Auschwitz; less than 300 survived. Among those who perished was their rabbi, J. Haberfeld.

DEPORTATIONS FROM THE BUDAPEST SUBURBS

0   miles   3

0   kilometres   5

Dunakeszi
200

Ujpest
10,000

Rakospalota
1,800

Csomor
70

Kistarcsa
75

Pestujhely
400

Rakosszentmihaly
660

Rakosliget
176

municipal border 1944

Budapest

Kobanya
4,000

Rakoscsaba
400

Kispest
4,000

Rakoskeresztur
200

Albertfalva
85

Pestszentlorinc
500

Pestszenterzsebet
3,000

Torokbalint
80

Csepel
700

Nagyteteny
140

Soroksar
150

Danube

Map 260

DEPORTATION, MASS MURDER AND REVOLT, JULY 1944

Shauliai *ghetto 'liquidated'*
(Shavli) 15 July

Kovno
8,000
1 July

Vilna

Ponary
19–25 July
3,000
2 July

Jewish partisan units 8 July

Baltic Sea

Stutthof

GREATER GERMANY

Majdanek *liberated 23 July*

Radom
the last **3,000**
slave labourers 26 July

Lublin

Ostrowiec
David Kempinski

Jewish partisan company led by Yehiel Grynszpan

Theresienstadt
4,000
deported six months earlier, gassed at Auschwitz 12 July

SILESIA
3 July Death march
6 July Death march

Auschwitz

Soviet forces

Dachau

S L O V A K I A

Csorna
650 *5 July*

Sopron
1,286
5 July

Koszeg (Güns)
117
4 July

Budapest

Szil
50
5 July

Papa
2,800
4 July

Mor
125

Dunaharaszti
100 *8 July*

Albertirsa
100

Monor
200

Paks
500

Debrecen
13,000
3–8 July

miles 80

kilometres 120

Tolna
120
6 July

Bonyhad
800 *6 July*

Mohacs

500 *5 July*

Decs
40

from Rhodes and Kos

© Martin Gilbert 1982

As Soviet forces approached Shauliai, Kovno, Vilna and Lublin during the first week of July, Jewish partisans were active behind the lines on all these fronts.

On July 2 the SS took the last 3,000 Jews of Vilna, labourers in a factory, and murdered them at Ponary *(above)*. Thousands were also killed at Shauliai, and Kovno, and thousands more evacuated to Stutthof and Dachau, as the Soviet forces drew near. At Ostrowiec, as the SS sent 2,000 slave labourers towards Auschwitz, some succeeded in breaking out and escaping.

On 4 July 1944 the Jews of Papa *(page 186)* were deported to Auschwitz *(above)*. In all, during that first week of July, 50,000 more Hungarian Jews were sent to their deaths *(opposite, above)*. Many of these

deportees lived in small communities to the south of Lake Balaton *(opposite, below)*. Then, on July 8 the Hungarian Government bowed to the growing international pressure, and ordered the deportations to be stopped. The Germans gave way. More than 437,402 Hungarian Jews had been deported; 300,000 were still alive on July 8, most of them in Budapest, where the deportations had been about to begin, having already reached the suburbs *(page 186)*.

Majdanek was entered by Soviet forces on July 23. The SS now accelerated the marches and evacuations away from Auschwitz *(above)*, while from France and Belgium *(opposite, above)*, as well as from Radom, the last few trains were still being sent into Auschwitz. Not only the final Hungarian

DISTANT DEPORTATIONS, JULY 1944

MORE HUNGARIAN DEPORTATIONS, 1–8 JULY 1944

deportees, but Jews from as far away as the islands of Kos and Rhodes were also still on their way to the gas chambers as more and more 'death marches' away from the camp were ordered, and hundreds of Jews were killed as men and women, weakened by hunger and ill-treatment, were marched westwards towards new labour camps.

In Yugoslavia, Jews fought among partisan units which were liberating larger and larger areas of the Balkans.

It was during these evacuations that Dachau, and soon also Bergen-Belsen, hitherto camps primarily for non-Jewish political prisoners, became camps into which tens of thousands of Jews were evacuated, mostly from the labour camp regions of the east, and in which, while not systematically murdered as in the eastern death camps, they perished in their hundreds from the brutality of the guards, and from starvation and disease.

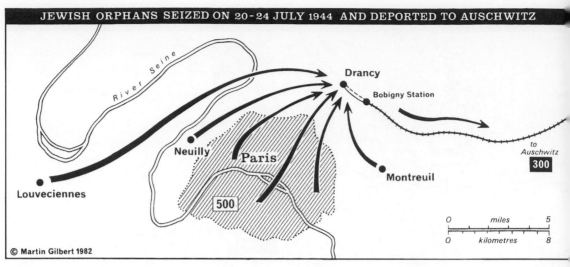

JEWISH ORPHANS SEIZED ON 20-24 JULY 1944 AND DEPORTED TO AUSCHWITZ

River Seine

Drancy

Bobigny Station

Neuilly

Paris

500

Louveciennes

Montreuil

to
Auschwitz
300

0   miles   5
0   kilometres   8

© Martin Gilbert 1982

BIRTHPLACES OF THIRTY-ONE OF THE CHILDREN DEPORTED ON 31 JULY 1944

BELGIUM

LUXEMBOURG

GERMANY

Longwy
Berthe Kerszbaum
aged 12   **Villerupt**
Arnold Nadel aged 14
Leon Nadel aged 9

Thionville
Mireille Korman
aged 12

Hayange
Jacqueline Korman aged 7
Hennette Korman aged 5

S A A R

F R A N C E

Metz

Alice Gliot aged 12
Louise Gliot aged 11
Adolf Gliot aged 10
Charles Gliot aged 7
Renée Grumberger aged 8
Jean Grumberger aged 7
Rolande Grumberger aged 6

Joseph Tabak aged 13
Jacques Tabak aged 7
Nathan Szklarz aged 12
Daniella Szklarz aged 6
Michelle Westreich aged 4

Forbach
Jacques Steinberg
aged 9
Madeleine Steinberg
aged 7

Sarreguemines
Leopold Ratz
aged 12
Liliane Ratz
aged 11

David Holz aged 13
Joseph Holz aged 12
Jacques Holz aged 11
Marianne Holz aged 9
Paul Holz aged 6
Emmanuel Holz aged 4

Odette Krieger aged 13
Genette Krieger aged 9
Nina Krieger aged 7

0   miles   15
0   kilometres   20

Nancy

© Martin Gilbert 1982

On 20 July 1944, while the Allies advanced towards Paris, the SS ordered the arrest of Jewish orphans in the Paris region. Within four days, 500 orphans had been seized, some 300 of whom were among a total of 1,300 Jews deported from Drancy to Auschwitz on 31 July 1944.

The map above, and the maps opposite, show the birthplaces and ages of 67 of these 1,300 deportees. On reaching Auschwitz, 800 of them were gassed, including all the children. Of the 500 adults selected for work in nearby labour camps, 350 survived the last ten months of the war.

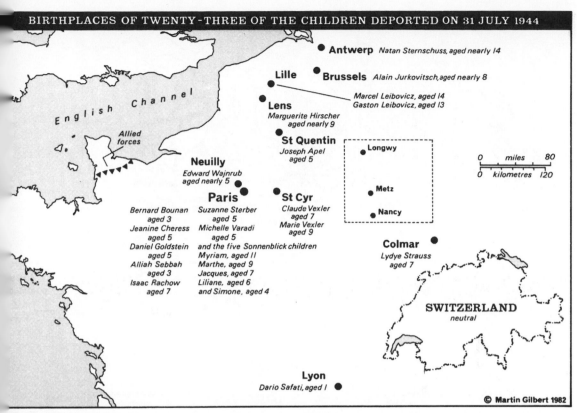

BIRTHPLACES OF TWENTY-THREE OF THE CHILDREN DEPORTED ON 31 JULY 1944

Antwerp *Natan Sternschuss, aged nearly 14*

Lille **Brussels** *Alain Jurkovitsch, aged nearly 8*

Marcel Leibovicz, aged 14
Gaston Leibovicz, aged 13

Lens
Marguerite Hirscher aged nearly 9

St Quentin
Joseph Apel aged 5

Longwy

English Channel

Allied forces

Neuilly
Edward Wajnrub aged nearly 5

Metz

Paris **St Cyr**
Claude Vexler aged 7
Marie Vexler aged 9

Nancy

Bernard Bounan aged 3
Jeanine Cheress aged 5
Daniel Goldstein aged 5
Alliah Sebbah aged 3
Isaac Rachow aged 7

Suzanne Sterber aged 5
Michelle Varadi aged 5
and the five Sonnenblick children
Myriam, aged 11
Marthe, aged 9
Jacques, aged 7
Liliane, aged 6
and Simone, aged 4

Colmar
Lydye Strauss aged 7

0 miles 80
0 kilometres 120

SWITZERLAND
neutral

Lyon
Dario Safati, aged 1

© Martin Gilbert 1982

BIRTHPLACES OF THIRTEEN MORE DEPORTEES, 31 JULY 1944

London

Ruth Mentzel aged 12 and her mother Charlotte, aged 34

Berlin

Milly Pomerance aged 50

Frankfurt

Drancy

Paris

Colmar

Auschwitz

Soviet forces

0 miles 300
0 kilometres 400

Lyon

Black Sea

Marseilles

Adriatic Sea

Claude Korssia aged 5 and his youngest sister Elise, aged 3

Allied forces

Behor Yeruchalmi aged 47

Tlemcen **Oran**
Mina Dahan aged 6

Gabrielle Korssia aged 14
Marcelle Korssia aged 7
Simone Korssia aged 9
and their mother Tama, aged 40
whose two youngest children had been born in Marseilles

RHODES

Jaffa
Eliezer Zlaskine aged 54

Mediterranean Sea

Cairo
Maurice Zeitoun aged 46

© Martin Gilbert 1982

THE ALLIED ADVANCE, 23 JUNE-25 AUGUST 1944

A LABOUR CAMP EVACUATION TO AUSCHWITZ, 22 JULY 1944

Between 23 June and 25 August 1944 both the Soviet and western Allied forces made considerable advances (*opposite, above*). As Bialystok, Lublin and Lvov were liberated, the Germans accelerated the evacuation of Jews away from the advancing Soviet forces.

As Russian troops approached Lublin, 1,200 Jews, many of them prisoners-of-war who had been captured in September 1939, were marched away on foot, westwards to Kielce, where 180 were killed. The survivors were then sent by train to Auschwitz, where 200 were gassed on arrival.

A similar death march and death train evacuation, during which more than 2,000 Jews died, started from Warsaw a week later (*above*). Those evacuated to Zychlin and then to Dachau were Jews who had been brought from Auschwitz to clear the rubble of the Warsaw ghetto. As this evacuation began, 50 of the slave labourers managed to escape into 'Aryan' Warsaw, and were to fight in the Warsaw uprising later that month (*page 193*).

Map 271

DEPORTATIONS, DEATH MARCHES AND REVOLT, AUGUST 1944

© Martin Gilbert 1982

North Sea

Baltic Sea

from Estonia

Stutthof

Ravensbrück

0 miles 100
0 kilometres 200

Soviet forces

Warsaw
uprising
1 August –
15 Sept

Lodz
70,000
6–30 August

Ostrowiec
labour camp
2,000
3 August

Buchenwald

Gross Rosen

Flossenburg

Auschwitz

Plaszow
evacuation begins

Drancy

Paris
51 17 August
uprising
15 – 25 August

Allied forces

Banska Bystrica

Mielec
slave labour camp
3,000
24 August

Gusen

Mauthausen

Novaky

Sered SLOVAKIA
uprising
26 August

Györ

Lyons
uprising
26 August **650**
11 August

Lake Balaton

death march August – October

several thousands
including the poet
Miklos Radnoti

Castres
uprising

Allied forces

Verona
222
2 August

Novi Sad

Belgrade

6,000

Marseilles

Mazamet
uprising

Pisa
7
1 August

Adriatic Sea

Bor
August death march

**Allied landing
15 August**

Allied forces

As the Allied armies advanced, the killing of Jews continued *(above)*, with deportations to Auschwitz from Paris, Lyons and Verona, as well as 70,000 sent to Auschwitz from Lodz, the last of the 'working' ghettos.

The evacuations away from Auschwitz were also gaining in intensity: hundreds died in deportation trains to Ravensbrück and Flossenbürg, Güsen and Mauthausen.

In Pisa the Nazis murdered the Catholic philanthropist Pardo-Roques and six Jews he had sheltered. Hundreds more Jews died

Map 272

SLAVE LABOUR CAMP EVACUATIONS, 28 AUGUST 1944

The front line on 8 August 1944

when the slave labour camps in Estonia *(above)* were evacuated by sea.

During August 1944 Jewish units, and individual Jews, were active in partisan activity in France. In the Warsaw uprising about 1,000 Jews in hiding, and escaped or liberated Jewish slave labourers, took part, including a Jewish battle unit commanded by Shmuel Kenigswein. During the Slovak revolt, a Jewish battalion, as well as hundreds of individual Jews took part in the capture of three major towns.

Map 273

MASSACRE, DEPORTATION AND EVACUATION, SEPTEMBER 1944

Narva
*liberated
21 September*

Klooga
3,000
19-23 September

Lake
Pskov

Lagedi
426

Soviet forces

Riga
*liberated
13 October*

North
Sea

Baltic Sea

25 September

1,019 *3 September*
2,087 *4 September*

HOLLAND

Hamburg
Neuengamme

Westerbork

Stutthof

5,000
*women
evacuated*

3,000
*women
evacuated*

Lodz

500
*men
evacuated*

Christianstadt

Kratzau

Soviet forces

Brussels
*liberated
3 September*

Theresienstadt
2,499
28 September
1,500
29 September

Auschwitz

*hundreds
women
evacuated*

500 *evacuated*

Nancy
*liberated
15 September*

Allied forces

Dachau

SWITZERLAND
neutral

Hungarian
fascist
forces

Csermo

Arad

*liberated
22 September*

Lugos
hundreds
*massacred
4 September*

| 0 | miles | 200 |
| 0 | kilometres | 300 |

Adriatic Sea

© Martin Gilbert 1982

As Allied forces liberated city after city, the murder of Jews continued. During September 1944 four trains reached Auschwitz from Holland and Theresienstadt *(above)*. Almost all the deportees, including all the old people and children, were gassed.

It was on one of these trains from Holland that Anne Frank, a Jewish girl whose parents had brought her to Holland as a refugee from Germany before the war, was most probably deported to Auschwitz. She later died at Bergen-Belsen.

Also during September 5,000 more women were evacuated out of Auschwitz to Stutthof, and 3,000 to Neuengamme. The photograph shows Himmler at Stutthof.

As Soviet forces approached Klooga, almost all the surviving slave labourers were

slaughtered, among them 1,500 Jews from Vilna, 800 Soviet prisoners-of-war and 700 Estonian political prisoners. Only 85 inmates survived.

In the slave labour camp at Lagedi *(above)* all the Jewish prisoners, including women and babies, were killed only a few hours before the Soviet troops arrived. In northern Transylvania, as Hungarian fascist units seized control, hundreds more Jews were massacred.

Meanwhile, from the many slave labour camps of German-occupied Latvia *(opposite)*, tens of thousands of Jews, many of them already deportees from Vilna and Dvinsk *(page 156)*, were being evacuated by ship to the Stutthof concentration camp region, as Soviet forces cut off the Gulf of Riga.

Map 274

SLAVE LABOUR CAMP EVACUATIONS, 25 SEPTEMBER 1944

Narva

Tallin (Reval)
Lagedi
Klooga

DAGO

ESTONIA

Lake Pskov

Baltic

Sea

OSEL

Gulf of Riga

Tartu (Dorpat)

Dondanga

Lenta

L A T V I A

Soviet forces

GOTTLAND

Sloka
Daugavgriva
Berze

Riga
Kaiserwald
Salaspils
Elvia Meibenes

Soviet forces

Dvinsk

Memel

L I T H U A N I A

Soviet forces

Vilna

Königsberg

Danzig
Stutthof

GREATER
GERMANY

EAST
PRUSSIA

Soviet forces

0 miles 80
0 kilometres 120

© Martin Gilbert 1982

Map 275

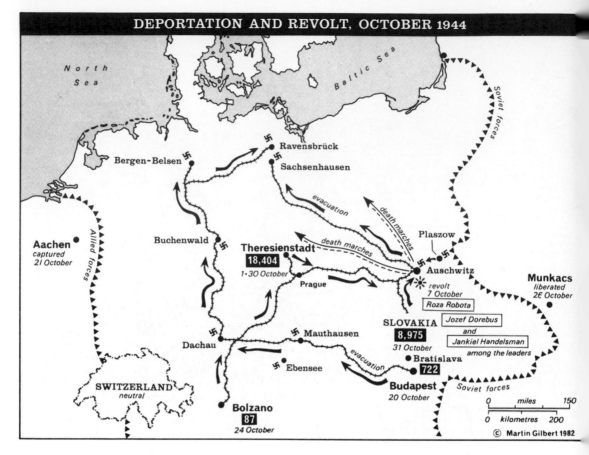

DEPORTATION AND REVOLT, OCTOBER 1944

North Sea

Baltic Sea

Soviet forces

Ravensbrück

Bergen-Belsen

Sachsenhausen

evacuation

death marches

Plaszow

Aachen
*captured
21 October*

Allied forces

Buchenwald

Theresienstadt
`18,404`
1-30 October

Prague

death marches

Auschwitz
*revolt
7 October*
`Roza Robota`

Munkacs
*liberated
26 October*

SLOVAKIA
`8,975`
31 October

`Jozef Dorebus`
and
`Jankiel Handelsman`
among the leaders

Dachau

Mauthausen

evacuation

Bratislava
`722`

Budapest
20 October

Soviet forces

SWITZERLAND
neutral

Ebensee

Bolzano
`87`
24 October

```
0        miles        150
0    kilometres    200
```

© Martin Gilbert 1982

Death marches and death train evacuations took place from Auschwitz, and also from Budapest, throughout October 1944. At the same time, Jews from northern Italy and Theresienstadt continued to be sent to Auschwitz, as were more than 8,000 Jews fom Slovakia, deported as a German reprisal against the Slovak revolt *(page 193)*. Among those deported from Slovakia on October 28 was Tobias Jakobovits, author of a history of the Jews of Bohemia and a member of the staff of the Jewish Museum in Prague; he was sent to his death together with the rest of the museum staff.

In Auschwitz, recently arrived Polish, Hungarian and Greek Jews who were being forced to drag the bodies of those gassed from the gas chambers to the crematoria, having secretly managed to gather some explosives from four Jewish girls working in a nearby munitions factory, blew up one of the four crematoria on 7 October 1944. All those who took part in the revolt were subsequently killed, except for a single Jew, Isaac Venezia, from Salonica, who managed to get back into the main camp. In the final

evacuation of Auschwitz *(page 202)*, he was among those sent to Ebensee, where he died of starvation.

Throughout November 1944 every day saw further towns liberated or captured by the Allies. In the west the Americans were on German soil. In the east the Russians had entered East Prussia, and they had captured the two islands at the mouth of the Gulf of Riga *(page 196)*.

In Auschwitz 8,000 more Jews were gassed during November *(opposite)*, before Himmler ordered the gassing to cease. The last gassings took place on November 28. Thousands of Jews were now sent away from Auschwitz by train to concentration camps and labour camps inside Germany. Among those camps wcre Dachau and Bergen-Belsen, which, while not serving as extermination camps, were nevertheless the scenes of increasing hardship, hunger, disease and brutality. One group of prisoners from Auschwitz was sent to Lieberose, where they were put to work building a special 'city' at Ullersdorf, to serve as a future rest home for German officers.

Map 276

EVACUATIONS AND DEATH MARCHES, NOVEMBER 1944

From Stutthof 12,000 Jews, including 4,000 women, were marched south-westward into Germany. Hundreds were killed, or died from exhaustion, on the march. From Piotrkow the last 400 slave labourers were sent to different camps. From Vamosmikola several thousand Jewish prisoners-of-war were sent on a death march across Germany to Luckenwalde. Hundreds died, or were shot, on the march.

On November 2 tens of thousands of Hungarian Jews were driven from Budapest, as Soviet forces approached the city. Whipped and shot by the SS, they were forced westwards towards Vienna: some 4,000 were saved by the intervention of Raoul

Wallenberg, a Swedish diplomat, but more than 10,000 died during six days of terror.

Amid these catastrophies, Jewish parachutists, recruited by the British in Palestine and dropped behind the German lines, had tried to make contact with the various Jewish partisan groups. One of these parachutists, a woman called Havivah Reik, took part in the final phases of the Slovak uprising, but was killed at Kremnicka. Another, Enzo Sereni, who had been captured in the German lines in Italy, was taken to Dachau and murdered. A third, Hanna Szenes, captured near Nagykanizsa on the Hungarian-Yugoslav border, was taken to Budapest, tortured, and shot.

Map 277

A DEATH MARCH FROM LIEBEROSE, DECEMBER 1944

Sachsenhausen
900 arrive
Oranienburg

miles 15

kilometres 20

River Oder

Falkensee
Falkensee

Spandau

Berlin

Wannsee
Potsdam

Waltersdorf

Schwielow See

Wusterhausen

Wildau
Kablow **2,600** *die on the march*

Storkow

Scharmutzel See

Fürstenwalde

Frankfurt-on-Oder

Glienicke

Buchow

Lindenberg

Beeskow

Bahrensdorf

Friedland

Günthersdorf

Gross Schwiedloch See

Luckenwalde

● **Ullersdorf**

3,500 *set off*

Lieberose

© Martin Gilbert 1982

In December 1944 the Jews who had been sent from Auschwitz to a camp at Lieberose *(page 198)* were evacuated again, forced to march on foot more than 100 miles to the concentration camp at Sachsenhausen *(above)*. More than 3,500 set off. Several hundred, too sick to leave the camp infirmary, were shot, and the building set on fire. The march continued in snow and slush, from first light to darkness. Each night the marchers were ordered to make a left turn, march 20 paces, and lie down. At dawn those who could not rise, or could only stumble, were shot. By the time the march reached its destination less than 900 were still alive.

On 6 January 1945 several hundred Jewish women had been taken by train from the Slovak forced labour camp at Sered to Ravensbrück. As the Soviet forces again moved westward, the remaining labour camps on Polish soil were likewise hastily evacuated *(opposite, below)*. At Skarzysko Kamienna, where 10,000 Jews had perished

in two years, some 5,000 slave labourers were evacuated by train to new camps. A few were able to run away in the confusion, and to hide until the Soviet forces arrived.

Conditions were no better once the evacuees reached their new camps inside Germany. Brutality, savage beatings, sadistic tortures, hunger, senseless hard labour, and shooting at the whim of the guards, were common to all the remaining camps, where overcrowding reached incredible proportion as the evacuations intensified.

The Allied armies were now ready for their final assault on the German heartland *(opposite, above)*. The first to advance, on 12 January 1945, were the Soviet forces. As they did so, the last 47 Jewish slave labourers at the former death camp at Chelmno, knowing that they were about to be shot by the SS as Soviet troops drew nearer, revolted, using a building to hold out in. The SS set fire to the building and then machine-gunned those who fled from it. Only one survived.

THE RED ARMY PREPARES TO ADVANCE, 12 JANUARY 1945

North Sea

Baltic Sea

Danzig
Stutthof

Ravensbrück
Stettin
Hamburg
Sachsenhausen
The Hague
Bergen-Belsen
Berlin
Chelmno
Warsaw
Lodz
Leipzig
Breslau
Skarzysko
Cologne
Gross Rosen
Czestochowa
Mielec
Brussels
Buchenwald
Auschwitz
Plaszow
Frankfurt
Prague
Zilina
Metz
Strasbourg
Sered
Tuttlingen
Dachau
Vienna
Belfort
Munich
Mauthausen
Budapest
Ebensee

SWITZERLAND
neutral

0   miles   150
0   kilometres   200
© Martin Gilbert 1982

Jasenovac

SLAVE LABOUR CAMP EVACUATIONS, AND REVOLT, 17 JANUARY 1945

Ravensbrück

Chelmno
revolt
the last **46** *killed*
1 *escaped*
17 January

Berlin

Warsaw

Soviet forces

River Oder

Lodz region
slave labour camps

Büchenwald

Gross Rosen

Czestochowa

Skarzysko Kamienna
slave labour camp
10,000 ◄ *killed*
5,000 ◄ *evacuated*

Mielec
slave labour camp

Prague

Plaszow
slave labour camp

0   miles   100
0   kilometres   150
© Martin Gilbert 1980

Map 280

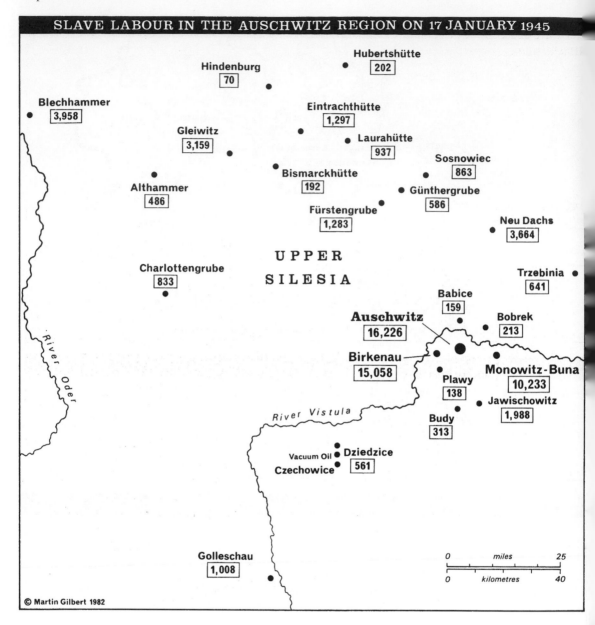

SLAVE LABOUR IN THE AUSCHWITZ REGION ON 17 JANUARY 1945

Hubertshütte
202

Hindenburg
70

Blechhammer
3,958

Eintrachthütte
1,297

Gleiwitz
3,159

Laurahütte
937

Sosnowiec
863

Bismarckhütte
192

Althammer
486

Günthergrube
586

Fürstengrube
1,283

Neu Dachs
3,664

UPPER

SILESIA

Charlottengrube
833

Trzebinia
641

Babice
159

Auschwitz
16,226

Bobrek
213

Birkenau
15,058

Monowitz-Buna
10,233

Plawy
138

Jawischowitz
1,988

River Vistula

Budy
313

Vacuum Oil Dziedzice
Czechowice   561

River Oder

miles   25

kilometres   40

Golleschau
1,008

© Martin Gilbert 1982

On 16 January 1945, shortly after the last slave labourers had been evacuated from Czestochowa, Soviet troops entered the city *(opposite, below)*. On January 17 the SS recorded *(above)* the number of slave labourers in the Auschwitz region: a total of more than 30,000 men and women. On the following day, January 18, orders were given for the immediate evacuation of all slave labour camps in Upper Silesia. The Jews were to go westward, at first on foot.

Hundreds died on these marches, or were shot as they walked. Many died because, too weak to rise after they had fallen down, they froze to death in the snow. The map opposite *(above)* gives the routes and numbers of only a few of these marches, and of the recorded deaths. Hundreds more died whose deaths were never recorded, or whose graves were never found. Several hundred escaped.

The lower map *(opposite)* shows the general direction of the train evacuations from 18 January 1945, and names 25 of the many dozens of camps to which the evacuees were sent. Many were forced to travel in open railway wagons, exposed to the full fury of winter, and hundreds died of starvation or exposure.

DEATH MARCH EVACUATIONS FROM THE AUSCHWITZ REGION, 18 JANUARY 1945

Blechhammer

to Gross Rosen

Gleiwitz

Neu Dachs
3,000

600
in 18 days

50

Mikolow

Janinagrube
800

Soviet front line on 18 January 1945

0 — miles — 8
0 — kilometres — 10

Neu Berun

Zory

Birkenau
1,500

Monowitz
1,000

Sweirklany

Rogozna   172

Cwiklice

Loslau   Wilchwy
43   5   Studionka

17 Auschwitz
3   2,500

Jastrzebia   Poreba   159   Miedzna
32   Mszana   Bzie   36   71   Jawischowitz
26   4   1,948
18

Dziedzice   200   *shot after evacuation*

© Martin Gilbert 1982

THE RED ARMY ADVANCE AND THE AUSCHWITZ REGION EVACUATIONS

North Sea

Baltic Sea

Memel
liberated 27 January

Neuengamme
Hamburg   Ravensbrück

Danzig   Stutthof

Bergen-Belsen   Salzwedel   Sachsenhausen

Gardelegen

Berlin

Dora

Warsaw

Cologne   Nordhausen

Buchenwald

British and United States forces

Ohrdruf   Rehmsdorf

Fulda

Soviet forces on 23 January 1945

Gross Rosen

Czestochowa
6,000
evacuated

Soviet forces on 15 January 1945

Flossenbürg

Loslau   Auschwitz
Birkenau   98,000
4,200   *evacuated*
shot 20 January

French forces

Schömberg

Schörzingen   Gusen
Spaichingen   Dachau
                Mauthausen
Tüttlingen

Munich   Vienna

Schlier   Gunskirchen
          Ebensee

SWITZERLAND
neutral

© Martin Gilbert 1982

0 — miles — 100
0 — kilometres — 150

Budapest
liberated 18 January

Map 283

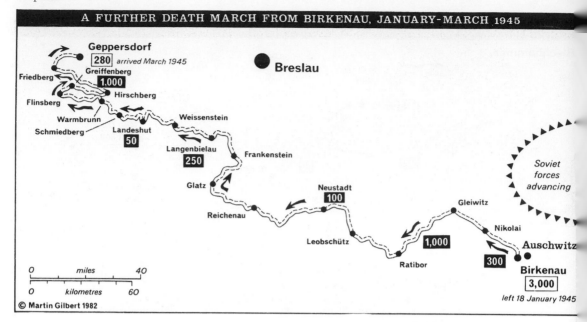

A FURTHER DEATH MARCH FROM BIRKENAU, JANUARY-MARCH 1945

Geppersdorf
280 arrived March 1945

Breslau

Greiffenberg
1.000

Friedberg

Hirschberg

Flinsberg

Weissenstein

Warmbrunn

Schmiedberg Landeshut
50

Langenbielau
250

Frankenstein

Glatz

Neustadt
100

Gleiwitz

Reichenau

Nikolai

Leobschütz

Soviet
forces
advancing

Auschwitz

1,000

Ratibor

300

Birkenau
3,000

0   miles   40

0   kilometres   60

© Martin Gilbert 1982

left 18 January 1945

Among the death marches from Birkenau was one which lasted for more than six weeks. Of the 3,000 who set out on foot, only 280 survived. The map above shows their route, and the numbers who died, or were shot, along the way.

The map opposite shows the route both of this march from Birkenau to Geppersdorf, and of five other evacuations which began in the last ten days of January 1945. The shortest was from Königsberg to the Baltic fishing village of Palmnicken. Most of the 3,700 marchers were Jewish women who had been working in one of the branches of Stutthof camp, in Königsberg itself. They were told that they were to be evacuated by sea. On the way, 700 were shot, some at the whim of the guards, others because they stumbled and fell. Then, as the marchers neared the shore, ostensibly to board the boat, the SS opened fire on them with machine-guns. The women were weak and unarmed. But still the will to live was strong in them, and they tried desperately to escape the withering fire. Three thousand were massacred. But about 60 escaped.

From Danzig, and from Stutthof, 29,000 Jews, most of them women, were evacuated by boat and train to camps in Germany. But only 3,000 survived the journey. Three days earlier, from Lamsdorf camp near Breslau, thousands of Jewish prisoners-of-war (see pages 21–2) had been sent, on foot, westwards towards Thuringia. Their march, like that of the Jews to Geppersdorf, took

more than six weeks, and hundreds died or were killed during its course.

The fifth evacuation shown here had an equally tragic course, but a less terrible ending. Over 100 Hungarian Jews from Auschwitz had earlier been sent to work in a quarry in Golleschau. On 21 January 1945 they too were evacuated, this time by train, from Golleschau. Sealed in two cattle trucks the Jews were shunted north, south, and west. No one on the route dared to open the trucks, which were labelled 'Property of the SS', and 20 of the Jews froze to death as the erratic journey continued. After six days the sealed wagons reached Zwittau, where they were detached from another train and left at the railway station. Learning of this, Oscar Schindler, a German Catholic who owned a number of factories, tried to get permission from the SS to shunt the wagons to his munitions factory at Brünnlitz. He was unsuccessful, but then decided to go personally to the railway station, where he found the bill of lading and wrote on the bottom: 'Final destination — Schindler Factory, Brünnlitz.' The wagons were sent on. When they reached his factory Schindler broke open the locks and released the Jews, giving them shelter, food and warmth, at the risk of his own life.

These were not the first Jews whom Schindler had saved. Earlier, he had brought to his factories prisoners from Plaszow, Gross Rosen and other camps, in theory to employ them as slave labour, but in fact to

Map 284

EVACUATION, MASSACRE AND RESCUE, 20-27 JANUARY 1945

protect them. One of these whom Schindler had saved earlier was Moshe Bejski, a young Polish Jew who was to become a Justice of the Supreme Court in Israel 35 years later. When Schindler died in October 1974, his body was taken to Jerusalem; at his funeral many of those whom he had saved walked in final homage to his burial place on the Mount of Olives.

On 27 January 1945, as Soviet troops entered Auschwitz-Birkenau, they found 648 dead inmates: Jews, Poles and Gypsies.

A FORTY-TWO DAY DEATH MARCH, 26 JANUARY - 11 MARCH 1945

Berlin

River Spree

River Oder

Neusalz *slave labour camp*
1,000 *women left, 26 January 1945*

Christianstadt
28 January

Muskau
1 February

18 February

S I L E S I A

River Elbe

River Neisse

Leipzig

Bautzen
28 February

Dresden

Breslau

Zinnwald
4 March

800
died or murdered on the march

Prague

Marienbad
7 March

Flossenbürg
200 *arrived on 11 March*

Weiden
10 March

0   miles   40
0   kilometres   60

© Martin Gilbert 1982

FROM DEATH MARCH TO DEATH TRAIN

Bergen-Belsen
arrived 24 March

Berlin

River Oder

Neusalz

Muskau

River Elbe

Bautzen

0   miles   60
0   kilometres   80

Nuremberg

Weiden

Marienbad

Prague

Flossenbürg
left 19 March

© Martin Gilbert 1982

One death march, lasting 42 days, consisted of 1,000 Jewish women who had been working as slave labourers at a camp at Neusalz. On 26 January 1945 they were ordered out of the camp and marched south westwards, accompanied by the beatings and shootings which had become a commonplace of death marchers. By the time the marchers reached Flossenbürg *(above)*, all but 200 had been killed. Eight days later the survivors were evacuated again, this time by train *(left)*, and several more had died by the time the train reached Bergen-Belsen.

On 18 February 1945, as the women deportees from Neusalz were crossing the River Spree, more than 500 Jews, hitherto protected because they were married to Christians, were seized throughout Germany and deported to Theresienstadt *(opposite)*. The photograph shows some of the hundreds of children who were sent to Theresienstadt.

Map 287

THE DEPORTATIONS CONTINUE, 18 FEBRUARY 1945

© Martin Gilbert 1982

Map 288

EVACUATION AND REVOLT, MARCH - APRIL 1945

Ravensbrück
9 women escape, caught and executed 30 March

Stettin

Danzig

Soviet forces advancing

Berlin

Leipzig

Lodz

Breslau *besieged*

500

Theresienstadt

Gross Rosen

Karlovy Vary

Prague

Flossenbürg

49

497 *shot* 3 April

Bratislava

Vienna

advancing

Ebensee
182 3 March

Koszeg (Güns) *slave labour camp*

Budapest

Soviet forces

Graz

Venice

Zagreb

Bologna

Jasenovac *revolt* 22 April

Belgrade

Allied front line

570 *killed*

80 *escape*

Florence

Yugoslav partisans

Baltic Sea

Adriatic Sea

0 miles 100
0 kilometres 150

© Martin Gilbert 1982

In March and April 1945 Soviet forces drove deep into Germany. But the desire to kill Jews, and to make use of Jewish slave labour, still dominated Nazi policy. In Bratislava, as Soviet troops approached, the Nazis murdered all 497 members of a Jewish slave labour battalion *(above)*.

From the concentration camp at Gross Rosen, 3,500 prisoners had been marched west and south, away from the advancing Russians. More than 500 died as they were forced through the rubble of Dresden to the concentration camp at Flossenbürg. A further 2,000 Jews from Gross Rosen were evacuated by train to Ebensee, one of the satellite camps of Mauthausen. In all, 49 died on the journey, and a further 182 during the disinfection procedure at the camp on the day of their arrival, 3 March 1945.

From the slave labour camp at Koszeg, where 3,000 Jews had died of hunger, disease, torture and execution in less than a year, the approach of the Russian army led to yet another death march, also to Ebensee, for the camp's 2,000 survivors *(opposite)*. For several weeks they were marched through the hills and mountains of Austria. Anyone who could not get to his feet at the start of the daily march was shot.

Until the summer of 1944 Koszeg had a small Jewish community of 117 people. They had been among the very last Hungarian Jews to be deported to Auschwitz, on 4 July 1944 *(page 187)*, two days before the deportations were brought to an end. Only 15 had survived. Among the dead was the rabbi of Koszeg, Isaac Linksz.

Later in 1944 Koszeg had seen the setting up of the slave labour camp which now, in March 1945, was itself being 'liquidated', in the Nazi terminology.

At Ravensbrück, north of Berlin, nine women who escaped were tracked down, and executed.

In the southernmost areas still under German control, less than 1,000 of Bosnia's 14,000 Jews were still alive, in the concentration camp at Jasenovac. There, on 22 April 1945, 600 prisoners, Jews and non-Jews, rose in revolt and attacked their guards. The guards had machine-guns and grenades. The prisoners had knives, sticks and bare hands. In all, 520 of the prisoners were killed: 80 escaped, of whom 20 were Jews.

The photograph is of a prisoner in Mauthausen who had decided to bring an end to his agony by running against the electrified wire. As more and more Jews and other prisoners were being brought into Mauthausen and its satellite camps the deaths there from brutality and starvation rose precipitately: more than 7,000 Jews died at Mauthausen in just over four months, 15,000 Gypsies, and more than 4,000 Soviet prisoners-of-war *(pages 219–20)*.

Map 289

A DEATH MARCH ACROSS AUSTRIA, MARCH-APRIL 1945

LOWER

River Danube

AUSTRIA

Vienna

UPPER

AUSTRIA

Mauthausen

Gunskirchen

2,000

Neusiedler Sea

Traun Sea

Ebensee

STYRIA

BURGENLAND

Koszeg
(Güns)
slave labour camp

O miles 20

O kilometres 30

© Martin Gilbert 1982

Map 290

FIVE EVACUATIONS, 1-3 APRIL 1945

North Sea

Baltic Sea

Hamburg

Neuengamme

Stettin

Bergen-Belsen

Sachsenhausen
left early April

Berlin

Soviet forces

British forces 1 April 1945

River Oder

Nordhausen
left 3 April

Artern
left early April

Kamenz

16 February – 15 April

American forces 1 April 1945

Dresden

Neustadt
arrived 22 April

Breslau
besieged

Chemnitz

Teplitz

Leitmeritz

Theresienstadt

Mainz

Sudeten mountains

Prague

Heilbronn **42** Crailsheim

Kochendorf
left 1 April
Poles, Czechs,
French, Russians
and Jews

Zobingen

Linz

Amstetten
left early
April

Ulm

Dachau

Wels

Melk

Hütten
47
Lake
Constance

Gmunden

Ebensee
arrived 18 April

Austrian Alps

Soviet forces

SWITZERLAND
neutral

| miles | 100 |
| kilometres | 160 |

0
0

© Martin Gilbert 1982

THREE EVACUATIONS, 3-4 APRIL 1945

From the first days of April it became clear that the Russian and western Allies would continue to advance until they met somewhere in the middle of Germany. But still Hitler hoped that the German army would be able to hold out in a mountainous area, either the Sudeten mountains or the Austrian Alps, and continue the war.

Two separate policies now drove the SS to prolong the agony of the death marches: the desire to prevent the Allies from liberating anyone who had been a witness of mass murder, and the wish to preserve for as long as possible a mass of slave labour for all the needs which confronted the disintegrating army: repairing roads and railway tracks, building up railway embankments, repairing bridges, excavating underground bunkers from which the battle could still be directed, preparing tank traps to check the Allied advance, and helping with the incredibly difficult work involved in preparing mountain fortresses deep underground.

Over and above these reasons, however, there remained the ever-present, all-pervading Nazi obsession that Jews were not human beings, that they must be made to suffer, and that it did not matter if they were to die, however cruel the circumstances. The death marches and death trains therefore continued, despite the increasing chaos on the roads and railways following the collapse of both the western and eastern fronts. The map on the left shows five such evacuations; the map on the right, three more, within less than a week.

With the rapid movement of armies, written records are scarce. The number of dead shown on these two maps represents only a fraction of the number of Jews who died from exhaustion, or brutality, in those four days.

Labour camps such as Ohrdruf had only been opened a few months earlier to enable a future army command centre to be built underground by tens of thousands of Jewish slave labourers who had been evacuated from the east. Now these same Jews were being evacuated again as American and British forces pressed in from the west. To go back east was impossible. Only north and south now lay open to traffic. And so thousands of Jews were taken by train to Bergen-Belsen, Dachau, Leitmeritz, Theresienstadt and Ebensee. In each of these camps conditions became so terrible, dominated by starvation and typhus, that hundreds died every day.

210

Map 292

AMERICAN TROOPS REACH OHRDRUF, 4 APRIL 1945

North Sea

Baltic Sea

Neuengamme

Ravensbrück

Bergen-Belsen

Sachsenhausen

Berlin

Soviet forces.

Gardelegen

River Oder

16 February to 15 April 1945

Allied forces. 4 April 1945

Mittelbau-Dora

Buchenwald

Ohrdruf
liberated 4 April 1945

Gross Rosen

Theresienstadt

Allied forces, 4 April 1945

Flossenbürg

© Martin Gilbert 1982

On 4 April 1945 United States troops reached the village of Ohrdruf *(above)*, where 4,000 camp inmates had died or been murdered in the previous three months, and where hundreds had been shot on the eve of the American arrival. Some of the victims were Jews, others Polish and Russian prisoners-of-war. All had been forced to build a vast underground radio and telephone centre, intended for the German army in the event of a retreat from Berlin.

The sight of the emaciated corpses created a wave of revulsion which spread back to Britain and the United States. General Eisenhower, who visited the camp, was so shocked that he sent photographs of the dead prisoners to Churchill, who at once arranged for several Members of Parliament to visit the camp.

On April 8 many Jewish inmates at Buchenwald, some of whom had only reached the camp from Auschwitz or Stutthof three months before, were marched out, leaving the non-Jewish prisoners to await the arrival of the Americans. The Jews were driven east, then south, to the concentration camp at Flossenbürg. Others, in camps at Aschersleben and Schönebeck, were driven south, then north again, then back south, first on foot and in trucks, then by train, to Leitmeritz. A third group was sent through the Sudeten mountains to Theresienstadt, 60 being murdered at the village of Buchau.

Map 293

FOUR FURTHER EVACUATIONS, 8-16 APRIL 1945

Soviet forces

Magdeburg

Schönebeck
left 12 April

Barby

River Elbe

Aschersleben
left 11 April

Zörbig

Bitterfeld

Delitzsch

Torgau

Leipzig

Colditz

Dresden

River Elbe

Buchenwald
left 8 April

Eisenberg

Weimar

Gera

Jena

Chemnitz

Weida

Freiberg

S A X O N Y

Leitmeritz

Theresienstadt

Johanngeorgenstadt
left 16 April

S U D E T E N L A N D

Plauen

Podersam

Hof

Karlsbad

Buchau
60

B A V A R I A

Eger

S U D E T E N L A N D

Marktredwitz

Bayreuth

Flossenbürg

Weiden

O   miles   30

O   kilometres   40

© Martin Gilbert 1982

Map 294

BRITISH TROOPS REACH BELSEN, 15 APRIL 1945

North Sea

Baltic Sea

Lübeck
Neuengamme
Hamburg
British forces
Bremen
Putlitz
Ravensbrück
Sachsenhausen
Stutthof
Soviet forces

Bergen-Belsen
liberated
15 April
Gardelegen

5,000 deaths
from weakness
and exhaustion
15-25 April
after liberation

Berlin

front line

18 April

Nordhausen
Mittlebau-Dora
Torgau

0   miles   100
0   kilometres   150

Ohrdruf   Buchenwald   Dresden   Soviet forces

liberated
11 April

American forces

15 April

Theresienstadt

Prague

Nuremberg
liberated
16 April

Flossenburg

Moravska
Ostrava

French forces

Stuttgart

Brno

Schömberg
Schörzingen
Spaichingen
Tuttlingen

Dachau

Mauthausen

Vienna

Munich

Günskirchen   liberated by Soviet forces
13 April

Ebensee

SWITZERLAND

© Martin Gilbert 1982

On 15 April 1945, eleven days after American troops had discovered the mass graves of Ohrdruf, British troops entered Belsen (*above*). Here the British found evidence of mass murder on an even vaster scale. Of 10,000 unburied bodies, most were victims of starvation. Even after liberation 500 inmates died each day from typhus and starvation; deaths which continued for more than a week after liberation.

Photographs, films and articles about Belsen circulated widely by the end of April, making so great an impact that the word 'Belsen' was to become synonymous with 'inhumanity'. For these were not reports of discoveries by other armies in the distant corners of the Reich, but of horrors as seen by men from London and Manchester, from the Midlands and the North of England, familiar enough with the horrors of war by April 1945, but shocked as they never

thought they could be by the sights that confronted them. 'There had been no food nor water for five days preceding the British entry', a British army review reported. 'Evidence of cannibalism was found. The inmates had lost all self respect, were degraded morally to the level of beasts. Their clothes were in rags, teeming with lice, and both inside and outside the huts was an almost continuous carpet of dead bodies, human excreta, rags and filth.'

Soldiers and nurses set to work to save those who could be saved. But even the arrival of food was too much for hundreds of the inmates, who died as a result of the 'richness' of the British army rations: dried milk-powder, oatmeal, sugar, salt and tinned meat.

On the same day that British troops entered Belsen, American troops entered yet another camp at Nordhausen, where

Map 295

DEATH MARCHES FROM RAVENSBRUCK AND SACHSENHAUSEN, 19-25 APRIL 1945

Neubrandenburg

Soviet forces advancing

Kölpinsee

Waren

Plauersee

Malchow

Plau

Müritzsee

Neu Strelitz

Fürstensee

Putlitz

Ravensbrück

17,000 women

Stolpsee

Pritzwalk

Wittstock

Zechlin

thousands

Dossow

thousands

Fretzdorf

Rheinsburg

hundreds

Rossow

Rogelin

Katerbow

Alt Ruppin

Lindow

hundreds

Walsleben

Grieben

Löwenburg

Neu Ruppin

Herzberg

Dretzsee

Beetz

Sommerfeld

hundreds

Sachsenhausen

40,000 men

Kremmen

Oranienburg

0 miles 15

0 kilometres 20

© Martin Gilbert 1982

hundreds of slave labourers were found, 'in conditions', as the United Stated Signal Corps recorded, 'almost unrecognizable as human. All were little more than skeletons: the dead lay beside the sick and dying in the same beds: filth and human excrement covered the floors. No attempt had been made to alleviate the disease and gangrene that had spread unchecked among the prisoners.'

At yet another camp, Gardelegen, the American troops found, in a huge open pit, the still burning logs on which the bodies of the dead had been cremated.

As the western Allies now had all the evidence they needed of Nazi atrocities, there could be no purpose in further evacuations. Nevertheless, on 15 April 1945, as the western and Soviet armies drew together, 17,000 women and 40,000 men were marched westwards from Ravensbrück and

Sachsenhausen (above). A Red Cross official who was present, by chance, as the marchers set off from Ravensbrück wrote in his report: 'As I approached them, I could see that they had sunken cheeks, distended bellies and swollen ankles. Their complexion was sallow. All of a sudden, a whole column of those starving wretches appeared. In each row a sick woman was supported or dragged along by her fellow-detainees. A young SS woman supervisor with a police dog on a leash led the column, followed by two girls who incessantly hurled abuse at the poor women.' Many hundreds died of exhaustion in the effort of the march. Hundreds more were shot by the wayside. The march was quite purposeless, except in the pain and death it caused. For the American and Russian troops had almost come together at Torgau in the centre of the Reich, and were to meet there on April 25.

Map 296

FRENCH FORCES REACH FOUR MASS MURDER SITES, 25 APRIL 1945

Free French forces 19 April 1945

ALSACE

River Neckar

Freudenstadt

Swabian Alps

Black Forest

River Rhine

Schömberg
1,771

Schörzingen
549

River Danube

Spaichingen
111

Freiburg

Donaueschingen
9

Tuttlingen
86

W U R T T E M B E R G

BADEN

Schaffhausen

River Rhine

Bodensee

Basel

miles 15
0
kilometres 20
0

S W I T Z E R L A N D
neutral

© Martin Gilbert 1982

In southern Germany it was the turn of French troops to stumble across the evidence of mass murder, and of recent killings. Even amid the beautiful spring fragrance of the Swabian Alps and the upper Danube, it was the stench of death which assailed them.

At four villages mass graves were found of Jews who had earlier been deported from camps and ghettos in the east. With typical Gestapo thoroughness, the names, ages and birthplaces of the victims had all been recorded. The map opposite *(above)* shows some of these birthplaces. The 39-year-old Peisach Rudnitzki had been born in distant Swieciany, where, in September 1941, nearly 4,000 Jews had been murdered, but where several hundred had managed to escape *(page 64),* including his own nephew, Yitzhak Rudnitzki, who survived the war as a partisan with the Red Army, and was later to become (as Yitzhak Arad) chairman of Yad Vashem, the holocaust memorial and archive in Jerusalem.

The Second World War was almost over. Yet no corner of the dwindling Reich was free from killing: on 25 April 1945, the day on which French forces reached Tüttlingen, six Jews were taken by the Gestapo at Cuneo, and shot *(opposite, above).*

Elsewhere, it was a day of historic importance: the meeting at Torgau of Russian and United States forces. Germany had been cut in half. A day later, the Germans evacuated the last survivors of Stutthof by sea to Lübeck *(opposite, below).* Hundreds died during the voyage. Four days later, while the evacuation ships were still at sea, Soviet troops entered Ravensbrück. In that one camp alone 92,000 Jews and non-Jews, most of them women and children, had been murdered in just over two years. But as the Soviet troops overtook the 'death marchers', several thousand were still alive.

That same day, 30 April 1945, Adolf Hitler committed suicide in Berlin.

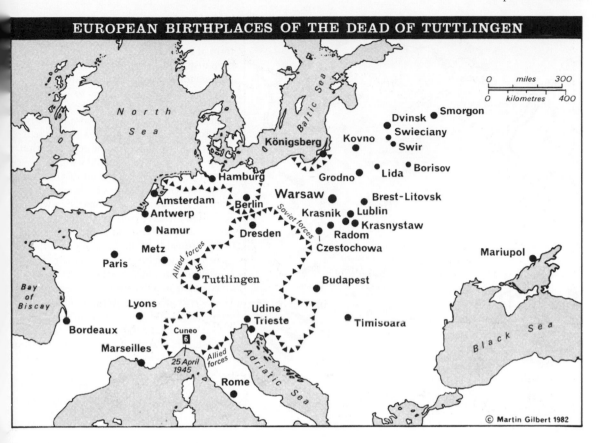

EUROPEAN BIRTHPLACES OF THE DEAD OF TUTTLINGEN

THE STUTTHOF SEA EVACUATION, 26 APRIL 1945

Map 299

THREE EVACUATIONS, APRIL - MAY 1945

Hamburg

Lübeck

Neuengamme
left early April

Ravensbrück
150 released
5 killed by
Allied
bombing

Stettin

Soviet forces

Berlin
occupied
2 May

American and Soviet
forces meet
25 April

Torgau

Nordhausen

Leipzig

Buchenwald

Rehmsdorf

Dresden

2,775
left
20 April

Theresienstadt

575
survived

1,200

Marienbad
1,000 27 April

Pilsen

Nuremberg

United States forces

0   miles   60
0   kilometres   80

Dachau
liberated
29 April

Munich

Mauthausen

Günskirchen

Schlier

Salzburg
captured
4 May

Ebensee
arrived 1 May 1945

Innsbruck
captured
3 May

© Martin Gilbert 1982

Shortly before American troops had
liberated Nordhausen on April 15, one last
train of concentration camp inmates had
been dispatched southwards from
Neuengamme, on the long and difficult
journey across the war zones, to Ebensee.

At the very moment when the German
army itself was made up of those formerly
unfit to serve, many of the guards on the
deportation trains and in the concentration
camps themselves remained the highly
trained criminal élite of the totalitarian state.
They also remained killers to the end: on 27
April 1945, during a death march in which
2,775 Jewish slave labourers were sent
eastward from Rehmsdorf, a satellite camp
of Buchenwald, 1,000 marchers were killed
by machine-gun fire and grenades at
Marienbad station. A further 1,200 were
killed as the march continued eastward to
Theresienstadt, where 500 were killed on
arrival. Only 75 of the marchers survived.

On April 28 the Red Cross arranged with
the SS for the transport of 150 Jewesses from
Ravensbrück to Sweden, the first of 3,500
Jewish and 3,500 non-Jewish women to be
transferred to safety in the last ten days of
the war *(page 223)*. On their way through
Germany, five of the women were killed
during an Allied air-raid.

On April 29 American forces entered
Dachau. The photographs opposite are
amoung thousands that were taken that
day, and in the following week. The top
photograph shows the camp as seen from
one of the guard towers. Hundreds of bodies
still lie in the perimeter ditch and in the open
space between the huts and the ditch. The
lower photograph, taken by an American
serviceman, shows the scene that confronted
the Allied troops. Some of the photographs
taken after the liberation of Dachau are
so terrible that they have never been
reproduced, nor have I felt able to reproduce
them here.

After the war Dachau was used as a
prison for Nazi war criminals, and at a series
of war crimes trials in the town of Dachau,
260 SS functionaries were sentenced to
death. The principal war criminals were tried
at Nuremberg in 1945 and 1946.

In the last year of the war more than
40,000 prisoners had died in Dachau,
of whom 80 per cent were Jews. At
Buchenwald, which American forces had
liberated two weeks earlier, on April 1,
56,549 had died of starvation, disease, or
from the deliberate sadism of the guards.

JEWS MURDERED IN MAUTHAUSEN, JANUARY - MAY 1945

NORWAY **1**

DENMARK **2**

HOLLAND **56**

ENGLAND **1**

LATVIA **5**

SOVIET UNION **25**

GERMANY **187**

POLAND **3,777**

BELGIUM **70**

LUXEMBOURG **4**

CZECHOSLOVAKIA

Mauthausen **135**

HUNGARY **3,214**

RUMANIA **16**

FRANCE **248**

ITALY **67**

YUGOSLAVIA **13**

BULGARIA **1**

GREECE **169**

TURKEY **1**

STATELESS **37**

Baltic Sea

Black Sea

Adriatic Sea

Mediterranean Sea

Aegean Sea

0 miles 300
0 kilometres 400

© Martin Gilbert 1982

FIFTEEN THOUSAND GYPSIES MURDERED IN MAUTHAUSEN, JANUARY - MAY 1945

HOLLAND **3**

POLAND **175**

SOVIET UNION **14,876**

LUXEMBOURG **14**

CZECHOSLOVAKIA **7**

Mauthausen

HUNGARY **1**

RUMANIA **6**

FRANCE **28**

CROATIA **2**

YUGOSLAVIA

ITALY **5**

SPAIN **1**

GREECE **3**

North Sea

Bay of Biscay

Adriatic Sea

Black Sea

Mediterranean Sea

Aegean Sea

0 miles 200
0 kilometres 300

©Martin Gilbert 1982

The last concentration camp to be liberated by the Americans was Mauthausen, together with its satellite camps at Gunskirchen and Ebensee *(pages 221–2)*. In just over four months, more than 30,000 people had been murdered at Mauthausen, or had died from starvation and disease. Jews and Gypsies *(left)*, formed the largest groups of those killed. But other groups had also been singled out by the Nazis for cruel deaths: homosexuals, Jehovah's Witnesses, Soviet prisoners-of-war, and tens of thousands of Spanish republicans. These Spaniards had been interned in France in September 1939, deported by the Germans to Mauthausen in 1940, and systematically worked to death in the stone quarry there, or shot at random, until only 3,000 remained alive by January 1945. Of these, 2,163 were killed in the last months *(opposite, below)*. The commandant of Mauthausen, Franz Ziereis, once boasted that he gave his son 50 Jews 'for target practice' as a birthday present.

All inmates at Mauthausen – Jews, Gypsies, homosexuals, religious prisoners, Russians and Spaniards – were subjected to the same vicious cruelties. Among those held in the camp was a British naval officer, Lieutenant Commander Pat O'Leary, GC, DSO. Leary's biographer, Vincent Brome, has recorded in *The Way Back*, published in London in 1968, how Leary 'became familiar with the gas lorries and the sight of prisoners loaded into them who died on the way to nowhere. He saw men kicked, strangled and beaten to death.'

On one occasion, Leary witnessed what happened when another prisoner, who had managed to escape, was recaptured; an SS guard, Leary recalled, 'launched a tremendous blow to the man's jaw. The prisoner's hand went up to ward off a second blow and the guard kicked him savagely in the stomach. As the man doubled up another sledgehammer blow hit his jaw. He fell down. "Up! Up!" The SS man kicked him to attention again. Then alternately he slogged his jaw and kicked his stomach, eight, nine, ten, eleven times, until one tremendous kick in the pit of the stomach brought blood gushing from the man's mouth; he screamed and fell down. The guard continued kicking him in the face, head, groin and legs. The twitching form at last lay quite inert and the pavement was quickly thick with blood.'

Such beatings were commonplace at Mauthausen: hundreds of prisoners being murdered each month by similar savagery.

HOMOSEXUALS MURDERED, JANUARY – MAY 1945

JEHOVAH'S WITNESSES MURDERED

INTERNEES AND PRISONERS-OF-WAR MURDERED

220

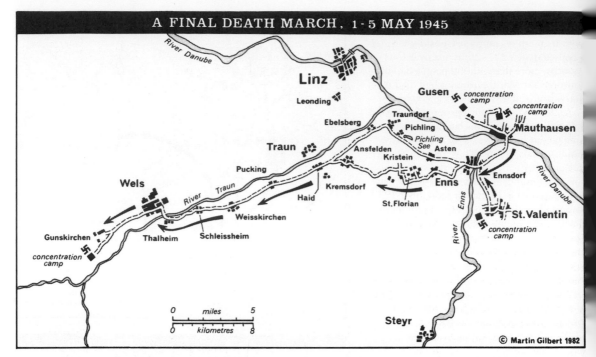

A FINAL DEATH MARCH, 1-5 MAY 1945

River Danube

Linz

Leonding

Traundorf

Ebelsberg

Pichling

Gusen
concentration
camp

concentration
camp

Mauthausen

Traun

Ansfelden

Kristein

Pichling
See

Asten

Pucking

Kremsdorf

Enns

Ennsdorf

River Enns

River Danube

Wels

River Traun

Haid

St.Florian

St.Valentin

Weisskirchen

concentration
camp

Gunskirchen

Thalheim

Schleissheim

concentration
camp

miles 5

kilometres 8

Steyr

© Martin Gilbert 1982

THE DEATH OF GEZA HAVAS, 5 MAY 1945

miles 40

kilometres 60

deported
to Germany
1944

Brno

evacuated to
Mauthausen
April 1945

Mauthausen

Linz

Bratislava

with other
Hungarian Jews,
interned in
various forced
labour camps,
1941-1944

Günskirchen
died a few hours
before the arrival of
the Allied forces,
5 May 1945

Vienna

River Danube

Neusiedler
Sea

Budapest

A U S T R I A

worked as a journalist
from 1936, aged 21.
Edited a collection of
essays on socialism

Lake Balaton

borders of 1937

Graz

H U N G A R Y

Nagykanizsa
born 1905

© Martin Gilbert 1982

Map 307

On 1 May 1945, as the American army approached Mauthausen, the last death marches of the war began, from Mauthausen itself, Gusen and St. Valentin, to Günskirchen (*opposite, above*). Hundreds of marchers fell to the ground as they marched, dying in the mud from sheer exhaustion.

Among those who reached Günskirchen alive was the Hungarian writer and journalist, Geza Havas. But on May 5, only a few hours before the Americans arrived, he died (*opposite, below*).

Starvation, disease and brutality continued to take their toll to the end. From one transport of 4,000 Hungarian Jews, brought earlier to Mauthausen from Auschwitz, and then marched to Günskirchen and Ebensee, only 300 were alive on the day of liberation. Of 1,000 Polish civilian workers, non-Jews, brought to Ebensee from Earsaw in September 1944, only 100 survived. At Ebensee, as the American armies approached, all 30,000 prisoners were ordered into a tunnel packed with explosives. As the historian of Mauthausen, Evelyn Le Chêne, has written: 'The prisoners, to a man, blankly refused. The SS guards were paralysed with indecision. The hordes of humans swayed and murmured. For the first time since their arrest, the prisoners who were not already dying saw the possibility that they might just survive the war. Understandably, they neither wished to be blown up in the tunnel, nor mown down by SS machine-guns for refusing. But they knew that in these last days, many of the SS had left and been replaced by Volksdeutche. A quick consultation with some of his command made it clear to the Commandant that they too were reluctant either to force the men into the tunnel, or to shoot them down. With the war all but over, they were thinking of the future, and the punishment they would receive for the slaughter of so many human beings was something they still wished – even with their already stained hands – to avoid. And so the prisoners won the day.'

When American troops reached Mauthausen, they found nearly 10,000 bodies in a huge communal grave. Of the 110,000 survivors, of whom 28,000 were Jews, more than 3,000 died after liberation (*right*). Some died because they were too weak or sick to be nursed back to health, others because they left the camp before they were strong enough to begin normal life again.

THE LAST LIBERATIONS, 4–8 MAY 1945

© Martin Gilbert 1982

222

Map 308

WOMEN SURVIVORS OF THE CAMPS DYING IN SWEDEN, MAY - NOVEMBER 1945

Stockholm

SWEDEN
● Karlstad
Norrköping

● Göteborg

● Halmstad
● Kalmar

Helsingborg

● Malmo

North Sea

Baltic Sea

Vilna
*Henia Azulanscha
aged 20*

Hamburg

Ravensbrück
7,000
*evacuated
28 April*

Warsaw
Rozika Rosenbaum aged 30

Lodz *Rachela Galster aged 40*

Amsterdam

Dresden
*Helena Hausmann
aged 20*

Sosnowiec
*Zofia Alterwein
aged 29*

Czestochowa *Bronislawa Dorfman aged 16*

Cracow *Cesia Kleiner aged 18*

*Lena Veffer
aged 21
Anna Watterman
aged 24
Eugelina Lissauer
aged 14
Rosette Bas
aged 20
Fre van Leer
aged 28*

Prague
*Anne Goldschmidt
aged 46
Gerda Fischelova
aged 23*

Lucenec
*Sara Ehrenfeld
aged 23*

Uzhgorod *Dina Rothstein aged 22*

Novoselitsa *Helen Abrahamovitsch
aged 22*

Beregszasz
Rozalia Katz aged 20

Györ
*Hedwig Gestettner
aged 25*

Budapest
*Ilona Delikat
aged 34
Erzsebet Kohn
aged 33
Judit Sandor aged
17*

Cluj (Kolozsvar)
*Sarolta Samu
aged 41
Ewa Aron
aged 17*

ITALY
*Regina Cepparo
aged 43*

Adriatic Sea

Belgrade
*Sara Krystik
age unknown*

Black Sea

© Martin Gilbert 1982

On 8 May 1945 the Allies accepted the unconditional surrender of Germany. More than eleven million civilians had been murdered in cold blood since the German invasion of Poland more than five years before. Among those eleven million were six million Jews *(page 231)*.

Czechs, Frenchmen, Greeks, Italians, Poles, Russians and Serbs had been among the millions of non-Jewish civilians killed in reprisal actions, and in mass executions. But only the Jews had been systematically searched out for death from every region, city, town, village and hamlet of German-dominated Europe. The Nazi aim was to ensure that not one single Jew survived, and 'Jew' was defined as anyone with Jewish parents, a single Jewish parent, or even a single Jewish grandparent.

Despite the Nazi intention, and as a result of the sudden collapse of the German armies, between 250,000 and 300,000 Jews survived the concentration camps and death marches. But the coming of the Allied victory could

not save tens of thousands of these 'survivors', who, as at Dachau, Belsen and Ebensee, were too weak and too sick to live more than a few days, weeks or months, despite all the care and attention lavished upon them, by their liberators. Also, as the historian Evelyn Le Chêne has written: 'Many died from sheer joy. They had lived on hope, on fear and on their nerves for so long that the sudden relaxation of tension, when it came, was too much for them.'

The map above gives the names, ages and birthplaces of 26 out of 3,500 Jewish women who, released from Ravensbrück after Red Cross intervention on April 28 1945 *(page 217)* and sent from there to Sweden, died in the Swedish towns shown here, between May and November 1945. The oldest was 46, the youngest, 14. These women all died after liberation, as had more than 5,000 prisoners at Belsen *(page 213)* and 3,000 at Mauthausen *(page 222)*. Others, amid the confusions and hardships of the immediate post-war world, slowly regained their strength.

Map 309

THREE YOUNG SURVIVORS REACH ULM

Among the survivors who reached western
Germany after the German surrender
in 1945 were several hundred children
who were taken to a children's home at
Ulm *(above)*. There, each child was
photographed, and such details as they could
recall were set down. Three of those children
are shown on the left.

Of Idel Levitan *(top)*, born in Lithuania,
the son of Micha and Mira Levitan, those
who questioned him noted: 'He was with his
parents in the Ghetto in Kovno. His parents
gave him to Christians. Parents were killed.
An aunt took him from the Christians, to
Lodz, from where he came with a Kibbutz
to Ulm, to the Children's Home.'

Of Renja From *(middle)*, born in Eastern
Galicia, the interviewer noted: 'She thinks
that at the outbreak of the war her mother
gave her to Poles. She knew then that she is
Jewish, but the Christians with whom she
was living forbad her to speak about it. She
learned that her mother was murdered by the
Germans and thrown into a ditch. She does
not remember her father. An acquaintance
of her family took her to Germany, to the
Children's Home at Ulm.'

Of Zlata Tauber, born in 1941, the
person who interviewed her wrote: 'She
does not remember her parents, she only
knows that she has been in Russia. One
brother is in Poland, but he does not want
to be Jew because of the persecutions they
had to go through. She therefore renounced
on him.'

SOME BIRTHPLACES OF DACHAU SURVIVORS

Baltic Sea

Borders of 1937

Gdynia

Bialystok

Mlawa

River Vistula

Gostynin

Klodawa

Kutno

Lodz

Mszczonow

Warsaw

Kalisz

Sieradz

Pabianice

Radom

Lublin

Belchatow

Piotrkow

Wielun

Szydlowiec

P O L A N D

Kielce

Sandomierz

Czestochowa

Zawierce

Bedzin

Olkusz

Sosnowiec

Radomysl

Auschwitz

Tarnow

Cracow

Bielsko

Nowy Targ

C Z E C H O S L O V A K I A

Kosice

Satoraljaujhely

Miskolc

Komarom

Esztergom

Eger

Hatvan

Vac

Jaszbereny

Sopron

Györ

Tatabanya

Budapest

Papa

Monor

Debrecen

Szombathely

H U N G A R Y

River Danube

Bekescaba

Lake Balaton

Nagykanizsa

Szeged

Kaposvar

Baja

Mako

Pecs

© Martin Gilbert 1982

MORE DACHAU SURVIVORS

North Sea

Baltic Sea

Riga

Vilna

Oszmiana

Kovno

Amsterdam

Berlin

Warsaw

Rotterdam

Lodz

Kiev

Przemysl

Beregszasz

Dachau

Vienna

Cluj

Budapest

Rome

Salonica

Corfu

Rhodes

Mediterranean Sea

© Martin Gilbert 1982

The map on the left and the map above show the birthplaces of most of the Jews who had been liberated by the Americans in Dachau. Gradually restored to physical health, many were still distressed. 'It seems to us', Dr. Zalman Grinberg told his fellow survivors at the end of 1945, 'that for the time being mankind does not understand what we have gone through and what we have experienced. We fear we will not be understood in future. We unlearned to laugh, we cannot cry any more, we do not understand our freedom yet, all this because we are still with our dead comrades . . . We belong in the mass-graves of those shot in Kharkov, Lublin and Kovno. We belong to the millions gassed and burned in Auschwitz and Birkenau. We belong to those tens of thousands tormented by milliards of lice, living in mud on a starvation diet, with coldness and despair as companions. We are not alive. We are dead!'

The photograph, taken after the liberation of Buchenwald, shows some of the survivors of death marches and evacuation trains (*maps 261, 271, 276, 279, 282, and 284*).

The majority of those who survived the Holocaust sought a new life beyond Europe. The map opposite gives the approximate number who went to the principal havens.

Map 312

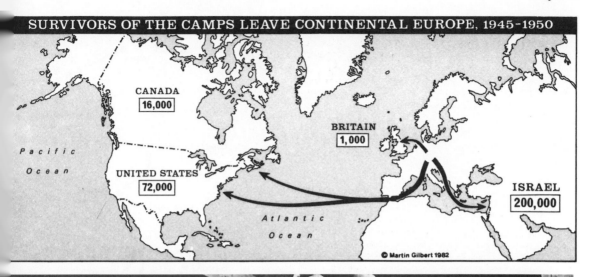

SURVIVORS OF THE CAMPS LEAVE CONTINENTAL EUROPE, 1945-1950

CANADA
16,000

BRITAIN
1,000

Pacific
Ocean

UNITED STATES
72,000

ISRAEL
200,000

Atlantic
Ocean

© Martin Gilbert 1982

Map 313

ONE MAN'S JOURNEY, 17 JANUARY - 24 OCTOBER 1945

Baltic Sea

Kovno

Vilna
17 January

Minsk
18 January

Baranowicze
19 January

Brest-Litovsk
21 January

Kowel
22 January

Przemysl
9 February

Rzeszow
26 February

Lvov
23 January and 31 January

Sanok
2 March

Stanislawow
27 January

Ungvar
5 March

Beregszasz
6 March

Satu Mare
8 March

Oradea Mare
9 March

Szombathely
11 July

Graz
12 July

Budapest
7 July

Cluj
10 March
and 2 June

Milan
15 August

Tarvisio
17 July

Mestre
22 July

Arad
5 July

Alba Julia
3 July

Padua
24 August

Bologna
13 September

Bucharest
11 March to
30 June

Adriatic Sea

Bari
15 September

to Palestine, 24 October

© Martin Gilbert 1982

miles 150

kilometres 250

Between 1944 and 1948 some 200,000 survivors left Europe for Palestine, then a British Mandate. Incredibly, the killing of Jews had continued in Poland for more than two years after Germany's surrender *(opposite)*. It was this Polish anti-semitic violence that gave a strong impetus to the 'Bricha', or flight of the Jews to Palestine. Thus, after the killing of two young Jews in Biala Podlaska, all 30 survivors left. In Lublin, Leon Felhendler, one of the leaders of the Sobibor revolt *(page 160)*, was likewise killed; also killed in Lublin, on 19 March 1946, was Chaim Hirschmann, one of only two survivors of Belzec death camp.

The flight to Palestine gained its culminating force with a pogrom in Kielce in which 41 Jews were killed. But the 'Bricha' itself had begun with each region's liberation. Thus, shortly after the liberation of Vilna, Dov Levin, a young Jew from Kovno who had fought with the Soviet partisans, embarked on a typical, but nevertheless remarkable journey *(above)*. The war ended while Levin was in Bucharest. But he continued his journey to Palestine.

Map 314

POST-WAR KILLINGS AND THE FLIGHT OF THE SURVIVORS, 1944-1948

North Sea

SWEDEN

Baltic Sea

BALTIC STATES

Hamburg

Stettin

Kovno
Vilna

Sokoly
Bialystok

POLAND   **1,000**   *Jews murdered between liberation and mid-1947*

Berlin

Boleslawiec   **8**

GERMANY

Warsaw

Biala Podlaska   **2**

Parczew   **4**

100,000

fled from Poland

Turek   **1**

Nachod

BOHEMIA

Kielce   **41**

Lublin   **2**

Piaski   **5**

VOLHYNIA

Ulm

Munich

Feldafing

AUSTRIA

SLOVAKIA

Snina

Mordy   **7**

Polaniec   **5**

UKRAINE

FRANCE

Salzburg

Bratislava   **16**

Skarzysko-Kamienna   **5**

BESSARABIA

Villach

Budapest   Diosgyor   **1**

Port de Bouc

Spezia

HUNGARY

BUKOVINA

Marseilles

Kunmadaras   **3**

RUMANIA

Le Ciotat

Sisak

YUGOSLAVIA

Bucharest

Adriatic Sea

Ancona

ITALY

Burgas

BULGARIA

Black Sea

Bari

GREECE

Athens

TURKEY

Mediterranean Sea

CYPRUS
British

0   *miles*   300

0   *kilometres*   500

PALESTINE
British Mandate

© Martin Gilbert 1982

Map 315

SURVIVORS, AND THOSE WHO RETURNED, 1945

NORWAY
1,000

FINLAND
2,000

SWEDEN

DENMARK
5,500

DANZIG
8,000

Memel

BALTIC STATES
25,000

WESTERN
SOVIET
UNION
300,000

HOLLAND
20,000

BELGIUM
40,000

GERMANY
330,000

POLAND
225,000

LUXEMBOURG
1,000

CZECHOSLOVAKIA
44,000

AUSTRIA
7,000

HUNGARY
300,000

RUMANIA
430,000

SWITZ.

FRANCE
200,000

ITALY
35,000

YUGOSLAVIA
12,000

BULGARIA
50,000

SPAIN

Frontiers
of 1937

ALBANIA
200

GREECE
12,000

CRETE
7

RHODES
161

© Martin Gilbert 1982

miles 250

kilometres 400

In addition to the 300,000 survivors of the concentration camps, over a million and a half European Jews survived Hitler's efforts to destroy them. Some were fortunate, as in Germany, to escape from Europe before the outbreak of war or, as in Hungary, that liberation came before the plans for their destruction could be completed. Others, as in Rumania, were saved when their Government, hitherto anti-Jewish, changed its policy in anticipation of an Allied victory. The Jews of Bulgaria were saved by the courage of the Bulgarian people *(page 140)*. The majority of the Polish Jews shown here survived because they found refuge in 1939 and 1940 in Soviet Central Asia. More than 20,000 French, Belgian and Dutch Jews had found refuge in Switzerland, Spain and Portugal. Denmark's Jews had been smuggled to safety in Sweden *(pages 153–4)*.

Some Jews everywhere, but particularly in France, Belgium, Holland and Italy, survived because the Germans took longer to deport them than time finally allowed: the Allied landings on continental Europe coming while deportations were still in progress. Other Jews all over Europe escaped deportation altogether because they were sheltered by individual non-Jews who risked their own lives to save Jews.

Map 316

NON-JEWS WHO HELPED SAVE JEWISH LIVES, 1939–1945

In every country of Europe, non-Jews saved Jewish lives during the Holocaust. Many risked their own lives to do so. This map shows the number of non-Jews recognized by the State of Israel since 1953 for saving Jews. The Polish figure – the largest – includes the members of an organization, known by its Polish initials ZEGOTA, which saved more than 4,000 Jews, 2,500 of them being Jewish children, under the supervision of a Polish Catholic, Irena Sendlerowa. The Norwegian figure includes a collective award to the members of the Norwegian resistance who helped smuggle Jews to neutral Sweden. One of the Danish awards is for the whole Danish people, who helped send almost all Denmark's Jews across the water to Sweden. The Turkish citizen shown, Selâhattin Ülkümen, was a diplomat who saved a number of Jews from deportation on the island of Rhodes. The Swedish figure includes the diplomat Raoul Wallenberg, and his colleague Per Anger, who saved many thousands of Jews in Budapest. Not shown on the map is an American, Varian Fry, who enabled Jews to leave France for the United States; a Chinese diplomat Feng Shan Ho, who gave exit visas for several thousand Jews in Vienna and an Armenian doctor, Dr. Ara Jeretzian, who saved more than forty Jews in Budapest.

In all, as the map opposite shows, more than 1,600,000 of the Jews who were alive in Europe in September 1939, were still alive in May 1945.

Map 317

JEWS MURDERED BETWEEN 1 SEPTEMBER 1939 AND 7 MAY 1945

FINLAND
11

NORWAY
728

— German Reich in 1937

—·—·— International Frontiers in 1937 (Northern Transylvania in 1940)

line of furthest German advance 1942

ESTONIA
1,000

LATVIA
80,000

North Sea

DENMARK
77

MEMEL
8,000

LITHUANIA
135,000

WHITE RUSSIA (BYELORUSSIA)

WESTERN RUSSIA

Baltic Sea

HOLLAND
106,000

BELGIUM
24,387

FREE CITY OF DANZIG
1,000

GERMANY
160,000

POLAND
3,000,000

VOLHYNIA

SOVIET UNION
1,000,000

English Channel

PODOLIA

GALICIA

RUTHENIA

BUKOVINA
124,632

UKRAINE

LUXEMBOURG
700

CZECHOSLOVAKIA
217,000

60,000

BESSARABIA

200,000

FRANCE
83,000

AUSTRIA
65,000

HUNGARY
267,800

NORTHERN TRANSYLVANIA
105,000

CRIMEA

ROMANIA
40,000

Black Sea

YUGOSLAVIA
60,000

ITALY
8,000

Adriatic Sea

7,122

4,221

MACE-DONIA

THRACE

Aegean Sea

Allied front line October 1943

ALBANIA
200

Mediterranean

KOS
120

RHODES
1,700

GREECE
65,000

CRETE
260

Sea

0   kilometres   400

0   miles   250

LIBYA
562

© Martin Gilbert 2008

231

By the most exact estimates of recent research, the number of Jews killed in Europe between September 1939 and May 1945 was nearly six million. This estimate is a minimum; the deaths shown opposite total just over 5,750,000, and are based on such country-by-country and region-by-region records as survive. These records are listed in the bibliography which follows.

Such a total, however, can never be complete. Thousands of infants and babies were murdered, by the Nazi killings squads in the autumn of 1941, for example, before their birth could be recorded for any 'statistical' purpose. Thousands more individuals, especially in the remoter villages of Poland, were 'added' to the deportation trains which left larger localities, without

any numerical register being made of their existence or fate. For several hundred Jewish communities throughout Europe, the most that the historical research of more than 35 years has been able to record is some phrase such as: 'the fate of this community is unknown'. Yet that community, perhaps of 100, or even 1,000 Jews, had existed in 1939, and had been destroyed by 1945.

Throughout Europe, the traveller to this day comes across monuments and gravestones to the victims. Stones mark the mass graves of individuals of whom nothing will be known: not their names, their ages, their birthplaces, nor indeed their total number. The photograph shows one such 'war grave', to 11 'unknown' Jews, killed in Austria in the early months of 1945.

232

Epilogue

An increasing number of visitors go each year to visit Holocaust-related sites. The maps that follow show the Warsaw and Theresienstadt ghettos, Majdanek, and Auschwitz I, II (Birkenau) and III (Buna-Monowitz). One of the two Theresienstadt maps shows the deportations into and out of Theresienstadt. I have also mapped the death camps of Belzec, Chelmno, Treblinka and Sobibor, and the main towns and villages in German-occupied Poland from which Jews were deported to them.

Map 318

PRINCIPAL DEPORTATIONS TO CHELMNO, DECEMBER 1941–MAY 1943

N

- Towns and villages from which Jews were deported to Chelmno

Rail and road deportation routes

Wloclawek
Radzejow
Brzesc Kujawski
Lubraniec
Piotrkow Kujawski
Izbica Kujawska
Sompolno
Chodecz
Gostynin
Gabin
Sanniki
Brdow
Krosniewice
Zychlin
Klodawa
Kolo
Kutno
River Warta
River Vistula
River Bzura
Chelmno
Grabow
Wladyslawow
Brudzew
Dabie
Leczyca
Tuliszkow
Ozorkow
Turek
Poddebice
Lodz
Kowale Panskie
Dobra
Uniejow
Brzeziny Lodzkie
Kozminek
River Ner
Lutomiersk
Warta
Pabianice
Sieradz
Zdunska Wola
Lask
Brzeziny
Zloczew
Belchatow
Lututow
River Warta
Wieruszow
Kielczyglow
Wielun
Boleslawiec
Siemkowice
Pajeczno
Praszka
Dzialoszyn

0   kilometres   30

0   miles   20

© Martin Gilbert 2008

235

Map 319

CHELMNO DEATH CAMP

Chelmno was in operation from 8 December 1941 until spring 1943, and again, when Jews from the Lodz ghetto were deported there in July and August 1944. More than 250,000 Jews were murdered there.

to Chelmno village

MAIN ROAD

to Kolo

Gas vans from Zawadki

1. Roadside memorial marker

2. Museum

3 Grave of executed Polish hostages

4. Monument-mausoleum

5. Old Jewish tombstones brought in the 1980s from the town of Turek

6. Site of children's barrack

7. Mass graves

8. Recently established memorials

9. Crematorium furnaces

© Martin Gilbert 2008

Map 320

PRINCIPAL DEPORTATIONS TO BELZEC, MARCH–DECEMBER 1942

Pilica
Wolbrom
Skawina
Dzialoszyce
Cracow
Makow
Wieliczka
Bochnia
Rabka
Brzesko
Nowy Targ
Dabrowa Tarnowska
Radomsyl
Zakliczyn
Tarnow
Tuchow
Debica
Mielec
Stary Sacz
Nowy Sacz
Pilzno
Ropczyce
Szczawnica
Biecz
Wielopole
Glogow
Sokolow
Kolbuszowa
Gorlice
Frysztak
Strzyzow
Rzeszow
Krynica
Jaslo
Niebylec
Blazowa
Zolynia
Krosno
Jasienica
Lancut
Dukla
Brzozow
Rymanow
Sanok
Radymno
Zagorz
Zaslaw
Przemysl nad
Olszanica
Ropienka

Jedlinia
Garbatka
Kazimierz
Wawolnica
Opole Lubelski
Lublin
Lubartow
Zawichost
Annopol
Sandomierz
Urzedow
Dzierkowice
Leczna
Tarnobrzeg
Krasnik
Zakrzowek
Baranow
Radomyslnad
Piaski
Sanem
Modliborzyce
Ulanow
Siennica
Goraj
Rozana
Frampol
Krasnystaw
Bilgoraj
Szczebrzeszyn
Izbica Lubelska
Krasniczyn
Zamosc
Lezajsk
Zwierzyniec
Tarnogrod
Dubienka
Jozefow
Komarow
Osada
Cieszanow
Tomaszow Lubelski
Hrubieszow
Tyszowce
Belzec Village
Laszczow
Belzec
Lubaczow
Uhnow
Niemirow
Rawa Ruska
Belz
Jaworow
Mosciska
Sokal
Zolkiew

Stary Sambor
Sambor
Rudki
Turka
Komarno
Lvov
Kamionka Strumilowa
Szczerzec
Busk
Boryslaw
Drohobycz
Mikolajow
Brody
Truskawiec
Rozdol
Olesko
Zydaczow
Bobrka
Sasow
Skole
Stryj
Chodorow
Narajow
Zloczow
Bolechow
Zurawno
Rohatyn
Zborow
Dolina
Bukaczowce
Pomorzany
Bursztyn
Brzezany
Jezierno
Bolszowce
Zbaraz
Podhajce
Tarnopol
Stanislawow
Mikulince
Skalat
Monasterzyska
Tlumacz
Buczacz
Chorostkow
Peczenizyn
Czortkow
Kopyczynce
Jablonow
Kolomyja
Tluste
Zablotow
Pistyn
Horodenka
Zabie
Zaleszczyki
Kuty
Korolowka
Kosow
Sniatyn
Roznow
Mielnica

0   kilometres   100
0   miles   60

● Towns and villages from which
● Jews were deported to Belzec,
   March to December 1942

↗ Rail and road deportation routes

© Martin Gilbert 2008

Map 321

BELZEC DEATH CAMP

Belzec was in operation from 17 March until 12 December 1942.
More than 600,000 Jews were murdered there.

Anti-tank ditch (1940)

Watchtower

Mass graves

Gas Chamber

Mass graves

Watchtower

Mass graves

'The Tube'

Central watchtower

Mass graves

Mass graves

Camp workshops

Camp garage

Undressing and haircutting barracks

Warehouses of the belongings of the victims

Anti-tank ditch (1940)

Ukrainian guards' compound

Gate house

Gallows

Main gate

Platform (ramp)

Wartime rail spur

Jewish slave labour barracks

Watchtower

① Present-day road into camp

to Lublin   Present-day | main railway line   to Lvov

to Belzec village and Lublin   Main road   Route 17   to Lvov

Between 1997 and 1999, archeologists from the Nicolas Copernicus University of Torun, led by Professor Andrzej Kola, drilled down into the earth at Belzec and found the locations of 33 mass graves. In the field of industrial slag laid down over the whole camp site in 2003 and 2004, darkly coloured areas of slag demarcate the locations of these mass graves. The remains of thousands of unburned bodies were found. Out of respect for the dead, the graves were not opened and the bodies were not exhumed. A memorial trench was dug through the site, a museum established, and, in the area of the railway ramps where the trains stopped to unload their human cargo, a memorial was built. It is based on the pyres that were constructed for the burning of the corpses from the mass graves. A new path completely encircles the camp. Along this path are inscribed, in cast-iron lettering, the names of the towns and villages from which Jews were deported to Belzec and murdered.

××××× Original inner camp perimeter

– – – – – Perimeter of present-day camp memorial area

Original buildings, no longer existing

Mass graves, located 1997 to 1999

① Present-day road into camp

© Martin Gilbert 2008

Map 322

PRINCIPAL DEPORTATIONS TO SOBIBOR, MAY 1942–OCTOBER 1943

Towns and villages from which Jews were deported to Sobibor, May 1942-October 1943

Rail and road deportation routes

For deportations from Holland to Sobibor, see map 198

River Bug

Slawatycze

Biala Podlaska

Wlodawa

Sobibor

Dubienka

GREATER

Chelm

Hrubieszow

Uchanie

Siedliszcze

Grabowiec

Leczna

Lubartow

Firlej

GERMANY

Gorzkow

Izbica Lubelska

Lysobyki

Michow

Lublin

Baranow

Zolkiewka

Ryki

Markuszow

Turobin

Konskowola

Wysokie

Deblin

Pulawy

Wawolnica

Zakrzowek

Belzyce

Urzedow

Modliborzyce

Opole

Dzierkowice

River Vistula

Jozefow

Annopol

0   kilometres   25

0   miles   15

© Martin Gilbert 2008

Map 323

SOBIBOR DEATH CAMP

Mass graves

Camp III

Cremation pyres

Memorial mound of ashes

Monuments (site of gas chamber)

Barracks where women's hair was cut off

'route to heaven'

Jewish 'death brigade' compound

Camp IV

Ammunition bunkers

to Wlodawa → *to Wlodawa →*

main railway line

Barracks for sorting clothing and luggage

Luggage store

Undressing area

Collection of money & valuables

Museum

Present-day Car Park

Inner Gate

Camp II

Orchard

Ukrainian compound

Watchtower

Garden

original site

site today

Ramp

Sobibor was in operation from April 1942 until a revolt of the Jewish slave labourers there in October 1943. More than 250,000 Jews were murdered there.

Commandant's office and living quarters 'The Merry Flea'

Water ditch

Camp I

Jewish slave labour camp compound

SS compound

Sobibor Railway Station

Ramp

	Roads today
	Buildings today
	Former buildings
××××	Camp perimeter
••••	Minefield
┼┼┼┼	Main railway (then and now)
┼┼┼┼┼	Narrow gauge railway (no longer exists) for taking sick and infirm Jews to gas chamber

Camp Gate

Escape route, 14 October 1943

0   metres   100

0   yards   100

to Chełm   *to Chełm*

© Martin Gilbert 2008

Map 324

JEWS DEPORTED INTO THERESIENSTADT, AND OUT OF THERESIENSTAD

Deportations into
Theresienstadt

Deportations out of
Theresienstadt,
to death camps

© Martin Gilbert 2008

More than 33,000 Jews died of starvation and disease inside Theresienstadt; a further 81,000 were deported 'to the east' where they were murdered. This map shows the numbers of Jews deported into Theresienstadt, country by country, between November 1941 and October 1944, and deportation out of Theresienstadt in 1943 and 1944.

After Auschwitz, the second largest number of Jews who were murdered after being deported from Theresienstadt were killed at Maly Trostenets, in German-occupied Byelorussia. Beginning on 10 May 1942, Jews were brought to Minsk every Tuesday and Friday from Theresienstadt, then driven by truck towards the village of Maly Trostenets. The trucks were mobile gas chambers; when they reached the camp all those inside them were dead. Of the one thousand Jews sent from Theresienstadt to Maly Trostenets on 25 August 1942, twenty-two of the younger men were taken to work at an SS farm. The rest were ordered into the gas vans. Of the twenty-two sent to the farm, only two survived the sadism of their overseers, escaping in May 1943 to join the partisans. One was killed in action against the Germans. One survived the war; he was the only survivor of the 23,503 Jews sent to Maly Trostenets.

Map 325

THE THERESIENSTADT GHETTO, NOVEMBER 1941–MAY 1945

More than 33,000 Jews died of starvation and disease inside Theresienstadt; a further 81,000 were deported 'to the east' where they were murdered, 44,693 of them at Auschwitz and 25,503 at Maly Trostenets, outside Minsk.

to Dresden

Ebergasse

17

14

Brunnenpark

16

Postgasse

18

13

15

19

35

Berggasse

to Prague

12

20

Stadtpark

SUDETEN
BARRACKS

11 2 1

Rathausgasse

3

CAVALRY
BARRACKS

Seestrasse

Bahnhofstrasse

Langestrasse

Marktplatz

Hauptstrasse

Parkstrasse

Wallstrasse

22

10

21

5

9

4

32

Neue Gasse

33

8 7 6

Westgasse

24

35

23

29

Badhausgasse

30

28

Jägergasse

25

31

Kleiner
Park

26

Südberg

34

Bäckergasse

27

to the
cemetery

Südstrasse

railway to
the main
Dresden-Prague line

1. Children's house and school
2. Post office, bank, theatre
3. Home for young people
4. Home for girls aged eight to sixteen
5. Tent for forced labour tasks (1,000 prisoners)
6. Ghetto shop used for clothing
7. Café, cabaret shows
8. SS Camp Command Headquarters
9. Housing for elderly Jews, Hospital
10. Jewish Ghetto Guard (100 men)
11. Infant school, kitchen, bakery
12. Homes for children and apprentices, and a library
13. Barracks of Czech gendarmes guarding perimeter
14. Craft workshops
15. SS dormitory and restaurant

16. SS Archives brought here from Berlin, 1943
17. Confiscated belongings sorted here
18. Women's barracks, concert performances, football in the yard
19. Housing for mothers and children under three years old
20. Playground for children; only allowed during the making of Nazi propaganda film
21. Central hospital, public baths, showers
22. Home for old and insane deportees

23. Disinfection centre, laundry, shower room
24. Joiners workshop
25. Jewish Council of Elders office and rooms; theatrical performances
26. Men's barracks
27. Bakery and central food store
28. Railway siding
29. Main women's barracks later used for deportees to Auschwitz
30. Barracks for very old deportees
31. Sports arena
32. Earliest deportees lived here
33. Jews with encephalitis housed here. Briefly a culture hall and synagogue during the making of Nazi propaganda film
34. Columbarium: urns with ashes placed here; the limit of mourners' journey
35. Allotments and a garden – these existed only during the making of Nazi propaganda film

© Martin Gilbert 2008

Map 326

PRINCIPAL DEPORTATIONS TO TREBLINKA, AUGUST 1942–AUGUST 1943

Bialystok

Mlawa

River Narew

Makow

Treblinka

Kosow
Lacki
Sterdyn

River Vistula

Jadow

Wyszogorod

Radzymin

River Bug

Wolomin

Wegrow

Sokolow

Stanislawow

Dobre

Warsaw

Minsk
Mazowiecki

Kaluszyn

Siedlce

Otwock

Biala
Podlaska

Karcew

Kolbiel

Siennica

Sobienie
Jeziory

Ludwisin

Latowicz

Serokomla

Miedzyrzec

Parysow

Stoczek

Lukow

River Vistula

Biala Rawska

Zelechow

Radzyn

Koluszki

Rawa
Mazowiecka

Ryki

Kock

Parczew

Ujazd

Kozienice

Deblin

Tomaszow
Mazowiecki

Drzewica

Przytyk

Gniewoszow

Piotrkow

Opoczno

Gnielniow

Radom

Zwolen

Lublin

Gorzkowice

Sulejow

Przysucha

Ciepielow

Kamiensk

Zarnow

Szydlowiec

Ilza

Chotcza
Nowa

Konskie

Skarzysko
Kamienna

Sienno

Radomsko

Przedborz

Suchedniow

Tarlow

Radoszyce

Cmielow

Krasnik

Wloszczowa

Kielce

Ostrowice

Ozarow

Czestochowa

Koniecpol

Checiny

Lagow

Opatow

Zarki

Jedzejow

Iwaniska

Sandomierz

Szczekociny

Chmielnik

Klimontow

Sedziszow

Pinczow

Staszow

Koprzywnica

Busko
Zdroj

Stopnica

Osiek

Wislica

Szczucin

	Towns and villages from which Jews were deported to Treblinka, August 1942 to August 1943
	Rail and road deportation routes

0 kilometres 50

0 miles 30

© Martin Gilbert 2008

Starting on 22 July 1942, for fifty-three days until 12 September, the SS deported 265,000 Jews from the Warsaw ghetto to Treblinka, an average of 5,000 each day. There were fewer than a hundred survivors. When the SS attempted to renew the deportations, first in January 1943 and then in April 1943, the surviving Jews of the ghetto rose in revolt (*see maps 183, 204 and 205*).

Map 327

TREBLINKA DEATH CAMP

to Treblinka main railway station

to Treblinka village

Modern entrance

Museum and Kiosk

■ former camp buildings

•–• former gates

Ä former watchtowers

Treblinka was in operation from 23 July 1942 until August 1943, when there was a revolt of the 850 Jewish slave labour camp inmates. More than 870,000 Jews were murdered there.

railway spur

Watchtower

Commandant's house

Main entrance

Watchtower

Camp perimeter

Ukrainian quarters

Administrative area

Jewish slave labour barracks

'Death Avenue'

Pyres where bodies were burned

Undressing and haircutting

Quarry Road

Rail spur (ramp)

'Station Square'

'Reception Square'

Watchtower

Watchtower

'Station' building

to Treblinka labour camp and quarry

Barracks for Jewish prisoners

Watchtower

Watchtower

Watchtower

© Martin Gilbert 2008

As Soviet forces approached Treblinka in autumn 1943, the SS destroyed the camp. So that no traces would remain, a farm was built on the site. Today it is a large field, on which are 17,000 memorial stones, inscribed with the name of a town or village from which Jews were deported to Treblinka and murdered. One stone carries the name of an individual: Janusz Korczak, the teacher who, with his assistants, chose to accompany his students from Warsaw, and died with them. In the centre of the field are a mass grave and a memorial with a large crack in it: a symbol of the evil that took place there.

Map 328

THE WARSAW GHETTO, NOVEMBER 1940–MAY 1943

Parysowski Square

Stawki

Muran-owska

Konwik-torska

Umschlagplatz

Mila 18

7

8

Stawki

Niska

Mila

Wolynska

Gesia

Jewish Cemetery

Okopowa

Marchlewskiego

Smocza

Esperanto

(Mordechaja Anielewicza)

Pawia

Dzielna

Nowolipki

Karmelicka

Zamenhofa

Lewartowskiego

Wolowa

Bonifaterska

Swietojerska

to Old Town

1

Warsaw Uprising Monument

Ghetto Uprising Monument

Krasinski Garden

Andersa

Nalewki

Dluga

Solidarnosci

Jewish Historical Institute

Pawiak Prison

Church of the Virgin

Tlomackie

Senatorska

Pawia

Dzielna

Nowolipki

3

2

Nowolipie

(Jana Pawła II)

(Solidarnosci)

Oria

Great Synagogue

Saxon Garden

5

Femina Cinema

Nazi headquarters for deportations

4

Leszno

Ogrodowa

Elektoralna

Chlodna

Zelazna

Krochmalna

Walicow

Grzybowska

Nozyk Synagogue

Krolewska

Prozna

Zielna

Marszalkowska

Towarowa

Chlodna

Ciepla

Twarda

Grzybowski Place

Factories where Jewish forced labourers worked:

1 Brushmakers'
2 Roerich
3 Fritz Schultz
4 Karl Georg Schultz
5 Big Toebbens
6 Small Toebbens
7 Transavia
8 Werterfassung

Zelazna

Cegalna (Pereca)

Prosta

Panska

Twarda

6

Rondo ONZ

Sliska

Sienna

Zlota

0   metres   250

0   yards   200

© Martin Gilbert 2008

—— Warsaw ghetto wall established in November 1940 (11 miles long). **STREET PLAN OF 2008**

Ghetto gates

Drastically reduced area of the ghetto, September 1942 to April 1943 (when the Warsaw ghetto revolt began)

Deportation railway siding (Umschlagplatz)

Map 329

MAJDANEK CONCENTRATION CAMP AND DEATH CAMP

←— to Lublin and Warsaw   Route 17 main road   to Zamosc and Lvov —→

(10)

(13)

(12)

(3)

Cremation pyres

(4)

(11)

(14)

Field I

(2)

(6) Laundry

Field II

As many as 80,000 Jews were murdered in Majdanek in 1943 and 1944 (50,000 of them Polish Jews, others from Slovakia, Bohemia and Moravia, Holland and Greece); among the Polish Jews murdered were several thousand who were deported to Majdanek after the Warsaw ghetto revolt had been crushed.

(5)

(1)

Field III
the only remaining Field

(15)

Field IV

(15)

(15)

(5)

Field V

(15)

Field VI

(7)

(9)

N

(8)

1. Dog kennels	7. New crematorium	13. SS doctor's house
2. Stores	8. Areas of mass executions	14. Present administration building
3. Baths and gas chambers	9. Mass execution pits	15. Planned extension, early to mid 1944
4. Selection yard	10. Commandant's house	I - VI Barracks ('Fields')
5. Guardhouse	11. SS Womens' quarters	▪ Watchtowers
6. Old crematorium	12. SS quarters and commandant's offices	Camp perimeter

© Martin Gilbert 2008

Map 330

RAILWAY DEPORTATION ROUTES OF JEWS TO AUSCHWITZ, 1942–1944

Between the summer of 1942 and late 1944 more than one million Jews were deported by train to Auschwitz and murdered there. This map shows the main railway deportation routes and some of the cities and towns from which Jews were deported to their deaths.

A German refugee from Frankfurt-on-Main, Anne Frank, was hidden in Amsterdam until she and those hidden with her were betrayed. Deported to Auschwitz in August 1944, she died in Belsen in March 1945, a month before Belsen was liberated.

© Martin Gilbert 2008

Map 331

AUSCHWITZ I, II AND III

N

from Cracow

Dwory
station

River Vistula

**Monowitz
slave labour
camp**
Auschwitz III

I.G.Farben
'Buna'
synthetic oil
and
rubber plant

*British
prisoners-of-war
camps*

from Cracow

River Przemsza

from Warsaw

River Sola

Auschwitz
town
(Oswiecim)

**Auschwitz
Main Camp**
*Auschwitz I
(see map 332)*

*from
Bielsko
Biala*

from Berlin

**Auschwitz
railway station**

**Union
factory**

**Rajska
village**

*from Zilina, Prague,
Vienna*

inner

outer perimeter

perimeter

Birkenau
*Auschwitz II
(see map 333)*

River Vistula

| 0 | kilometres | 2 |

| 0 | mile | 1 |

© Martin Gilbert 2008

Map 332

AUSCHWITZ MAIN CAMP (AUSCHWITZ I)

Visitors' car park

N

to Auschwitz station

rail spur

27

l   f   24

i   j   21 20 19 18 17 16 14 13

m   n   o

k

h

11 10   7   6   5   4

g

road to Bielsko-Biala

road to Oswiecim town

Camp Commandant's Office   Camp Commandant's House

River Sola

| 0 | metres | 100 |
| 0 | yards | 100 |

a. Entrance
b. Reception building for new prisoners
c. Stores, warehouse, workshops
d. SS Guardroom
e. Entrance gate inscribed 'Arbeit macht frei' (work makes you free)
f. Place where camp orchestra played
g. Wall of Death, where prisoners were executed by shooting
h. Gravel pit, site of executions
i. Warehouse for belongings taken from deportees. The poison gas canisters were also stored here

j. Laundry
k. Assembly Square (Appelplatz)
l. Camp kitchen
m. SS hospital
n. Gas chamber and Crematorium (Crematorium I)
o. Political section (Camp Gestapo)
p. SS garages, stables and stores

Block 4: Extermination exhibition
Block 5: Exhibition of material evidence of crimes
Block 6: Exhibition of everday life of prisoners
Block 7: Exhibition of living and sanitary conditions
Block 10: Exhibition of sterilization experiments

Block 11: Death block exhibition
Block 13: Denmark and Germany exhibitions
Block 14: National exhibition, formerly Soviet exhibition
Block 16: Czechoslovak exhibition
Block 17: Yugoslavia and Austria exhibition
Block 18: Hungarian and Bulgarian exhibitions
Block 19: Prisoners' hospital
Block 20: Prisoners' hospital
Block 21: Prisoners' hospital
Block 24: Museum archive
Block 27: Exhibition, 'Suffering and struggle of Jews'

■ Brick perimeter wall   ■ Watchtowers

© Martin Gilbert 2008

Map 333

BIRKENAU (AUSCHWITZ II)

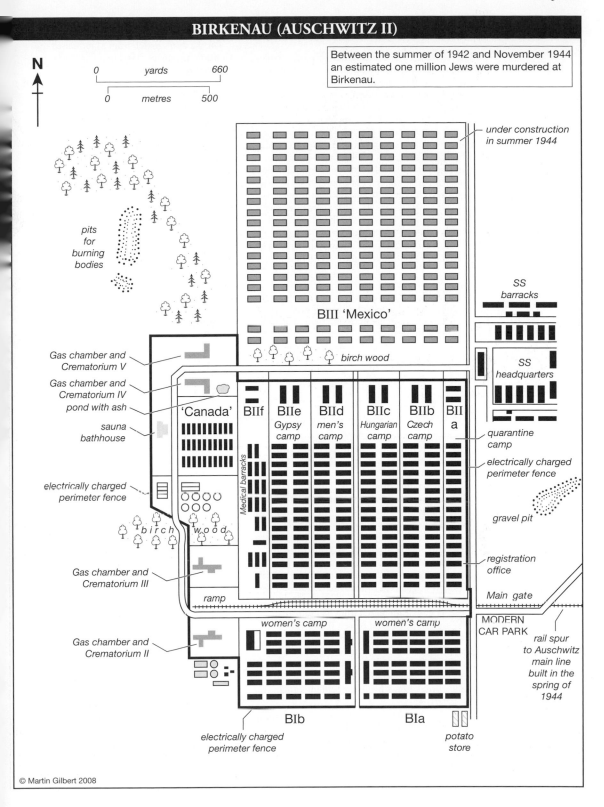

N

| 0 | yards | 660 |
| 0 | metres | 500 |

Between the summer of 1942 and November 1944 an estimated one million Jews were murdered at Birkenau.

under construction in summer 1944

pits for burning bodies

BIII 'Mexico'

SS barracks

SS headquarters

birch wood

Gas chamber and Crematorium V

Gas chamber and Crematorium IV

pond with ash

'Canada'

BIIf

BIIe
Gypsy camp

BIId
men's camp

BIIc
Hungarian camp

BIIb
Czech camp

BII a

quarantine camp

electrically charged perimeter fence

sauna bathhouse

Medical barracks

electrically charged perimeter fence

birch wood

gravel pit

Gas chamber and Crematorium III

registration office

ramp

Main gate

Gas chamber and Crematorium II

women's camp

women's camp

MODERN CAR PARK

rail spur to Auschwitz main line built in the spring of 1944

BIb

BIa

electrically charged perimeter fence

potato store

© Martin Gilbert 2008

Bibliography

I have restricted this bibliography to those works which I have personally consulted in assembling the facts for this Atlas, and have indicated against particular titles those specific maps for which the title was of service. I have also indicated those sources which provided comprehensive material on deportations and other facts incorporated on the maps. To avoid any danger of exaggeration, whenever two sources conflict in the precise number of those murdered in any instance, I have chosen the lower figure. For example, in the case of the Nazi killing squad massacre at Rowne in November 1941, page 81, where contemporary German sources indicate a death toll of at least 18,000, while one recent Jewish source has had reason to estimate that the figure could be as high as 22,000, I have retained the lower figure.

Unpublished sources

The unpublished sources which contained material for individual maps included the following eye-witness testimonies in the archives of Yad Vashem, Jerusalem:

the deportations from Germany to Poland in 1938 (map 19), testimony of Theodor Hatalgy 03/3206;

the Hajerat-M'Guil labour camp in the Sahara (map 59), testimony of Avraham Alfassi, 03/963;

the Jassy death train (map 73), testimony of Binyamin Rabinovitz, 03/897;

the deportation from Norway to Auschwitz (map 164), testimony of Dr L. Eitinger, a German refugee doctor, 01/255;

the deportation from Corfu to Auschwitz (map 250), testimony of Eliahu Uschman, 03/3041;

the deportation from Rhodes to Auschwitz (map 261), testimony of Hanna Zironi, 03/3171;

the deportation of Jews from Albania to Bergen-Belsen (map 230), testimony of Yisrael Teitelbaum, 03/3252;

the Warsaw to Zychlin death march (map 269), testimony of Henech Abramovitch, M I/E, 1605/1489;

the 42-day death march from Neusalz (map 285), testimony of Alisa Besser, 03/3394;

the Stutthof death camp and death marches (map 298), testimony of Pninna Sela, 03/638;

the Palmnicken massacre (map 284), testimony of Celina Moskowitz, 03/1108;

the rescue of Jews by Oskar Schindler (map 284), 01/164;

the post-war murder of Jews in Poland (map 314), at Sokoly near Bialystok, testimony of Icchak Szajder, and at Skarzysko-Kamienna, M 11/B, 244 and M1/PZ;10/632.

For a general guide to all European localities, deportations, slave labour camps, resistance, escape to the partisans, and death marches of the period, I consulted Yehuda Bauer (editor), *Guide to Unpublished Materials of the Holocaust Period*,

volume 3, Jerusalem 1975; volume 4, Jerusalem 1977 and volume 5, Jerusalem 1979.

For the death march from Mauthausen to Gunskirchen (map 305), I found important material on a single-sheet map, 'Weg des Todesmarsches Mauthausen-Gunskirchen', in the Yad Vashem archives, O 15/23–1–4.

For many of the other death marches between June 1944 and May 1945 (maps 290, 291, 292 and 299), I drew on material in 'Vol. 2, Death Marches (Marches de la Mort), Routes and Distances', issued on 28 May 1946 by the Intelligence Section of the UNRRA Central Tracing Bureau.

For the location of mass murder sites, revolts and slave labour camps in eastern Poland, now western White Russia (including maps 88, 98 and 216), I was fortunate to be able to consult 'The Jewish Underground in the Ghettos of Western Byelorussia during the Holocaust', a doctoral thesis submitted by Dr Shalom Cholawski to the Senate of the Hebrew University of Jerusalem in December 1977.

The fate of the Jews of Bessarabia (map 78) is described in 'The Rumanian Jewry between 23.8.1944 and 31.12.1947', a doctoral thesis submitted by Dr Jean Ancel to the Senate of the Hebrew University of Jerusalem in September 1979.

For further details of the slave labour camps in the Sahara (map 59), I consulted the letter and documents submitted by Dr E. Schaefer to the Wiener Library, London, 16 April 1958.

Other unpublished materials from which I have drawn material include:

'Treatment of Jews in Upper Silesia', 6 May 1938, a report by R. F. O'N Bashford, the British Vice-Consul in Breslau, copy in Foreign Office papers 371/21635 (map 8);

'Concentration, Work and Punishment Camps in the British Zone, I Germany, II Austria', Foreign Office papers 371/57528 (map 278): lists camps known to have existed between 1939 and 1945 in the British Zones of Germany and Austria, with notes on location, type of camp, and conditions inside the camps;

'Jews in Nazi Europe, February 1933 to November 1941', memorandum submitted to the Inter-American Jewish Conference, Balitmore, Maryland, 23 November 1941, by the Institute of Jewish Affairs (including maps 43, 44 and 52): includes a list of 27 towns and villages from which Jews were expelled in German-occupied Poland, 19 localities to which the Jews of Cracow were expelled, and 21 cities and towns in which ghettos had been established, with the number of Jews in each;

'List of Persons Imprisoned in Terezin/Theresienstadt', Czechoslovak Relief Action, London, March 1945 (alphabetical list of names, ages and last domicile);

'Tableaux Recapitulatif des Israelites et Tziganes deportés du camp de rassemblement de Malines vers les camps d'Extermination de Haute ilesie', Brussels 28 November 1977 (lists 25 deportations from Belgium to Auschwitz, with dates and details, and 4 deportations elsewhere: also 11 attempts at escape, with dates);

'Overzicht van de uit Nederland Gedeporteerde Joden', Rijksinstituut voor Oorlogsdocumentatie (Netherlands State Institute for War Documentation), Amsterdam n.d. (lists 68 deportations from Holland to Auschwitz, 19 to Sobibor, 7 to Theresienstadt and 8 to Bergen-Belsen, with dates and numbers of those deported).

'German Extermination Camps – Auschwitz and Birkenau', issued by the Executive Office of the President, War Refugee Board, Washington D.C., 26 November 1944 (includes the report of four escapees from Birkenau, Rudolf Vrba and Alfred Wetzler, 33 pages, and Czeslaw Mordowicz and Arnost Rosin, 6 pages).

The Palestine High Commissioner's comment at the time of the 'Struma' disaster (map 103) is in his telegram No. 257, Most Secret, in the Colonial Office papers, London, reference 733/446/76021.

I based the map on page 240 (map 313) on Dov Levin's diary of his journey from Vilna to Palestine, and on his letter to me of 3 July 1980.

I obtained further information used in this Atlas in conversation in Jerusalem on 23 December 1980 with:

Shmuel Krakowski, recollections of the evacuation of Dziedzice (map 281), and of the Rehmsdorf to Theresienstadt evacuation (map 299).

Judge Moshe Bejski, recollections of the Schindler Jews (map 284).

Hadassa Modlinger, recollections of the evacuation from Ravensbrück to Sweden (map 299).

I received further spoken testimony from:

Hugo Gryn, the Ruthenian deportations (map 255) and the Lieberose death march (map 277), in conversation in London, 11 January 1979, and from

Leon Pommers, the escape of Jews across the Trans-Siberian railway, (map 69) in conversation in Jerusalem, 14 May 1979.

I am also grateful to Alexander Pechersky, the leader of the revolt at Sobibor (map 222), for his letter of recollections, sent from Rostov-on-Don, on 16 December 1980.

I have based two maps (maps 310 and 311), on 'Sharit Ha-Platah', 5 volumes, Dachau 26 June 1945 (names, birthplaces and dates of birth of survivors in the former concentration camps). Volume 1, revised Munich 1946, covers Dachau; volume 2, Buchenwald and others; volume 3, Bergen-Belsen, Salzwedel, Gardelegen and Theresienstadt; volume 4, Linz, Buchenwald (children aged 16–17), Dachau, Braunschweig, Mannheim, Mauthausen, Innsbruck, Celle, Regensburg; volume 5, Feldafing, Dachau, Allauch and others.

The map on page 224 (map 292) was based in part on 'Atrocities and other conditions in Concentration Camps in Germany', Report of the Committee Request by Gen. Dwight D. Eisenhower through the Chief of Staff, Gen. George C. Marshall, to the Congress of the United States, 79th Congress, 1st Session, Document No. 40, Washington 15 May 1945.

Published documents

Two principal published sources from the point of view of German policy and practice are the *Trial of the Major War Criminals before the International Military Tribunal: Official Text*, 42 volumes, Nuremberg 1947–1949 and the *Trial of War Criminals Before the Nuremberg Military Tribunals under Control Council Law No. 10*, 15 volumes, Washington D.C., 1949–1953.

There is also a comprehensive guide to more than 3,000 of the documents submitted at the Nuremberg Trials in Jacob Robinson and Henry Sachs (editors), *The Holocaust, The Nuremberg Evidence, Part One: Documents*, Jerusalem 1976. I have plotted details on the maps from many of these documents, reference L, NG, NO, NOKW, PS, RF and D, and in particular from the documents dated:

26 October 1938, expulsion of Polish Jews from Germany, reference NG 2014 (map 19);

8 November 1938, report of explusion of Polish Jews from Germany, NG 2010 (map 19);

27 February 1940, statistics of Warthegau expulsions, NO 5348 (map 43);

29 February 1940, further statistics of Warthegau expulsions, NO 5402 (map 43);

28 March 1940, Stettin and Schneidemühl deportations to Lublin region, NG 2490 (map 37);

31 October 1940, report of 6,504 German Jews deported to the Pyrenees, NG 4934 (map 49);

3 July 1941, only 2,000 Jews left in Siauliai, NO 4537 (map 73);

7 July 1941, 400 Jews killed in Riga, NO 2935 (map 73);

13 July 1941, 500 Jews being shot every day in Vilna, NO 2937 (map 73);

27 August 1941, murder of 11,000 Hungarian Jews at Kamenets Podolsk, PS 197 (map 74);

27 August 1941, 4,000 Jews killed in Jassy, NG 4962 (map 74);

3 September 1941, 300 Jews shot at Ananayev, NOKW 1702 (map 86);

19 September 1941, *Einsatzkommando A*, reports 46,692 Jews killed in Lithuania in less than three months, NO 3149 (map 87);

19 September 1941, 1,303 Jews killed at Berdichev, NO 3149 (map 86);

2 October 1941, report of 33,771 Jews killed at Babi Yar on 29 and 30 September 1941, NO 3137 (map 86);

11 October 1941, 449 shot in Belgrade area in three days, NOKW 497 (map 86);

13 October 1941, death of Dutch Jews in Mauthausen NG 2710 (map 90);

15 October 1941, *Einsatzgruppe A,* reports having killed 125,000 Jews and 5,000 non-Jews, L 180;

24 October 1941, deportation of 50,000 Reich

Jews to Riga and Minsk, PS 3921 (map 92);

26 October 1941, Jews shot in Odessa, NO 3403 (map 86);

29 October 1941, 8,000 Jews shot at Mariupol, NOKW 1529 (map 86);

1 November 1941, 7,000 Jews murdered at Borisov, NOKW 3146 (map 94);

3 November 1941, *Einsatzgruppe C,* reports on killing of 75,000 Jews, NO 3157;

14 November 1941, *Einsatzgruppe B,* reports on killing of 45,000 Jews, NO 2825;

19 November 1941, 10,000 Jews killed in Dnepropetrovsk, NO 2832 (map 94);

25 November 1941, 1,200 Buchenwald inmates deported to Bernberg, NO 907 (map 94);

30 November 1941, 14 Jews killed at Armyansk, NOKW 1532 (map 94);

8 December 1941, report of 15,000 Jews killed in Rovno (Rowne) a month earlier, NO 2827 (map 94);

12 December 1941 'shooting on the spot' a solution in Serbia, NG 3354 (map 96);

12 December 1941, *Einsatzgruppe D,* reports killing 55,000 Jews, NO 2828;

14 December 1941, killing of 76 Jews at Karasubazar, NOKW 2029 (map 96);

end 1941-early 1942, the 'Jaeger report' on *Einsatzgruppe A* killings in Lithuania and Latvia, totalling 137,346 deaths, listed under men, women and children, between July 4 and 25 November 1941, PS 2273;

1 January 1942, killings at Simferopol on previous day, NOKW 2231;

14 January 1942, Estonia 'cleared of Jews' and 26,900 Jews killed in Riga, NO 3279 (map 98);

17 January 1942, 22 Jewish partisans shot at Evpatoria, NOKW 1524 (map 102);

20 January 1942, minutes of Wannsee Conference, NG 2586 G(7) (maps 99 and 100);

28 February 1942, 36 Jews executed at Feodosiya, NOKW 1862 (map 102);

8 April 1942, murder of 91,678 Jews in the Crimea, NO 3338 and NO 3359 (map 102);

1 May 1942, 22 Jews executed at Feodosiya, NOKW 1717 (map 102);

1 May 1942, Warthegau extermination 'in progress', NO 246 (map 117);

30 May 1942, Dr Clauberg proposes medical experiments at Auschwitz, NO 211 (map 122);

9 June 1942, despatch of a gas van from Belgrade to Riga, PS 501 (map 127);

30 June 1942, report of 52,000 Slovak Jews already deported, NG 4553 (map 126);

9 July 1942, deportations from Belgium, NG 002 (map 134);

6 August 1942, Dr Clauberg requests second sterilization unit for Auschwitz, NO 210 (map 122);

11 August 1942, Hungarian protests against anti-Jewish measures, NG 1856 (map 238);

20 August 1942, Italian refusal to deport Croat Jews, NG 2368 (map 89);

27 August 1942, 95,000 Jews executed in Baranowicze district, and 6,000 escape to partisans, NG 1315 (map 224);

3 September 1942, 27,069 French Jews already deported, RF 1227;

11 September 1942, reports of 17,000 Dutch Jews already deported, NG 2631;

18 September 1942, Jews to receive no meat, meat products or eggs in Greater Germany, NG 1651;

24 September 1942, further Italian refusal to deport Croat Jews, NG 3165;

25 September 1942, Rumanian Jews deported from France, NG 1971 (map 155);

3 October 1942, Jewish resistance groups in Germany reported to the Ministry of Justice in Berlin, NG 683;

20 November 1942, third Italian refusal to deport Croat Jews, NG 2345;

6 December 1942, forced labour in Tunisia, NG 2099 and NG 3150 (map 188);

18 February 1943, report of 86,632 Jews murdered in Minsk, NO 3339 (map 193);

4 March 1943, planned deportation of Croat Jews, NG 2348 (map 205);

16 May 1943, the Stroop report on the destruction of the Warsaw ghetto, PS 1061 (map 204);

7 June 1943, Dr Clauberg reports sterilization rate at Auschwitz of 1,000 women a day, by a single physician with assistants, NO 212 (map 206);

7 June 1943, pro-Jewish demonstrations in Sofia, NG 2357 (map 197);

21 June 1943, Jewish skeleton collection plans for Strasbourg, NO 091 (map 208);

30 June 1943, total of 434,329 Jews deported from Galicia by 27 June 1943, L 018 (map 206);

5 July 1943, six Jews shot earlier at Heraklion, NOKW 2907 (map 208);

15 July 1943, order to deport all 800 Jews still alive in Croat concentration camps, NG 2413 (map 208);

4 October 1943, Danish resistance to deportation of Jews, NG 3920 (map 213);

17 October 1943, Jews arrested in Rome, NO 315 (map 221);

2 November 1943, 73 Jews and 30 Jewesses from Auschwitz to Natzweiler, for a collection of Jewish skeletons, NO 086 (map 208);

6 April 1944, arrest of Jewish children in children's homes, and deportation to Drancy, RF 1235;

14 April 1944, report of deportation of Greek Jews on 23–25 March 1944, NOKW 2520 (map 232);

23 April 1944, deportation of Hungarian Jews to start on 15 May 1944, NG 2233 (map 240);

28 April 1944, Corfu deportation plans, NOKW 1985 (map 250);

4 May 1944, progress of ghettoization and deportation plans for Ruthenia (200,000 ghettoized) and Transylvania (110,000 to be ghettoized), NG 2262 (map 240);

8 June 1944, statistics of Hungarian deportations, NG 5620 (map 241);

16 June 1944, renewal of Slovak deportations, NG 2261 (map 251);

3 July 1944, deportations from Rhodes, NOKW 795 and NOKW 1802 (map 261);

10 September 1944, Jewish forced labourers, ,000 in all, at Bor, NOKW 981 (map 273);

15 October 1944, order for destruction of ewish skeleton collection at Strasbourg, NO 807 map 208);

27 October 1944, deportation of total of 37,402 Jews from Hungary reported, NG 5573 map 260);

22 January 1945, Stutthof death march orders, NO 3796 (map 284);

25 January 1945, Stutthof death march schedule, NO 3792 (map 284);

23 May 1945, testimony of Franz Ziereis, Commandant at Mauthausen, NO 1973 (map 300);

18 March 1946, affidavit by Baron van Lamsweerde on the Rehmsdorf to Theresienstadt death march, D924 (map 299);

6 June 1947, affidavit by Paul Blobel on Unit 1005 to obliterate traces of mass graves, NO 3829 (map 217);

23 October 1947, eye-witness account of gas vans used in Riga, NO 5511 (map 127).

Single sheet maps

Among the historical atlases and maps consulted were several single-sheet maps on specific themes, including:

Jean Ancel, *Transnistria Inclusiv Provinciile Afectate De Deportari Masive,* Jerusalem, n.d. (the Transnistrian camps and death marches) maps 78 and 80;

Dokumentaãná Akcia, *Deportácia Îidov zo Slovenska,* Bratislava, June 1948 (deportation routes and numbers from Slovak towns and villages) maps 126 and 128;

Herbert Froboess, *Deutschland 1945,* Munich n.d. (location of concentration camps and sub-camps in Greater Germany, including the Natzweiler and Mauthausen sub-camps) map 278;

Dr Gollert, Die Territoriale Verteilung der Juden in Warschau nach Polizeikommissariaten, Volkszahlung vom 24 Februar 1940 (gives percentage of Jews throughout Warsaw, before the expulsions into the ghetto) map 55;

C. Jablonski, *Podzialy Administracyjne Wojewodztwa Lodzkeigo i Obszarow Przyleglych 1939–1945r.,* Lodz 1972 (wartime administrative boundaries of the Lodz region) map 42;

Edward Kossoy, *Judenvernichtung im Donauraum,* Munich, n.d. (deportation routes with dates and numbers, from Austria, Slovakia, Bukovina, Ruthenia, Transylvania, Banat, Bacska and Serbia, with inset of concentration, labour and internment camps in Italy);

Edward Kossoy, *Polen,* Munich, n.d. (concentration camps and labour camps throughout Poland, with insets on France, Transnistria, North Africa, Upper Silesia, and Warsaw region);

Edward Kossoy, *Polen und Balticum am Ende des sweiten Weltkrieges,* Munich, n.d. (death camps, concentration camps, slave labour camps, deportation routes with dates and number, from the General Government, the Baltic States, Upper Silesia, Danzig-West Prussia, East Prussia and the Warthegau);

League of Nations, *Territory of Saar Basin,* scale 1:100,000, 3 May 1919 (map provided as annex 2 to the Treaty of Versailles), London 1919, map 7;

Militärgeographischen Institut in Wien, single sheet maps of western Russia (borders of 1914), reprinted Vienna 1940, scale 1:200,000;

Mitteleuropa in der ersten Hälfte des Jahres 1945 n.d. (concentration camps and their satellite camps, with front lines on 1 April, 14 April and 6 May 1945, and the dates on the liberation of the camps maps 290 to 294 and map 307;

Lieutenant Popescu, *Transnistria,* 1.43, maps 78 and 80.

Zidovske Pracovne Tabory A Strediska Na Slovensku, Bratislava, 5 July 1943 (locates Jewish labour camps in Slovakia) map 216.

Atlases

Several Atlases provided historical as well as geographical information not obtainable elsewhere, among them:

O. A. Beloglazova (editor) *Atlas S.S.S.R.,* Moscow 1954;

Wladyslaw Czaplinski and Tadeusz Ladogorski, *Atlas Historyczny Polski,* Warsaw 1968;

Deutscher Generalatlas, 1:200,000, Stuttgart 1967–1968;

George Goodall (editor), *Philips' International Atlas,* 5th edition, Liverpool 1945 (includes the boundaries of German-occupied Poland, plates 53–54, of German-occupied Czechoslovakia, plates 59–60, and of Hungarian-occupied Transylvania, plates 63–64);

Dimitri Kosev and others, *Atlas po Bulgarska Istoria,* Sofia 1963;

Janusz Lopatto (editor), *Samochodowy Atlas Polski 1:500,000,* Warsaw 1979 (road Atlas of Poland, 34 map spreads, town plans and gazetteer);

Dr Oswald Muris, *Hansa Weltatlas,* Leipzig 1943 (includes the European frontiers of September 1943, and the internal administrative divisions of Greater Germany);

T. Dodson Stamps and Vincent J. Esposito, *A Military History of World War II: Atlas,* West Point 1953 (168 campaign maps, including 7 maps on the Polish campaign, 5 maps on the Balkan campaign, 22 maps on the war in eastern Europe, 26 maps on the war in western Europe, 15 maps on the war in North Africa and 16 maps on the operations in Italy).

Books and articles

There are now nearly five hundred 'memorial' books on the destroyed Jewish communities of Europe; including more than 400 for Poland, 20 for Rumania, 13 for Russia, 5 for Lithuania, 4 for Czechoslovakia, 4 for Germany, 1 for Yugoslavia (Sombor), 1 for Greece (Salonica) and 1 for Latvia.

I have tried to make the fullest possible use of these books, some of which are listed in the bibliography, and to which there is, up to 1973, a comprehensive guide in David Bass, 'Bibliographical List of Memorial Books Published in the years 1943–1972', in *Yad Vashem Studies,* ix, Jerusalem 1973, pages 273–321.

The Bulletin of the Jewish Historical Institute in Warsaw, founded in 1951, contains many important articles on the fate of Polish Jewry. Of particular value are the tables of deportations from towns, villages and hamlets throughout Poland, prepared by Tatiana Berenstein (Berensztyn), Danuta Dabrowska, Adam Rutkowski and Szymon Datner, and which I have listed in the bibliography of published works.

For the basic historical facts of more than a thousand separate communities overtaken by the Holocaust, as well as for the country-by-country entries, and a specific Holocaust section, each with its own bibliography, I have used Cecil Roth (editor in chief), *Encyclopaedia Judaica,* Jerusalem 1972, 16 volumes. The individual community entries in these sixteen volumes are being substantially supplemented by the Yad Vashem project, *Pinkas Hakehillot Encyclopaedia of Jewish Communities,* of which the following six volumes have already been published and which provide detailed information on the life and destruction of several hundred of the communities plotted in this Atlas:

Rumania, volume 1, Jerusalem 1969;
Germany-Bavaria, Jerusalem 1972 (including maps 108 and 109);
Hungary, Jerusalem 1976;
Poland: the Communities of Lodz and its Region, Jerusalem 1976;
Poland: Eastern Galicia, Jerusalem 1980;
Rumania, volume 2, Jerusalem 1980.

Other published works which proved indispensable in the preparation of this Atlas were:
Activité des Organisations Juives en France sous L'Occupation, Paris 1947.
S. Adler-Rudel, 'The Evian Conference on the Refugee Question', in *Leo Baeck Institute Year Book* xiii, 1968, pages 235–73.
Reuben Ainsztein, Jewish Resistance in Nazi-Occupied Eastern Europe, London 1974.
Henry Allainmet, Auschwitz en France: La Vérité sur le seul camp d'Extermination en France, Le Struthof, Paris 1974 (about Natzweiler).
American Jewish Committee, *The Jews in Nazi Germany: A Handbook of Facts Regarding the Present Situation,* New York 1935 (documents on anti-Jewish measures and the text of laws affecting the Jews).
Jacob Apenszlak (editor), *The Black Book of Polish Jewry,* New York 1943.
Jacob Apenszlak and Moshe Polakiewicz, *Armed Resistance of the Jews in Poland,* New York 1944.
Yitzhak Arad, *Ghetto in Flames: the Struggle and Destruction of the Jews in Vilna in the*

Holocaust, Jerusalem 1980 (lists all murder 'actions' in Vilna between 1941 and 1944).
Yitzhak Arad, *The Partisan,* New York 1979 (the story of Swieciany, Vilna, and Jewish partisan activity).
Schlomo Aronson, Beginnings of the Gestapo System: the Bavarian model in 1933, New Brunswick, New Jersey 1969.
Z. Asaria, Zur Geschichte der Juden in Osnabrueck, Osnabrück 1969.
K. J. Ball-Kaduri, 'Berlin is "Purged" of Jews: The Jews in Berlin in 1943', in *Yad Vashem Studies,* v, Jerusalem 1963, pages 271–316 (includes lists of 11 deportations from Berlin to Auschwitz between 12 January and 12 March 1943, and 8 to Theresienstadt between 12 January and 17 March 1943).
Yehuda Bauer *Flight and Rescue: Brichah,* New York 1970 (map 314).
Yehuda Bauer, 'Rescue Operations Through Vilna', in *Yad Vashem Studies,* ix, Jerusalem 1973, pages 215–223 (map 69).
Arieh L. Bauminger, *Roll of Honour,* 2nd edition, Tel Aviv 1971 (non-Jews who saved Jews).
Norman H. Baynes (editor) *Hitler's Speeches,* 2 volumes, London 1941.
Wladyslaw Bednarz, Das Vernichtungslager zu Chelmno am Ner, Warsaw 1946.
Tatiana Berenstein, 'Eksterminacja Zydow w Galicji 1941–1943' *Biuletyn Zydowskiego Instytutu Historycznego,* number 61, Warsaw, 1967 (12 statistical tables of the ghettoization, deportation and destruction in 139 Jewish communities in Eastern Galicia between 1941 and 1943).
Tatiana Berenstein, 'Martyrologia, opór i zaglada ludnosci zydowskiej', in *Biuletyn Zydowskiego Instytutu Historycznego,* number 21, pages 56–83, Warsaw 1957 (10 statistical tables listing the size, deportation and destruction of Jewish communities in the Lublin district between 1939 and 1944).
Adolf Berman, 'The Fate of Jewish Children in the Warsaw Ghetto', in Yisrael Gutman and Livia Rothkirchen (editors), *The Catastrophe of European Jewry,* Jerusalem 1976, pages 400–421.
Blackbook of Localities whose Jewish Population was Exterminated by the Nazis, Yad Vashem, Martyrs' and Heroes' Remembrance Authority, Jerusalem 1965 (lists the number of Jews town by town and village by village, according to the pre-war census returns, in Poland, Germany, Yugosalvia, Austria, Hungary, Rumania, Greece, Czechoslovakia, Holland, Norway, Luxembourg, Estonia, Latvia, Lithuania and the Soviet Union).
Nachman Blumenthal (editor), Yizkor Baranow: A Memorial to the Jewish Community of Baranow, Jerusalem 1964.
Joseph Borkin, *The Crime and Punishment of I. G. Farben,* New York 1978 (slave labour at Auschwitz-Monowitz, based on the published Nuremberg War Crimes Trials records).
Randolph L. Braham, *The Destruction of*

ungarian Jewry: A Documentary Account, 2
*o*lumes, New York 1963 (documents on German
*d*eportation policy, with facsimiles).

Randolph L. Braham, The Politics of Genocide:
*th*e Holocaust in Hungary, 2 volumes, New York
*1*981.

Randolph L. Braham, *Hungarian-Jewish
St*udies, 3 volumes, New York 1966, 1969, 1973.

Randolph L. Braham, 'The Kamenets Podolsk
*a*nd Delvidek Massacres: Prelude to the Holocaust
*i*n Hungary', in *Yad Vashem Studies,* ix, Jerusalem
*1*973, pages 133–156.

B. Brilling (editor), *Westfalia Judaica.*

Zvie A. Brown and Dov Levin, The Story of an
*U*nderground: the resistance of the Jews of Kovno
*(*Lithuania) in the Second World War, Jerusalem
*1*962.

T. Brustin-Berenstein, 'Deportacje i Zaglada
*S*kupisk Zydowskich w Dystrykcie Warszawskim'
*i*n *Biuletyn Zydowskiego Instytutu Historycznego,*
*n*umber 3, Warsaw 1952 (11 statistical tables of
*t*he ghettoization, deportation and destruction of
*J*ews in Warsaw, and of Jewish communities
*t*hroughout the Warsaw region).

Tadeusz Bystrycki (general editor) *Skorowidz
M*iejscowsci Rzeczpospolitej Polskiej, 4 volumes,
*W*arsaw and Przemysl, 1934 (lists the location of all
*t*owns, villages and hamlets in inter-war Poland).

Frederick B. Chary, The Bulgarian Jews and the
*F*inal Solution, 1940–1944, Pittsburgh 1972 (map
197).

Marta Cohen (editor and translator), *Hanna
Senesh: Her Life and Diary,* London 1971 (map
276).

Congrès Juif Mondial, Section de Roumanie,
Commission d'Etudes, *Le Massacre des Juifs de
Jassy,* Bucharest 1946 (photographs and
documents of the town and train massacres,
June-July 1941) (map 73).

Danuta Czech, 'Deportation und Vernichtung
der griechischen Juden', in *Hefte von Auschwitz,*
II, 1970 (lists 19 train deportations to Auschwitz
from Salonica between 20 March and 18 August
1943 and two from Athens and Corfu on 11 April
and 30 June 1944).

Danuta Czech, 'Kalendarium der Ereignisse im
Konzentrationslager Auschwitz-Birkenau', in
Hefte von Auschwitz, numbers 2–9, Oswiecim,
1959–64 (records all deportation trains reaching
Auschwitz between March 1942 and November
1944, with dates, and the fate of those on them).

D. Dabrowska, 'Zaglada Skupisk Zydowskich
w "Kraju Warty" w okresie Okupacji
Hitlerowskiej' in *Biuletyn Zydowskiego Instytutu
Historycznego,* number 13, Warsaw 1955 (16
statistical tables of the ghettoization, deportation
and destruction in the city of Lodz and other
towns and villages of the Warthegau).

Szymon Datner, 'Eksterminacja Zydow w
Okregu Bialostockim', in *Biuletyn Zydowskiego
Instytutu Historycznego,* number 60, Warsaw
1966 (8 statistical tables of the ghettoization,
deportation and destruction in Bialystok and the
Bialystok region), see in particular map 168.

Szymon Datner, *Las Sprawiedliwych* (the forest
of the righteous), Warsaw 1968 (the story of
non-Jewish Poles who helped Jews in Poland).

Szymon Datner, *Walka i zaglada bialostockiego
ghetta,* Lodz 1946 (the Bialystok ghetto revolt)
(map 210).

Szymon Datner, 55 Dni (i.ix-15. x 1939)
Wehrmachtu w Polsce, Warsaw 1967 (map 29).

A. de Cocatrix, *The Number of Victims of the
National Socialist Persecution,* International
Tracing Service, Arolsen, 12 April 1977.

Louis de Jong, 'The Netherlands and Auschwitz'
in *Yad Vashem Studies,* vii, Jerusalem 1968, pages
39–55.

Lucjan Dobroszycki, 'Restoring Jewish Life in
Post-War Poland', in *Soviet Jewish Affairs,* volume
3, number 2, London 1973 (details of Jews killed
by Poles after liberation) (map 316).

Giuliana Donati, *Deportazione Degli Ebrei
Dall' Italia,* Milan, March 1975 (lists 14
deportations from Italy to Auschwitz, and 7 other
deportations, between 16 September 1943 and 14
December 1944, with the fate of the deportees).

Giuliana Donati, Ebrei in Italia: Deportazione,
Resistenza, Florence 1975.

S. M. Dubnow, *History of the Jews in Russia
and Poland from the earliest times until the
present day,* 3 volumes, Jewish Publication Society
of America reprint, Philadelphia 1946 (map 3).

Krzysztof Dunin-Wasowicz, 'Zydowscy
wiezniowie KL Stutthof', *Biuletyn Zydowskiego
Instytutu Historycznego,* number 63, Warsaw
1967 (lists 26 deportations of Jews into Stutthof
between 29 June 1944 and 14 October 1944; and
14 deportations of Jewish men, women and
children out of Stutthof between 21 July 1944 and
12 December 1944).

Dr Max Freiherr du Prel, *Das General-
Gouvernement,* Würzburg 1942 (preface dated
Vienna, 10 March 1942: a 404-page German
survey of the General Government, with maps and
photographs).

Georges Dunand, *Ne perdez pas leur trace!,*
Neuchatel 1951 (the fate of the Jews of Bratislava,
by an eye-witness between September and
December 1944).

Ralph Durand, *Guernsey under German Rule,*
London 1946.

Stanislaw Duszak, *Majdanek,* Lublin 1980.

Helmut Eschwege, 'Resistance of German Jews
against the Nazi Regime', *Leo Baeck Institute Year
Book* xv, 1970, pages 143–180.

Liliana Picciotto Fargion, L'occupazione tedesca
e gli ebrei di Roma: documenti e fatti, Milan 1979.

Benjamin B. Ferencz, Less Than Slaves: Jewish
Forced Labor and the Quest for Compensation,
Cambridge Massachusetts, 1979.

M. R. D. Foot, S. O. E. in France: An Account
of the British Special Operations in France
1940–1944, London 1966.

Josef Fraenkel (editor), The Jews of Austria,
Essays on their Life, History and Destruction,
London 1967.

Philip Friedman, *Roads to Extinction: Essays on*

the Holocaust, New York and Philadelphia 1980 (includes essays on the destruction of the Jews of Lvov, the Gypsies, and Jewish resistance).

Glówna Komisja Badania Zbrodni Hitlerowskich w Polsce, *Obozy hitlerowskie na ziemiach polskich 1939–1945: Informator encyklopedyczny,* Warsaw 1979 (lists 5,877 labour camps, ghettos, concentration camps and other mass murder and atrocity sites with a comprehensive bibliography for each of these localities).

Dr Branko Gostl (and others), editors, Federation of Jewish Communities in Yugoslavia *Spomenica 1919–1969,* Belgrade 1969.

Günter Grass (and others), Danzig 1939: Treasures of a Destroyed Community, New York 1980.

Yisrael Gutman, 'The Genesis of Resistance in the Warsaw Ghetto', in *Yad Vashem Studies,* ix, Jerusalem 1973, pages 29–70.

Yisrael Gutman, *The Jews of Warsaw 1939–1943 Ghetto-Underground-Uprising,* Jerusalem 1977 (in Hebrew) (lists the monthly deaths from starvation in Warsaw in 1941 and 1942).

Yisrael Gutman and Efraim Zuroff (editors), *Rescue Attempts During the Holocaust,* Jerusalem 1977 (proceedings of the second Yad Vashem International Historical Conference, Jerusalem, 8–11 April 1974).

Gideon Hausner, *Justice in Jerusalem,* New York 1966 (the Eichmann Trial, narrative and extracts from evidence).

Heinz Heger, *The Men with the Pink Triangle,* London 1980 (memoirs of a homosexual at Sachsenhausen and Flossenbürg, with an historical introduction by David Fernbach).

Celia S. Heller, On the Edge of Destruction: Jews of Poland Between the Two World Wars, New York 1977 (map 12).

I. Heller and Z. Vajda, *The Synagogues in Hungary,* New York 1968.

Raul Hilberg, *The Destruction of the European Jews,* Chicago 1961 (New Viewpoints edition, New York 1973).

Raul Hilberg (editor), Documents of Destruction, Germany and Jewry 1933–1945, London 1972.

Sir John Hope-Simpson, The Refugee Problem: Report of a Survey, London 1939.

International Committee of the Red Cross, Documents relating to the work of the International Committee of the Red Cross for the benefit of civilian detainees in German Concentration Camps between 1939 and 1945, Geneva 1965 (contains an eye-witness account of the evacuations from Ravensbrück and Sachsenhausen in April 1945) (map 295).

Jewish Black Book Committe, *The Black Book: the Nazi Crime Against the Jewish People,* New York, 1946 (a Soviet source for German war crimes against Jews and others).

Albert Kalme, Total Terror: An Exposé of Genocide in the Baltics, New York 1951.

Abraham I. Katsh (editor and translator), *The*

Warsaw Diary of Chaim A. Kaplan, New York 1965.

Robert Katz, *Death in Rome,* London 1967 (th Ardeatine caves massacre of 24 March 1944) (ma 233).

Yitzhak Katznelson, *Vittel Diary (22.5.43–16.9.43),* Kibbutz Lohamei Haghettaot, Israel 1972 (map 231).

Donald Kenrick and Gratton Puxon, *The Destiny of Europe's Gypsies,* London 1972 (map 182).

Joseph Kermish, 'The Warsaw Ghetto Uprising in the Light of a hitherto Unpublished Official German Report', in *Yad Vashem Studies,* ix, Jerusalem 1973, pages 7–27.

Serge Klarsfeld, Additif au Mémorial de la Déportation des Juifs de France, Paris 1981.

Serge Klarsfeld, *Le Mémorial de la Déportation des Juifs de France,* Paris 1978 (lists dates of each deportation from France, executions in France, and the names of all deportees and others killed) (see in particular maps 51, 113, 114, 136, 148 to 150, 155, 159, 169 to 172, 243 to 147, 153 and 263 to 266).

David Knout, Contribution à l'historie de la Résistance Juive en France 1940–1944, Paris 1947.

Edward Kossoy, *Handbuch zum Entschädigungsverfahren,* Munich 1958 (details of camp numbers and regional origin of deportees at Auschwitz, Dachau and elsewhere; a note of Jewish names in all European languages, and the date of all Jewish holy days during the war; also Displaced Persons camps, reparations, and emigrant ships to Palestine).

Yehezkiel Korn, Jewish Agricultural Settlement in the Crimea, 1922–1947, Jerusalem 1973 (in Hebrew) (map 102).

Shmuel Krakowski, 'The Fate of Jewish Prisoners of War in the September 1939 Campaign' in *Yad V ashem Studies,* volume xii, Jerusalem 1977 (maps 32 and 35).

Shmuel Krakowski, *Jewish Armed Resistance in Poland 1942–1944,* Jerusalem 1977 (in Hebrew).

David Kranzler, Japanese, Nazis and Jews: the Jewish Refugee Community of Shanghai, 1938–1945, New York 1976 (map 16).

Kriegstagebuch des Oberkommandos der Wehrmacht, 4 volumes, Frankfurt-am-Main, 1965 (dates on which the German army captured, and then lost, towns and territory: volume 1, 1 August 1940 to 31 December 1941; volume 2, 1942; volume 3, 1943; volume 4, 1944–45, edited respectively by Hans-Adolf Jacobsen, Andreas Hillgruber, Walther Hubatsch and Percy Ernest Schramm).

Gedalia Lachman, 'The Destruction of Skala', in Max Mermelstein-Weidenfeld (chairman, editorial committee), *Skala,* Tel Aviv 1978.

Isaac Landman (editor), *The Universal Jewish Encyclopaedia,* 10 volumes, New York 1939 (contains details of anti-Jewish violence through eastern Europe during the 1930s) (maps 10 to 12).

Jehuda-Gyula Lang, *A Pápai Zsidóság Emlékkönyve,* Tel Aviv 1973 (lists the villages and

...ames the deportees from Papa and the Papa ...gion) (map 258).

I. M. Lask (editor), *The Kalish Book,* Tel Aviv ...968 (maps 44 and 54).

Evelyn Le Chêne, *Mauthausen: The History of a ...eath Camp,* London 1971 (maps 300 to 304).

Eugene Levai, Black Book on the Martyrdom of ...ungarian Jewry, Zurich 1948.

Liberated Jews Arrived in Sweden in 1945, 2 ...olumes, Malmö 1946 (includes list of Jewish ...efugees dying in Sweden in 1945, part 1 ...zechoslovakians, part 2 Dutchmen, part 3 ...ungarians, part 4 Italians, part 5 Poles, part 6 ...umanians, part 7 Stateless formerly Germans, ...nd part 8 Yugoslavs) (map 308).

Liste Alphabetique des Personnes, en majorité ...sraelites, Deportées Par Les Convois Partis du ...amp de Rassemblement de Malines entre le 4 ...out 1942 et le 31 Juillet 1944, 3 volumes, ...russels, 1 July 1954.

Dora Litani, 'The Destruction of the Jews of ...dessa in the Light of Rumanian Documents', *Yad ...ashem Studies,* vi, Jerusalem 1967, pages ...35–154.

Czeslaw Madajczyk (editor), *Zamojszczyzna ...onderlaboratorium SS,* 2 volumes, Warsaw 1979 ...documents on the expulsion and massacre of ...oles in the Zamosc province) (map 179).

Ber Mark, *Uprising in the Warsaw Ghetto,* New ...ork 1975 (map 204).

Albert Menasche, Birkenau (Auschwitz II), ...Memoirs of an eye-witness, how 72,000 Greek ...ews Perished, New York, 1947.

Sybil Milton (translator and editor), *The Stroop ...eport: The Jewish Quarter of Warsaw Is No ...More!* facsimile edition, New York 1979 (map ...204).

S. Moldawer, *The Road to Lublin,* New York ...1940 (map 37).

Michael Molho, *In Memoriam: Hommage aux ...Victimes Juives des Nazis en Grèce,* Salonica 1973 ...lists numbers of Greek Jews murdered, ...community by community) (maps 196 and 232).

Werner Nachman and Heinrich Freund, *Sie Sind ...Nicht Vergessen,* Mannheim, n.d. (the deportation ...of Jews from the Saar, Baden and the Palantinate ...to Gurs, in October 1940) (maps 49 and 50).

Donald L. Niewyk, *The Jews in Weimar ...Germany,* Baton Rouge, Louisiana 1980.

Albert Nirenstein, A Tower from the Enemy: ...Contributions to a History of Jewish Resistance in ...Poland, New York 1959.

Miram Novitch, Le Passage des Barbares: ...Contribution à l'Histoire de la Déportation et de la ...Résistance des Juifs Grecs, Nice, n.d.

Miriam Novitch (editor), Sobibor: Martyrdom ...and Revolt, Documents and Testimonies, New ...York 1980 (map 222).

Miklos Nyiszli, Auschwitz: A Doctor's Eye-...witness Account, New York 1960.

Opinia, Warsaw, 25 July 1946, page 7 (lists ...those killed in the Kielce pogrom).

Wila Orbach, 'The Destruction of the Jews in ...the Nazi-Occupied Territories of the USSR', in

Soviet Jewish Affairs, volume 6, no. 2, 1976 (lists localities with Jewish death tolls).

Nissan Oren, 'The Bulgarian Exception: a Reassessment of the Salvation of the Jewish Community', in *Yad Vashem Studies,* vii, Jerusalem 1968, pages 83–106 (map 197).

Papers Concerning the Treatment of German Nationals in Germany, Command Paper 6120 of 1939, Germany No. 2 of 1939, London 1939 (treatment of German Jews in German concentration camps, 1933–1939).

Edmond Paris, Genocide in Satellite Croatia: A Record of Racial and Religious Persecution, Chicago 1961.

Robert O. Paxton, Vichy France: Old guard and New Order, 1940–1944, London 1972.

Stanislaw Piotrowski, *Hans Frank's Diary,* Warsaw 1961.

Republic of Poland, Ministry of Foreign Affairs The German Occupation of Poland, Extract of Note addressed to the Governments of the Allied and Neutral Powers on May 3, 1941, London 1941.

Polish Ministry of Information, *The German New Order In Poland,* London 1942.

Walter Poller, Medical Block, Buchenwald: the Personal Testimony of Inmate 996, Block 36, London 1961.

Bernard Postal and Samuel H. Abramson, *The Traveler's Guide to Jewish Landmarks of Europe,* New York 1971.

Werner Präg and Wolfgang Jacobmeyer (editors), *Das Diensttagebuch des deutschen Generalgouverneurs in Polen, 1939–1945,* Stuttgart 1975 (contains Hans Frank's speeches to his officials on ridding the General Government of Jews).

Miklós Radnóti, *The Witness* (selected poems, translated from the Hungarian by Thomas Orszag-Land), London 1977 (map 271).

Leyzer Ran (editor), *Jerusalem of Lithuania Illustrated and Documented,* 3 volumes, New York 1974 (the story of the Jews of Vilna through photographs).

Jacques Ravine, La Résistance Organisée des Juifs en France 1940–1944, Paris 1973.

Gerald Reitlinger, The Final Solution: The Attempt to Exterminate the Jews of Europe 1939–1945, London 1953.

Eugen Rosenfeldt, *Tuttlingen,* Tuttlingen 1947 (maps 296 and 297).

Herbert Rosenkranz, *Verfolgung und Selbstbehauptung Die Juden in Österreich 1938–1945,* Vienna 1978 (details of all emigration and deportations from Austria).

Ryszard Rosin (editor), *Zbrodnie Hitlerowskie w Lodzi i Województwie Lódzkim,* Lodz 1942 (Nazi crimes in Lodz and the Lodz region).

Henryk Ross, The Last Journey of the Jews of Lodz Litzmannstadt, Tel Aviv 1950.

Livia Rothkirchen, The Destruction of Slovak Jewry: A Documentary History, Jerusalem 1961.

Royal Institute of International Affairs, *Chronology of the Second World War,* London 1947.

Yitskhok Rudashevski, The Diary of the Vilna Ghetto, June 1941-April 1943, Tel Aviv 1973 (map 202).

A. Rutkowski, 'Zaglada Zydow w dystrykcie radomskim', Biuletyn Zydowskiego Instytutu Historycznego, number 15, Warsaw 1955 (13 statistical tables of the ghettoization, deportation and destruction in the Radom district, including the cities of Radom and Kielce, between 1939 and 1945).

Ernst Schäfer (editor), Ravensbrück, Berlin 1960 Rabbi Israel Schepansky, Holocaust Calendar of Polish Jewry, New York, July 1974 (in Hebrew).

Gertrude Schneider, Journey Into Terror: Story of the Riga Ghetto, New York 1979.

A. J. Sherman, Island Refuge: Britain and Refugees from the Third Reich 1933–1939, London 1973 (map 15).

Du?an Sindik (editor), Secanja Jevreja na Logor Jasenovac, Belgrade 1972 (memoirs of Jews in the Jasenovac camp).

Derrick Sington, Belsen Uncovered, London 1946 (map 294).

Tadeusz Skutnik, Stutthof: Informator historyczny, Gdansk 1979

George H. Stein, The Waffen S.S., Hitler's Elite Guard at War 1939–1945, London 1966

Zosa Szajkowski, Analytical Franco-Jewish Gazetteer 1939–1945, New York 1966.

Zosa Szajkowski, Jews, Wars and Communism, 2 volumes, New York 1972 and 1974.

Zvi Szner (editor) Extermination and Resistance: Historical Records and Source Material, volume 1, Kibbutz Lohamei Haghettaot, Israel 1958.

Arieh Tartakower and Kurt R. Grossman, The Jewish Refugee, New York 1944 (maps 15 and 16).

Totenbuch Theresienstadt, Vienna 1971, volume 1, 'Deportierte Aus Osterreich' (lists 50 deportations into Theresienstadt between 21 June 1942 and 15 April 1945, and 66 deportations out of Theresienstadt, with numbers and destinations between 9 January 1942 and 28 October 1944).

Michael Tregenza, 'Belzec Death Camp', in Th Wiener Library Bulletin, 1977, volume xxx, page 8–25.

Germaine Tillion, Ravensbrück, Garden City, New York, 1975.

Max Ungar (printer), Mauthausen 8.8.1939–5.5.1945, Vienna n.d.

Dr A. Ungerer (editor), Verzeichnis von Ghettos, Zwangsarbeitslagern, und Konzentrationslagern, Munich 1953 (lists date of establishment of ghettos in Poland and also expulsions, labour camps and concentration camps).

Zorach Warhaftig, Uprooted: Jewish Refugees and Displaced Persons After Liberation, New York, November 1946 (maps 312 and 315).

Leon Weliczker Wells, The Janowska Road, New York 1963 (maps 222 and 223).

Janusz Wieczorek (editor), Scenes of Fighting and Martyrdom Guide: War Years in Poland, 1939–1945, Warsaw 1968 (town-by-town and locality-by-locality notes of monuments to Nazi atrocities in Poland, post-1945 boundaries).

Mary H. Williams (editor), Chronology 1941–1945, United States Army in World War II, Special Studies, Washington 1960.

Leni Yahil, The Rescue of Danish Jewry, Philadelphia 1969 (map 213).

The Yellow Spot, the outlawing of half a million human beings, London 1936 (documents on anti-Jewish measures in Germany between 1933 and 1935, introduction by the Bishop of Durham date 12 February 1936) (map 6).

Yitzhak Zuckerman, 'The Jewish Fighting Organization – Z.O.B. – its Establishment and Activites', written in Warsaw in March 1944, published in Yisrael Gutman and Livia Rothkirchen (editors), The Catastrophe of European Jewry, Jerusalem 1976, pages 518–548 (map 131).

ndex of Places

ompiled by the author

vith map numbers)

Index of Individuals

compiled by the author

(with map numbers)

Lange, Jacob, 21
Langer, Mandel, 178
Le Chêne, Evelyn, 222, 223
Leibel, Claire, 133, 134
Leibel, Nelly, 133, 134
Leibel, Pauline, 133, 134
Leiber, Frajdla, 107
Leibovicz, Gaston, 190
Leibovicz, Marcel, 190
Leon, Isaac, 165
Leon, Sadie, 122
Levin, Dov, 227
Levis, Jenny, 131
Levitan, Idel, 224
Levitan, Micha, 224
Levitan, Mira, 224
Levy, Denise, 176
Levy, Rudolf, xii
Lewin, Jankel, 164
Lewinsztejn, Nathan, 142
Lichtenstein, Abraham, 131
Liebeskind, Adolf, 127
Linder, Jakub, 127
Lindow, Rosita, 176
Linkever, Hirsch, 131
Linksz, Isaac, 207
Lion, Octave, 131
Lippman, Henry, 155
Liskin, Max, 131, 132
Lismann, Hermann, 142
Liss, Maurice, 165
Lissauer, Eugelina, 223
Lissman, Hermann, xii
Loewy, M., 47
Lopatin, Dov, 106
Lucas, Lucie, 131
Luft, Anda, 136
Lust, Lieba, 35
Lustiger, Aaron, 135
Lustiger, Gisele, 135

M

Majtek, Michael, 103, 104, 118
Makline, Kiva, 133
Malinsky, Rose, 131
Malkevich, M. P., 80
Maltz, Mrs., 131
Mandel, Eugen, 47
Mandel, Vijoslav, 47
Mandelevitch, Githel, 134
Marx, Suzanne, 122
Matem, Haim, 178
Mayer, Anna, 108
Mayer, Cecile, 36
Mayer, Djamba, 108
Mayer, Djoia, 108
Mayer, Emanuel, 36
Mayer, Eva, 36
Mayer, Freda, 36
Mayer, Johanna, 36
Mayer, Joseph, 36
Mayer, Julius (aged 27), 36
Mayer, Julius (aged 54), 36

Mayer, Julius (aged 56), 36
Mayer, Laura, 36
Mayer, Lehmann, 36
Mayer, Maier, 36
Mayer, Marcel, 108
Mayer, Marie, 36
Meyer, Max, 36
Mayer, Meta, 36
Mayer, Michel, 36
Mayer, Mina, 36
Mayer, Rosalie, 36
Mayer, Salo, 36
Mayer, Selma, 36
Meichel, Jacqueline, 98
Meissl, David, 47
Menache, Jacques, 164
Menasse, Yvette, 131, 132
Mentzel, Charlotte, 190
Mentzel, Ruth, 190
Mires, Abraham, 131
Misrachi, Joseph, 125
Mitrani, Bellina, 108
Mnouchine, Lazare, 82
Modiano, Pola, 122, 165
Moscovitch, Rosa, 131
Moscowitz, Solomon, 125
Moseri, Hugo, 131
Moszkowicz, Daniel, 151
Moszkowicz, tinette, 98
Moucatel, Isaac, 165
Moucatel, Robert, 165

N

Nadel, Arnold, 189
Nadel, Leon, 189
Neumann, Abraham, 91
Navon, Albert, 164
Navon, Jean, 164
Navon, Odette, 164
Navon, Sol, 164
Newer, Jean, 142
Newer, Victor, 142
Neumann, Caroline, 134
Nicholas II, tsar of Russia, 57
Ninio, Avram, 108
Ninio, Daniel, 108
Ninio, Esther, 108
Ninio, Moshe, 108
Ninio, Rebecca, 108
Niwesz, Eva, 114
Nusbaum, Heniek, 127
Nusbaum, Mundek, 127

O

O'Leary, Pat, 220

P

Papo, Elizer, 108
Pechersky, Alexander, 160
Perl, Micheline, 98
Perlestein, Robert, 155

Pesah, Moses, 167
Pétain, Marshal Philippe, 43
Piekmann, Nicolas, 131
Pijade, Mosha, 46
Pinto, Mazeltow, 122
Pomerance, Milly, 190
Poulios, Magalta, 121
Poznanski, Albert, 98
Preston, Thomas, 50
Prins, Dick, 114, 142
Prins, Jacob, 114, 142
Propper, Mijo, 47
Prussak, Ida, 131, 132

Q

Quaziz, Georges, 175

R

Rachow, Isaac, 190
Radnoti, Miklos, xii
Rakcine, Salomon, 165
Rathenau, Walter, 2
Ratz, Leopold, 189
Ratz, Liliane, 189
Reik, Havivah, 198
Reiss, Frieda, 133
Reznik, Pinchas, 114, 176
Rikow, Mordeschil, 47
Ringelblum, Emanuel, xii, 166
Robota, Roza, 197
Rodblat, Josef, 80
Roncalli, Angelo (later Pope John
   XXIII), 140
Roosevelt, Theodore, 57
Rosenblatt, Rozika, 223
Rosenblatt, Gad, 102
Rosenburg, Nicole, 98
Rosenburg, Ryuwen, 122
Rosenbusch, Maximilian, 33
Roth, Alexander, 47
Roth, Germaine; 133
Roth, M., 47
Roth, Pierre, xiii, 133
Rothstein, Dina, 223
Roubenstein, George, 122
Rozio, Joseph, 121
Rubin, Betty, 131
Rubin, David, 80
Rubin, Moise, 114
Rubinstein, Victor, 178
Rudashevski, Yitskhok, xii, 143
Rudnitzki, Peisach, 215
Rudnitzki, Yitzhak (Yitzhak
   Arad), 215

S

Saal, Isaac, 164
Sabatkowski, Hayyim, 129,
   130
Sabatkowski, Herske, 130
Sabatkowski, Mordekhai, 130